Lyndon Ambrose Smith

Recent School Law Decisions

Lyndon Ambrose Smith
Recent School Law Decisions
ISBN/EAN: 9783744666961
Printed in Europe, USA, Canada, Australia, Japan
Cover: Foto ©Suzi / pixelio.de

More available books at **www.hansebooks.com**

SCHOOL LAW OF VIRGINIA,

CONSTITUTION OF THE STATE,

AND THE LAWS GOVERNING STATE AND NATIONAL
INSTITUTIONS OF LEARNING,

CODIFIED FOR THE

INFORMATION AND USE OF SCHOOL OFFICERS,

BY THE

Superintendent of Public Instruction.

RICHMOND:
PRINTED FOR THE BOARD OF EDUCATION.
1883.

PREFACE.

This revised edition of the School Law has been prepared by the Superintendent of Public Instruction, by order of the State Board of Education, for the use and information of school superintendents and district school trustees. Whilst the text of the Code of 1873, as amended by subsequent legislation, including many entirely new sections, is closely followed, the scheme of the compilation has been radically changed, and, I believe, for the better. Starting with the Constitution of our State, I have endeavored to arrange all the subsequent legislation affecting the public school system, inaugurated by that instrument, in logical order without regard to the relative position occupied by the sections in the Code and various acts in which they are found, every section having its proper reference to the Code or the acts from which it has been taken. As this is intended as a means of giving information to the school world, I thought it proper to give succinctly the rules governing every institution in the State, supported, either in whole or in part, by State annuity, with the steps necessary to be taken to gain admission therein. Having experienced great difficulty with the old compilation, owing to its multiplying sections by sub-sections, I have discarded all such divisions, and have given each section, however unimportant, its proper number, running from one on through the book; and have indexed it by subjects, pages, and sections; so that every section has its number, and there can be no confusion in referring to it.

Beginning with page 123 will be found the Regulations which have been adopted from time to time by the Board of Education, by virtue of authority vested in it by law.

This edition of the School Law is prepared merely as a matter of convenience for school officers, and has no authority independent of the acts from which it is compiled.

A sufficient number of copies for the use of boards of school trustees will be forwarded to the city and county superintendents, who will be required to receipt to the Board of Education for the number of copies supplied; and upon their failure so to do, the value of the books delivered will be deducted from their salaries. The superintendent shall deliver to the clerk of each board of school trustees in his county *three copies*, one for each member thereof, taking his receipt therefor, which he shall enter upon his record-book. The district clerk shall mark the name of his district in large letters on each of said copies, and shall deliver one to each member of the board, taking his receipt therefor, which he shall duly enter upon the record-book of the district; and the district clerk shall be responsible to the board, or his successor in office, for each of said books so delivered, and each member shall be responsible to the district clerk for the proper care of the copy delivered to him; and any trustee whose term shall expire and who shall not be re-appointed, or who shall die, resign, or be removed, shall, by representative or in person, deliver to said clerk, in good order, the book for which he receipted.

R. R. FARR,
Superintendent of Public Instruction.

CONTENTS.

	PAGE.
State Constitution,	1
Of Public Free Schools for the Counties and of the Literary Fund,	31
University of Virginia,	72
Virginia Military Institute,	81
The Institution for the Deaf and Dumb and the Blind,	89
Virginia Agricultural and Mechanical College,	92
Hampton Normal and Agricultural Institute,	97
Miller Manual Labor School of Albemarle,	101
Virginia Normal and Collegiate Institute,	105
United States Military Academy,	110
United States Naval Academy	113
Normal College in Nashville,	116
Of Public Free Schools in the Cities and Towns,	118
Regulations of the Board of Education,	123

STATE CONSTITUTION.

Whereas, the delegates and representatives of the good people of Virginia, in convention assembled, on the twenty-ninth day of June, in the year of our Lord one thousand seven hundred and seventy-six, reciting and declaring, that whereas George the Third, King of Great Britain and Ireland, and elector of Hanover, before that time entrusted with the exercise of the kingly office in the government of Virginia, had endeavored to pervert the same into a detestable and insupportable tyranny, by putting his negative on laws the most wholesome and necessary for the public good; by denying his governors permission to pass laws of immediate and pressing importance, unless suspended in their operation for his assent, and, when so suspended, neglecting to attend to them for many years; by refusing to pass certain other laws, unless the persons to be benefitted by them would relinquish the inalienable right of representation in the legislature; by dissolving legislative assemblies repeatedly and continually, for opposing with manly firmness his invasions of the rights of the people; when dissolved, by refusing to call others for a long space of time, thereby leaving the political system without any legislative head; by endeavoring to prevent the population of our country, and for that purpose obstructing the laws for naturalization of foreigners: by keeping among us, in time of peace, standing armies and ships of war; by affecting to render the military independent of and superior to the civil power; by combining with others to subject us to a foreign jurisdiction, giving his assent to their pretended acts of legislation for quartering large bodies of armed troops among us; for cutting off our trade with all parts of the world; for imposing taxes on us without our consent; for depriving us of the benefit of the trial by jury; for transporting us beyond the seas for trial for pretended offences; for suspending our own legislatures, and declaring themselves invested with power to legislate for us in all cases whatsoever; by plundering our seas, ravaging our coasts, burning our towns, and destroying the lives of our people; by inciting insurrection of our fellow-subjects with the allurements of forfeiture and confiscation; by prompting our negroes to rise in arms amongst us—those very negroes whom, by an inhuman use of his negative, he had refused us permission to exclude by law; by endeavoring to bring on the inhabitants of our frontiers the merciless Indian savages, whose known rule of warfare is an undistinguished destruction of all ages, sexes, and conditions of existence; by transporting hither a large army of foreign mercenaries to complete the work of death, desolation and tyranny, then already begun, with circumstances of cruelty and perfidy unworthy the head of a civilized nation; by answering our repeated petitions for redress with a repetition of our injuries; and finally by abandoning the helm of government and declaring us out of his allegiance and protection; by which several acts of misrule, the government of this country, as before exercised under the crown of Great Britain, was totally dissolved—did, therefore, having maturely considered the premises, and viewing with great concern the deplorable condition to which this once happy country would be reduced unless some regular, adequate mode of civil policy should be speedily adopted, and in compliance with the recommendation of the general congress, ordain and declare a form of government of Virginia:

And whereas, a convention, held on the first Monday in October, in the year one thousand eight hundred and twenty-nine, did propose to the people of this commonwealth an amended constitution, or form of government, which was ratified by them.

And whereas, the general assembly of Virginia, by an act passed on the fourth of March, in the year one thousand eight hundred and fifty, did provide for the election, by the people, of delegates to meet in general convention, to consider, discuss, and propose a new constitution, or alterations and amendments to the existing constitution of this commonwealth; and by an act passed on the thirteenth of March, in the year one thousand eight hundred and fifty-one, did further provide for submitting the same to the people for ratification or rejection; and the same having been submitted accordingly, was ratified by them:

And whereas, the general assembly of Virginia, by an act passed on the twenty-first day of December, in the year one thousand eight hundred and sixty-three, did provide for the election, by the people, of delegates to meet in general convention, to consider, discuss, and adopt alterations and amendments to the existing constitution of this commonwealth, the delegates so assembled did, therefore, having maturely considered the premises, adopt a revised and amended constitution as the form of government of Virginia:

And whereas, the congress of the United States did, by an act passed on the second day of March, in the year one thousand eight hundred and sixty-seven, and entitled "an act to provide for the more efficient government of the rebel states," and by acts supplementary thereto, passed on the twenty-third day of March, and the nineteenth day of July, in the year one thousand eight hundred and sixty-seven, provide for the election, by the people of Virginia, qualified to vote under the provisions of said acts, of delegates to meet in convention, to frame a constitution or form of government for Virginia, in conformity with said acts; and by the same acts did further provide for the submitting of such constitution to the qualified voters for ratification or rejection:

We, therefore, the delegates of the good people of Virginia, elected, and in convention assembled, in pursuance of said acts, invoking the favor and guidance of Almighty God, do propose to the people the following constitution and form of government for this commonwealth:

ARTICLE I.

BILL OF RIGHTS.

A declaration of rights, made by the representatives of the good people of Virginia, assembled in full and free convention; which rights do pertain to them and their posterity, as the basis and foundation of government.

1. That all men are by nature equally free and independent, and have certain inherent rights, of which, when they enter into a state of society, they cannot, by any compact, deprive or divest their posterity, namely, the enjoyment of life and liberty, with the means of acquiring and possessing property, and pursuing and obtaining happiness and safety.

2. That this state shall ever remain a member of the United States of America, and that the people thereof are a part of the American Nation, and that all attempts, from whatever source or upon whatever pretext, to dissolve said union or to sever said nation, are unauthorized and ought to be resisted with the whole power of the state.

3. That the constitution of the United States, and the laws of Congress passed in pursuance thereof, constitute the supreme law of the land, to which paramount allegiance and obedience are due from every citizen, anything in the constitution, ordinances or laws of any state to the contrary notwithstanding.

4. That all power is vested in, and consequently derived from, the people; that magistrates are their trustees and servants, and at all times amenable to them.

5. That government is, or ought to be, instituted for the common benefit, protection and security of the people, nation or community; of all the

various modes and forms of government, that is best which is capable of producing the greatest degree of happiness and safety, and is most effectually secured against the danger of maladministration; and that when any government shall be found inadequate or contrary to these purposes, a majority of the community hath an indubitable, inalienable, and indefeasible right to reform, alter or abolish it, in such manner as shall be judged most conducive to the public weal.

6. That no man, or set of men, are entitled to exclusive or separate emoluments or privileges from the community but in consideration of public services; which, not being descendible, neither ought the offices of magistrate, legislator, or judge to be hereditary.

7. That the legislative, executive, and judicial powers should be separate and distinct; and that the members thereof may be restrained from oppression, by feeling and participating the burthens of the people, they should, at fixed periods, be reduced to a private station, return into that body from which they were originally taken, and the vacancies be supplied by frequent, certain and regular elections, in which all or any part of the former members to be again eligible or ineligible, as the laws shall direct.

8. That all elections ought to be free, and that all men having sufficient evidence of permanent common interest with, and attachment to the community, have the right of suffrage, and cannot be taxed or deprived of their property for public uses, without their own consent, or that of their representatives so elected, nor bound by any law to which they have not in like manner assented, for the public good.

9. That all power of suspending laws, or the execution of laws by any authority, without consent of the representatives of the people, is injurious to their rights and ought not to be exercised.

10. That in all capital or criminal prosecutions, a man hath a right to demand the cause and nature of his accusation, to be confronted with the accusers and witnesses, to call for evidence in his favor, and to a speedy trial by an impartial jury of his vicinage, without whose unanimous consent he cannot be found guilty; nor can he be compelled to give evidence against himself; that no man be deprived of his liberty, except by the law of the land or the judgment of his peers.

11. That excessive bail ought not to be required, nor excessive fines imposed, nor cruel and unusual punishment inflicted.

12. That general warrants, whereby an officer or messenger may be commanded to search suspected places without evidence of a fact committed, or to seize any person or persons not named, or whose offence is not par-

ticularly described and supported by evidence, are grievous and oppressive, and ought not to be granted.

13. That in controversies respecting property, and in suits between man and man, the trial by jury is preferable to any other, and ought to be held sacred

14. That the freedom of the press is one of the great bulwarks of liberty, and can never be restrained but by despotic governments, and any citizen may speak, write and publish his sentiments on all subjects, being responsible for the abuse of that liberty.

15. That a well-regulated militia, composed of the body of the people trained to arms, is the proper, natural, and safe defence of a free state; that standing armies, in time of peace, should be avoided as dangerous to liberty, and that in all cases the military should be under strict subordination to, and governed by, the civil power.

16. That the people have a right to uniform government; and, therefore, that no government separate from, or independent of, the government of Virginia ought to be erected or established within the limits thereof.

17. That no free government, or the blessings of liberty, can be preserved to any people but by a firm adherence to justice, moderation, temperance, and virtue, and by a frequent recurrence to fundamental principles.

18. That religion, or the duty which we owe to our Creator, and the manner of discharging it, can be directed only by reason and conviction, not by force or violence; and, therefore, all men are equally entitle to the free exercise of religion according to the dictates of conscience; and that it is the mutual duty of all to practise christian forbearance, love, and charity towards each other.

19. That neither slavery nor involuntary servitude, except as lawful imprisonment may constitute such, shall exist within this state.

20. That all citizens of the state are hereby declared to possess equal civil and political rights and public privileges.

21. The rights enumerated in this bill of rights shall not be construed to limit other rights of the people not therein expressed.

The declaration of the political rights and privileges of the inhabitants of this state is hereby declared to be a part of the constitution of this commonwealth, and shall not be violated on any pretence whatever.

ARTICLE II.

DIVISION OF POWERS.

The legislative, executive, and judiciary departments shall be separate and distinct, so that neither exercise the powers properly belonging to either of the others; nor shall any person exercise the power of more than one of them at the same time, except as hereinafter provided.

ARTICLE III.

ELECTIVE FRANCHISE AND QUALIFICATIONS FOR OFFICE.

SEC. 1 Every male citizen of the United States, twenty-one years old, who shall have been a resident of the state twelve months, and of the county, city, or town in which he shall offer to vote, three months next preceding any election, shall be entitled to vote for members of the general assembly, and all officers elected by the people: provided that no officer, soldier, seaman, or marine of the United States army or navy, shall be considered a resident of this state by reason of being stationed therein: and provided, also, that the following persons shall be excluded from voting:

First. Idiots and lunatics.

Second. Persons convicted of bribery in any election, embezzlement of public funds, treason, felony, or petit larceny.

Third. No person who, while a citizen of this state, has since the adoption of this constitution, fought a duel with a deadly weapon, sent or accepted a challenge to fight a duel with a deadly weapon, either within or beyond the boundaries of this state, or knowingly conveyed a challenge, or aided or assisted in any manner in fighting a duel, shall be allowed to vote or hold any office of honor, profit or trust, under this constitution.

SEC. 2. All elections shall be by ballot, and all persons entitled to vote shall be eligible to any office within the gift of the people, except as restricted in this constitution.

SEC. 3. All persons entitled to vote and hold office, and none others, shall be eligible to sit as jurors.

SEC. 4.* No voter, during the time of holding any election at which he is entitled to vote, shall be compelled to perform military service, except in time of war or public danger, to work upon public roads, or to attend any court as suitor, juror or witness; and no voter shall be subject to arrest, under any civil process, during his attendance at elections, or in going to or returning from them.

Oath of Office.

SEC. 5.* *All persons, before entering upon the discharge of any function*

---
*Change of the numbers of sections 5 and 6 to 4 and 5 rendered necessary by the striking out of section 4, Article III.

as officers of this state, must take and subscribe the following oath or affirmation:

"*I, —— ——, do solemnly swear (or affirm), that I will support and maintain the constitution and laws of the United States, and the constitution and laws of the state of Virginia; that I recognize and accept the civil and political equality of all men before the law, and that I will faithfully perform the duty of —— to the best of my ability: So help me God.*"

[The Schedule embraced in amendments to this article, ratified on the 7th of November, 1876, is in these words:

SCHEDULE.

2. That all elections held subsequent to the ratification of these amendments by the people before the adjournment of the next regular session of the legislature, held after such ratification, shall be had and conducted under and in accordance with the election laws and registration laws which may be in force at the time of such ratification, unless the same shall have been sooner amended or repealed by the general assembly.]

ARTICLE IV.

EXECUTIVE DEPARTMENT.

Governor.

SEC. 1. The chief executive power of this commonwealth shall be vested in a governor. He shall hold office for a term of four years, to commence on the first day of January next succeeding his election, and be ineligible to the same office for the term next succeeding that for which he was elected, and to any other office during his term of service.

SEC. 2. The governor shall be elected by the voters at the times and places of choosing members of the general assembly. Returns of elections shall be transmitted, under seal, by the proper officers, to the secretary of the commonwealth, who shall deliver them to the Speaker of the House of Delegates on the first day of the next session of the general assembly. The Speaker of the House of Delegates shall, within one week thereafter, in presence of a majority of the Senate and House of Delegates, open the said returns, and the votes shall then be counted. The person having the highest number of votes shall be declared elected; but if two or more shall have the highest and an equal number of votes, one of them shall be chosen governor by the joint vote of the two houses of the general assembly.

Contested elections for governor shall be decided by a like vote, and the mode of proceeding in such cases shall be prescribed by law.

SEC. 3. No person except a citizen of the United States shall be eligible to the office of governor; and if such person be of foreign birth, he must have been a citizen of the United States for ten years next preceding his election; nor shall any person be eligible to that office unless he shall have attained the age of thirty years, and have been a resident of this state for three years next preceding his election.

SEC. 4. The governor shall reside at the seat of government; shall receive five thousand dollars for each year of his service, and while in office shall receive no other emolument from this or any other government.

SEC. 5. He shall take care that the laws be faithfully executed; communicate to the general assembly at every session the condition of the commonwealth; recommend to their consideration such measures as he may deem expedient, and convene the general assembly, on application of two-thirds of the members of both houses thereof, or when, in his opinion, the interest of the commonwealth may require it. He shall be commander-in-chief of the land and naval forces of the state; have power to embody the militia to repel invasion, suppress insurrection, and enforce the execution of the laws; conduct, either in person or in such manner as shall be prescribed by law, all intercourse with other and foreign states; and during the recess of the general assembly, to fill, *pro tempore*, all vacancies in those offices for which the constitution and laws make no provision; but his appointments to such vacancies shall be by commissions, to expire at the end of thirty days after the commencement of the next session of the general assembly. He shall have power to remit fines and penalties in such cases and under such rules and regulations as may be prescribed by law, and except when the prosecution has been carried on by the House of Delegates; to grant reprieves and pardons after conviction; to remove political disabilities consequent upon conviction for offences committed prior or subsequent to the adoption of this constitution and to commute capital punishment; but he shall communicate to the general assembly, at each session, particulars of every case of fine or penalty remitted, of reprieve or pardon granted, and of punishment commuted, with his reasons for remitting, granting, or commuting the same.

SEC. 6. He may require information in writing from the officers in the executive department upon any subject relating to the duties of their respective offices; and may also require the opinion, in writing, of the attorney-general upon any question of law connected with his duties.

SEC. 7. Commissions and grants shall run in the name of the commonwealth of Virginia, and be attested by the governor, with the seal of the commonwealth annexed.

SEC. 8. Every bill which shall have passed the Senate and House of Delegates, and every resolution requiring the assent of both branches of the general assembly, shall, before it becomes a law, be presented to the governor; if he approves, he shall sign it; but if not, he shall return it with his objections, to the house in which it shall have originated, who shall enter the objections at large on their journal and proceed to reconsider it. If, after such consideration, two-thirds of the members present shall agree to pass the bill or joint resolution, it shall be sent, together with the objections, to the other house, by which it shall likewise be reconsidered, and, if approved by two-thirds of the members present, it shall become a law, notwithstanding the objections of the governor. But in all such cases the votes of both houses shall be determined by ayes and noes, and the names of the members voting for and against the bill or joint resolution shall be entered on the journal of each house respectively. If any bill or resolution shall not be returned by the governor within five days (Sundays excepted) after it shall have been presented to him, the same shall be a law in like manner as if he had signed it, unless the legislature shall, by their adjournment, prevent its return, in which case it shall not be a law.

Lieutenant-Governor.

SEC. 9. A lieutenant-governor shall be elected at the same time and for the same term as the governor, and his qualification and the manner of his election, in all respects, shall be the same.

SEC. 10. In case of the removal of the governor from office, or of his death, failure to qualify, resignation, removal from the state, or inability to discharge the powers and duties of the office, the said office with its compensation, shall devolve upon the lieutenant-governor; and the general assembly shall provide by law for the discharge of the executive functions in other necessary cases.

SEC. 11. The lieutenant-governor shall be President of the Senate, but shall have no vote except in case of an equal division; and while acting as such, shall receive a compensation equal to that allowed to the Speaker of the House of Delegates.

Secretary of the Commonwealth, Treasurer, and Auditor

SEC. 12. A secretary of the commonwealth, treasurer, and auditor of public accounts, shall be elected by the joint vote of the two houses of the general assembly, and continue in office for the term of two years, unless sooner relieved. The salary of each shall be determined by law.

SEC. 13. The secretary shall keep a record of the official acts of the governor, which shall be signed by the governor and attested by the secretary; and when required, he shall lay the same, and any papers, minutes and vouchers pertaining to his office, before either house of the general assembly; and shall perform such other duties as may be prescribed by law. All fees received by the secretary shall be paid into the treasury.

SEC. 14. The powers and duties of the treasurer and auditor shall be such as are now or may hereafter be prescribed by law.

SEC. 15. There may be established in the office of the secretary of state, a bureau of statistics and a bureau of agriculture, chemistry and geology, under such regulations as may be prescribed by law.

SEC. 16. The general assembly shall have power to establish a bureau of agriculture and immigration, under such regulations as may be prescribed.

Board of Public Works.

SEC. 17. There shall be a board of public works, to consist of the governor, auditor, and treasurer of the commonwealth, under such regulations as may be prescribed by law.

ARTICLE V.

LEGISLATIVE DEPARTMENT.

SEC. 1. The legislative power of this commonwealth shall be vested in a general assembly, which shall consist of a Senate and House of Delegates.

SEC. 2. The House of Delegates shall be elected biennially by the voters of the several cities and counties, on the Tuesday succeeding the first Monday in November, and shall, from and after the Tuesday succeeding the first Monday in November, eighteen hundred and seventy-nine, consist of not more than one hundred and not less than ninety members.

SEC. 3. From and after the same date, the Senate shall consist of not less than thirty-three nor more than forty members. They shall be elected for the term of four years—for the election of whom the counties, cities and towns shall be divided into districts. Each county, city and town of the respective districts shall, at the time of the first election of its delegate or delegates under this amendment, vote for one or more senators. The senators first elected under this amendment, in districts bearing odd numbers, shall vacate their offices at the end of two years; and those elected in districts bearing even numbers, at the end of four years; and vacancies occurring by expiration of term shall be filled by the election of senators for the full term.

SEC. 4. An apportionment of senators and members of the House of Delegates shall be made at the regular session of the general assembly next preceding the Tuesday after the first Monday in November, eighteen hundred and seventy-nine or sooner. A reapportionment shall be made in the year eighteen hundred and ninety-one, and every tenth year thereafter.

Qualification of senators and delegates.

SEC. 5. Any person may be elected senator who, at the time of election, is actually a resident within the district, and qualified to vote for members of the general assembly according to this constitution; and any person may be elected a member of the House of Delegates who, at the time of election is actually a resident within the county, city, town, or election district, qualified to vote for members of the general assembly according to this constitution. But no person holding a salaried office under the state government shall be capable of being elected a member of either house of the general assembly. The removal of any person elected to either branch of the general assembly, from the city, county, town, or district for which he was elected, shall vacate his office.

Powers and duties of the general assembly.

SEC. 6. The general assembly shall meet once in two years, and not oftener, unless convened by the governor, in the manner prescribed in this constitution. No session of the general assembly, after the first under this amendment, shall continue longer than ninety days, without the concurrence of three-fifths of the members elected to each house; in which case the session may be extended for a further period, not exceeding thirty days. Neither house, during the session of the general assembly, shall, without the consent of the other, adjourn for more than three days, nor to any other place than that in which the two houses shall be sitting. A majority of the members elected to each house shall constitute a quorum to do business; but a smaller number may adjourn from day to day, and shall have power to compel the attendance of absent members in such manner and under such penalty as each house may prescribe.

SEC. 7. The House of Delegate shall choose its own Speaker; and in the absence of the lieutenant-governor, or when he shall exercise the office of governor, the Senate shall choose from their own body a president *pro tempore;* and each house shall appoint its own officers, settle its own rules of proceeding, and direct writs of election for supplying intermediate vacancies, but if vacancies shall occur during the recess of the general assembly, such writs may be issued by the governor, under such regulations as may be prescribed by law. Each house shall judge of the election, qualification and returns of its members; may punish them for disorderly behavior, and, with the concurrence of two-thirds, expel a member.

SEC. 8. The members of the general assembly shall receive for their services a salary, to be ascertained by law, and paid out of the public treasury; but no act increasing such salary shall take effect until after the end of the term for which the members of the House of Delegates voting thereon were elected; and no senator or delegate, during the term for which he shall have been elected, shall be appointed to any civil office of profit under the commonwealth which has been created, or the emoluments of which have been increased during such term, except offices filled by election by the people.

SEC. 9. Bills and resolutions may originate in either of the two houses of the general assembly, to be approved or rejected by either, and may be amended by either house, with the consent of the other.

SEC. 10. Each house of the general assembly shall keep a journal of its proceedings, which shall be published from time to time; and the yeas and nays of the members of either house, on any question, shall, at the desire of one-fifth of those present, be entered on the journal. No bill shall become a law until it has been read on three different days of the session in the house in which it originated, unless two-thirds of the members in that house shall otherwise determine.

SEC. 11. The members of the general assembly shall, in all cases except treason, felony, or breach of the peace, be privileged from arrest during the sessions of their respective houses; and for any speech or debate in either house they shall not be questioned in any other place They shall not be subject to arrest, under any civil process, during the sessions of the general assembly, nor for fifteen days next before the convening and after the termination of each session.

SEC. 12. The whole number of members to which the state may at any time be entitled in the House of Representatives of the United States, shall be apportioned as nearly as may be, amongst the several counties, cities and towns of the state, according to their population.

SEC. 13. In the apportionment, the state shall be divided into districts, corresponding in number with the representatives to which it may be entitled in the House of Representatives of the congress of the United States, which shall be formed respectively, of contiguous counties, cities and towns; be compact, and include, as nearly as may be, an equal number of population.

Sec. 14. The privilege of the writ of *habeas corpus* shall not be suspended, unless when, in cases of invasion or rebellion, the public safety may require it. The general assembly shall not pass any bill of attainder, or any *ex post facto* law, or any law impairing the obligation of contracts, or any law whereby private property shall be taken for public uses without just compensation, or any law abridging the freedom of speech or of the press. No man shall be compelled to frequent or support any religious worship, place or ministry whatsoever, nor shall any man be enforced, restrained, molested or burthened in his body or goods, or otherwise suffer, on account of his religious opinions or belief, but all men shall be free to profess, and by argument to maintain, their opinion in matters of religion, and the same shall in nowise affect, diminish or enlarge their civil capacities. And the general assembly shall not prescribe any religious test whatever, or confer any peculiar privileges or advantages on any sect or denomination, or pass any law requiring or authorizing any religious society, or the people of any district within this commonwealth, to levy on themselves or others any tax for the erection or repair of any house of public worship, or for the support of any church or ministry, but it shall be left free to every person to select his religious instructor, and to make for his support such private contract as he shall please.

Sec. 15. No law shall embrace more than one object, which shall be expressed in its title, nor shall any law be revived or amended with reference to its title, but the act revived, or the section amended, shall be re-enacted and published at length.

Sec. 16. The governor, lieutenant-governor, judges and all others offending against the state, by maladministration, corruption, neglect of duty, or other high crime or misdemeanor, shall be impeachable by the House of Delegates, and be prosecuted before the Senate, which shall have the sole power to try impeachment. When sitting for that purpose, they shall be on oath or affirmation, and no person shall be convicted without the concurrence of two-thirds of the members present. Judgment, in case of impeachment, shall not extend further than to removal from office, and disqualification to hold and enjoy any office of honor, trust or profit under the commonwealth; but the party convicted shall, nevertheless, be subject to indictment, trial, judgment, and punishment according to law. The

Senate may sit during the recess of the general assembly for the trial of impeachment.

SEC. 17. The general assembly shall not grant a charter of incorporation to any church or religious denomination, but may secure the title to church property to an extent to be limited by law.

SEC. 18. No lottery shall hereafter be authorized by law; and the buying, selling or transferring of tickets or chances in any lottery, shall be prohibited.

SEC. 19. No new county shall be formed with an area of less than six hundred square miles; nor shall the county or counties from which it is formed be reduced below that area; nor shall any county having a population less than ten thousand, be deprived of more than one-fifth of such population; nor shall a county having a larger population, be reduced below eight thousand But any county, the length of which is three times its mean breadth, or which exceeds fifty miles in length, may be divided at the discretion of the general assembly In all general elections, the voters in any county, not entitled to separate representation, shall vote in the same election district.

SEC. 20. The general assembly shall confer on the courts the power to grant divorces, change the names of persons, and direct the sale of estates belonging to infants and other persons under legal disabilities, but shall not, by special legislation, grant relief in such cases, or in any other case of which the courts or other tribunals may have jurisdiction.

SEC. 21. The general assembly shall provide for the annual registration of births, marriages, and deaths.

SEC. 22. The manner of conducting and making returns of elections, of determining contested elections, and of filling vacancies in office, in cases not specially provided for by this constitution, shall be prescribed by law; and the general assembly may declare the cases in which any office shall be deemed vacant, where no provision is made for that purpose in this constitution.

SEC. 23. The legislature shall have power to provide for the government of cities and towns, and to establish such courts therein as may be necessary for the administration of justice.

SEC. 24. The general assembly shall have power, by a two-thirds vote, to remove disabilities incurred under clause third, section one, article third, of this constitution, with reference to duelling.

NOTE.—For Schedule in act for submission to the people of amendments to this article, *vide* Acts 1875–6, page 92.

ARTICLE VI.

JUDICIARY DEPARTMENT.

SEC. 1. There shall be a supreme court of appeals, circuit courts, and county courts. The jurisdiction of these tribunals, and the judges thereof, except so far as the same is conferred by this constitution, shall be regulated by law.

SEC. 2. The supreme court of appeals shall consist of five judges, any three of whom may hold a court. It shall have appellate jurisdiction only, except in cases of *habeas corpus, mandamus,* and prohibition. It shall not have jurisdiction in civil cases where the matter in controversy, exclusive of costs, is less in value or amount than five hundred dollars, except in controversies concerning the title or boundaries of land, the probate of a will, the appointment or qualification of a personal representative, guardian, committee, or curator; or concerning a mill, roadway, ferry, or landing; or the right of a corporation or of a county to levy tolls or taxes, and except in cases of *habeas corpus, mandamus,* and prohibition, or the constitutionality of a law: provided that the assent of a majority of the judges elected to the court shall be required, in order to declare any law null and void by reason of its repugnance to the federal constitution, or to the constitution of this state.

SEC. 3. Special courts of appeals, to consist of not less than three nor more than five judges, may be formed of the judges of the supreme court of appeals and of the circuit courts, or any of them, to try any cases on the docket of said court, in respect to which a majority of the judges thereof may be so situated as to make it improper for them to sit on the hearing of the same; and also to try any cases on the said docket which cannot be otherwise disposed of with convenient dispatch.

SEC. 4. When a judgment or decree is reversed or affirmed by the supreme court of appeals, the reasons therefor shall be stated in writing and preserved with the records of the case.

SEC. 5. The judges shall be chosen by the joint vote of the two houses of the general assembly, and shall hold their office for a term of twelve years; they shall, when chosen, have held a judicial station in the United States, or shall have practiced law in this or some other state for five years.

SEC. 6. The officers of the supreme court of appeals shall be appointed by the said court, or by the judges thereof in vacation. Their duties, compensation, and tenure of office shall be prescribed by law.

SEC. 7. The supreme court of appeals shall hold its sessions at two or more places in the state, to be fixed by law.

SEC. 8. At every election of a governor, an attorney-general shall be elected by the qualified voters of this commonwealth. He shall be commissioned by the governor, perform such duties and receive such compensation as may be prescribed by law, and shall be removable in the manner prescribed for the removal of judges.

Circuit Courts.

SEC. 9. The state shall be divided into sixteen judicial circuits, as follows:

1. The counties of Norfolk, Princess Anne, Nansemond, Isle of Wight, Southampton, Surry, and the city of Norfolk shall constitute the first circuit.

2. The counties of Sussex, Greensville, Brunswick, Prince George, Dinwiddie, Nottoway, Chesterfield, and the city of Petersburg shall constitute the second circuit.

3. The counties of Mecklenburg, Lunenburg, Charlotte, Amelia, Powhatan, Prince Edward, Buckingham, and Cumberland shall constitute the third circuit.

4. The counties of Halifax, Pittsylvania, Henry, Patrick, Franklin, and the town of Danville shall constitute the fourth circuit.

5. The counties of Bedford, Campbell, Appomattox, Amherst, Nelson, and the city of Lynchburg shall constitute the fifth circuit.

6. The counties of Albemarle, Fluvanna, Culpeper, Goochland, Madison, Greene, and Orange shall constitute the sixth circuit.

7. The county of Henrico and the city of Richmond shall constitute the seventh circuit.

8. The counties of Accomac, Northampton, York, Elizabeth City, Warwick, James City, New Kent, Charles City, and the city of Williamsburg shall constitute the eighth circuit.

9. The counties of Lancaster, Northumberland, Mathews, Middlesex, Gloucester, King William, Essex, and King and Queen shall constitute the ninth circuit.

10. The counties of Westmoreland, Spotsylvania, Caroline, Hanover, Stafford, King George, Richmond and Louisa shall constitute the tenth circuit.

11. The counties of Loudoun, Fauquier, Fairfax, Prince William, Rappahannock, and Alexandria shall constitute the eleventh circuit.

12. The counties of Frederick, Clarke, Warren, Page, Shenandoah, and Rockingham shall constitute the twelfth circuit.

13. The counties of Augusta, Rockbridge, Bath, Highland, and Alleghany shall constitute the thirteenth circuit.

14. The counties of Botetourt, Roanoke, Montgomery, Floyd, Giles, and Craig shall constitute the fourteenth circuit.

15. The counties of Carroll, Grayson, Wythe, Pulaski, Bland, and Tazewell shall constitute the fifteenth circuit.

16. The counties of Smyth, Washington, Lee, Scott, Wise, Russell, Buchanan, and Dickenson shall constitute the sixteenth circuit.

SEC. 10. The general assembly may rearrange said circuits or any of them, and increase or diminish the number thereof, when the public interests shall require it.

SEC. 11. For each circuit a judge shall be chosen by the joint vote of the two houses of the general assembly, who shall hold his office for a term of eight years, unless sooner removed in the manner prescribed by this constitution. He shall, when chosen, possess the same qualifications of judges of the supreme court of appeals; and during his continuance in office shall reside in the circuit of which he is judge.

SEC. 12. A circuit court shall be held, at least twice a year by the judges of each circuit, in every county and corporation thereof wherein a circuit court now is or may hereafter be established. But the judges may be required or authorized to hold the courts of their respective circuits alternately, and the judge of one circuit to hold court in any other circuit.

County Courts.

SEC. 13. In each county of this commonwealth there shall be a court called the county court, which shall be held monthly by a judge learned in the law of the state, and to be known as the county court judge: provided that counties containing less than eight thousand inhabitants shall be attached to adjoining counties for the formation of districts for county judges. County court judges shall be chosen in the same manner as judges of the circuit courts. They shall hold their office for a term of six years, except the first term under this constitution, which shall be three years, and during their continuance in office they shall reside in their respective counties or districts. The jurisdiction of said courts shall be the same as that of the existing county courts, except so far as it is modified by this constitution, or may be changed by law.

Government of Cities and Towns.

SEC. 14. For each city or town in the state containing a population of five thousand, shall be elected, on the joint vote of the two houses of the general assembly, one city judge, who shall hold a corporation or hustings court of said city or town, as often, and as many days in each month, as may be prescribed by law, with similar jurisdiction, which may be given by law, to the circuit courts of this state, and who shall hold his office for a term of six years: provided that in cities or towns containing thirty thousand inhabitants there may be elected an additional judge, to hold courts of probate and record, separate and apart from the corporation or hustings courts, and perform such other duties as shall be prescribed by law.

SEC. 15. Also the following enumerated officers, who shall be elected by the qualified voters of said cities or towns: One clerk of the corporation or hustings court, who shall also be the clerk of the circuit court, except in cities or towns containing a population of thirty thousand or more; in which city or town there may be a separate clerk for the circuit court, who shall hold his office for a term of six years.

SEC. 16. One commonwealth's attorney, who shall be the commonwealth's attorney for the circuit court, and shall hold his office for a term of two years.

SEC. 17. One city sergeant, who shall hold his office for a term of two years.

SEC. 18. One city or town treasurer, whose duties shall be similar to those of county treasurer, and shall hold his office for a term of three years.

SEC. 19. One commissioner of the revenue.

SEC. 20. There shall be chosen by the electors of every city, a mayor, who shall be the chief executive officer thereof, and who shall see that the duties of the various city officers are faithfully performed. He shall have power to investigate their acts, have access to all books and documents in their offices, and may examine them and their subordinates on oath. The evidence given by persons so examined, shall not be used against them in any criminal proceedings. He shall also have power to suspend or remove such officers, whether they be elected or appointed, for misconduct in office or neglect of duty, to be specified in the order of suspension or removal; but no such removal shall be made without reasonable notice to the officer complained of, and an opportunity afforded him to be heard in his defence. All city, town, and village officers, whose election or appointment is not provided for by this constitution, shall be elected by the electors of such cities, towns, and villages, or of some division thereof, or appointed by such authorities thereof as the general assembly shall designate. All other officers whose election or appointment is not provided for by this constitution and all officers whose offices may be hereafter created by law, shall be elected by the people, or appointed, as the general assembly may direct. Members of common councils shall hold no other office in cities, and no city officer shall hold a seat in the general assembly. The general assembly, at its first session after the adoption of this constitution, shall pass such laws as may be necessary to give effect to the provisions of this article. General laws shall be passed for the organization and government of cities, and no special act shall be passed, except in cases where, in the judgment of the general assembly, the object of such act cannot be attained by general laws. Nothing in this article shall affect the power of the general assembly over quarantine, or in regard to the port of Norfolk, or the interest of the state in the lands under water and within the jurisdiction or boundaries of any city, or to regulate the wharves, piers, or slips in any city. All laws or city ordinances in conflict with the provisions of the preceding sections, shall be void from and after the adoption of this constitution.

SEC. 22. All regular elections for city or town officers, under this article, shall be held on the fourth Thursday in May, and the officers elect shall enter upon their duties on the first day of July succeeding.

General Provisions.

SEC. 22. All the judges shall be commissioned by the governor, and shall receive such salaries and allowances as may be determined by law, the amount of which shall not be diminished during their term of office. Their terms of office shall commence on the first day of January next following their appointment; and they shall discharge the duties of their respective offices from their first appointment and qualification under this constitution until their terms begin.

SEC. 23. Judges may be removed from office by a concurrent vote of both houses of the general assembly, but a majority of all the members elected to each house must concur in such vote, and the cause of removal shall be entered on the Journal of each house. The judge upon whom the general assembly may be about to proceed, shall have notice thereof, accompanied by a copy of the causes alleged for his removal, at least twenty days before the day on which either house of the general assembly shall act thereon.

SEC. 24. Judges of the supreme court of appeals, and judges of the circuit courts, shall not hold any other office of public trust during their continuance in office.

SEC. 25. Judges, and all other officers elected or appointed, shall continue to discharge the duties of their offices after their terms of service have expired, until their successors have qualified.

SEC. 26. Writs shall run "in the name of the commonwealth of Virginia," and be attested by the clerks of the several courts. Indictment shall conclude "against the peace and dignity of the commonwealth."

ARTICLE VII.

COUNTY ORGANIZATION.

SEC. 1. There shall be elected by the qualified voters of the county, one sheriff, one attorney for the commonwealth, who shall also be the commonwealth's attorney for the circuit court; one county clerk, who shall also be the clerk of the circuit court, except that in counties containing fifteen thousand inhabitants, there may be a separate clerk for the circuit court; one county treasurer, and so many commissioners of the revenue as may be provided by law; and there shall be appointed, in a manner to be provided by law, one superintendent of the poor, and one county surveyor; and there shall also be appointed, in the manner provided for in article eight, *one superintendent of schools*. All regular elections for county officers shall be held on the fourth Thursday in May; and all officers elected *or appointed*, under this provision, shall enter upon the duties of their offices on the *first day of July next succeeding their election, and shall hold their respective offices for the term of four years*, except that county and circuit court clerks shall hold offices for six years.

SEC. 2. Each county of the state shall be divided into so many compactly located magisterial districts as may be deemed necessary, not less than three: provided, that after these have been formed no additional districts shall be made containing less than thirty square miles; each magisterial district shall be known as —— magisterial district of —— county. In each district there shall be elected one supervisor, three justices of the peace, one constable, and one overseer of the poor, who shall hold their respective offices for the term of two years. All regular elections for magisterial district officers shall take place on the fourth Thursday in May, and all officers so elected shall enter upon the duties of their respective offices on the first day of July next succeeding their election. The supervisors of the district shall constitute the board of supervisors for that county, whose duty it shall be to audit the accounts of the county, examine the books of the commissioners of the revenue, regulate and equalize the valuation of property, fix the county levies for the ensuing year, and perform any other duties required of them by law.

School Districts.

SEC. 3. *Each magisterial district shall be divided into so many compactly located school districts as may be deemed necessary: provided, that no school district shall be formed containing less than one hundred inhabitants. In each school district there shall be elected or appointed, annually, one school trustee, who shall hold his office three years: provided, that at the first election held under this provision, there shall be three trustees elected, whose terms shall be one, two and three years respectively.*

SEC. 4.* *The general assembly at its first session after the adoption of this constitution, shall pass such laws as may be necessary to give effect to the provisions of this article. But nothing in this article shall be construed as prohibiting the general assembly from providing by law for any additional officers in any city or county.*

SEC. 5.† *Sheriffs shall hold no other office. They may be required by law to renew their security, and in default of so doing, their offices shall be declared vacant. Counties shall never be made responsible for the acts of the sheriffs.*

NOTE.—For schedule in act for submitting to the people the amendments to Article VII, *vide* Sessions Acts, 1874, page 211.

ARTICLE VIII.

EDUCATION.

SEC. 1. *The general assembly shall elect, in joint ballot, within thirty days after its organization, under this constitution, and every fourth year thereafter, a superintendent of public instruction. He shall have the general supervision of the public free school interest of the state, and shall report to the general assembly for its consideration, within thirty days after his election, a plan for a uniform system of public free schools.*

SEC. 2. *There shall be a board of education, composed of the governor, superintendent of public instruction, and attorney-general, which shall appoint and have power to remove, for cause and upon notice to the incumbents, subject to confirmation by the Senate, all county superintendents of public free schools. This board shall have, regulated by law, the management and investment of all school funds, and such supervision of schools of higher grades as the law shall provide.*

SEC. 3. *The general assembly shall provide by law, at its first session under this constitution, a uniform system of public free schools, and for its*

---

*Change in number of section 5 of Article VII to 4 rendered necessary by the striking out of section 4.

†Change in number of section 6 of Article VII to 5 rendered necessary by the striking out of section 4.

gradual, equal, and full introduction into all the counties of the state, by the year 1876, or as much earlier as practicable.

SEC. 4. *The general assembly shall have power after a full introduction of the public free school system, to make such laws as shall not permit parents and guardians to allow their children to grow up in ignorance and vagrancy.*

SEC. 5. *The general assembly shall establish, as soon as practicable, normal schools, and may establish agricultural schools and such grades of schools as shall be for the public good.*

SEC. 6. *The board of education shall provide for uniformity of text-books and the furnishing of school-houses with such apparatus and library as may be necessary, under such regulations as may be provided by law.*

SEC. 7. *The general assembly shall set apart, as a permanent and perpetual literary fund, the present literary funds of the state, the proceeds of all public lands donated by congress for public school purposes, of all escheated property, of all waste and unappropriated lands, of all property accruing to the state by forfeiture, and all fines collected for offences committed against the state, and such other sums as the general assembly may appropriate.*

SEC. 8. *The general assembly shall apply the annual interest on the literary fund, the capitation tax provided for by this constitution for public free school purposes, and an annual tax upon the property of the state of not less than one mill nor more than five mills on the dollar, for the equal benefit of all the people of the state, the number of children between the ages of five and twenty-one years, in each public free school district, being the basis of such division. Provision shall be made to supply children attending the public free schools with necessary text-books in cases where the parent or guardian is unable, by reason of poverty, to furnish them. Each county and public free school district may raise additional sums by a tax on property for the support of the public free schools. All unexpended sums of any one year in any public free school district shall go into the general school fund for re-division the next year: provided, that any tax authorized by this section to be raised by counties or school districts shall not exceed five mills on a dollar in any one year, and shall not be subject to a redivision, as hereinbefore provided in this section.*

SEC. 9. *The general assembly shall have power to foster all higher grades of schools under its supervision, and to provide for such purpose a permanent educational fund.*

SEC. 10. *All grants and donations received by the general assembly for educational purposes shall be applied according to the terms prescribed by the donors.*

SEC. 11. *Each city and county shall be held accountable for the destruction of school property that may take place within its limits by incendiaries or open violence.*

SEC. 12. *The general assembly shall fix the salaries and prescribe the duties of all school officers, and shall make all needful laws and regulations to carry into effect the public free school system provided for by this article.*

ARTICLE IX.

MILITIA.

SEC. 1. The militia of this state shall consist of all able-bodied male persons between the ages of eighteen and forty-five years, except such persons as hereafter may be exempted by the laws of the United States or of this state; but those who belong to religious societies whose tenets forbid them to carry arms, shall not be compelled to do so, but shall pay an equivalent for personal service; and the militia shall be organized, armed and equipped, and trained, as the general assembly may provide by law.

SEC. 2. The legislature shall provide by law for the encouragement of volunteer corps of the several arms of the service, which shall be classed as the active militia; and all other militia shall be classified as the reserve militia, and shall not be required to muster in time of peace.

ARTICLE X.

TAXATION AND FINANCE.

SEC. 1. Taxation, except as hereinafter provided, whether imposed by the state, county, or corporate bodies, shall be equal and uniform, and all property, both real and personal, shall be taxed in proportion to its value, to be ascertained as prescribed by law. No one species of property, from which a tax may be collected, shall be taxed higher than any other species of property of equal value.

SEC. 2. No tax shall be imposed on any of the citizens of this state for the privilege of taking or catching oysters from their natural beds with tongs in the waters thereof; but the amount of sales of oysters so taken by any citizen, in any one year, may be taxed at a rate not exceeding the rate of taxation imposed upon any other species of property.

SEC. 3. The legislature may exempt all property used exclusively for state, county, municipal, benevolent, charitable, educational and religious purposes.

SEC. 4. The general assembly may levy a tax on income in excess of six hundred dollars per annum, and upon the following licenses, viz: the sale of ardent spirits, theatrical and circus companies, menageries, jugglers, itinerant peddlers, and all other shows and exhibitions for which an entrance fee is required; commission merchants, persons selling by sample, brokers and pawn-brokers, and all other business which cannot be reached by the *ad valorem* system. The capital invested in all business operations shall be assessed and taxed as other property. Assessments upon all stock shall be according to the market value thereof.

SEC. 5. *The general assembly may levy a tax not exceeding one dollar per annum, on every male citizen who has attained the age of twenty-one years, which shall be applied exclusively in aid of public free schools;* and counties and corporations shall have power to impose a capitation tax, not exceeding fifty cents per annum, for all purposes.

SEC. 6. The general assembly shall provide for a reassessment of the real estate of this state in the year 1869, or as soon thereafter as practicable, and every fifth year thereafter; provided, in making such assessment, no land shall be assessed above or below its value.

SEC. 7. No debt shall be contracted by this state except to meet casual deficits in the revenue, to redeem a previous liability of the state, to suppress insurrection, repel invasion, or defend the state in time of war.

SEC 8. The general assembly shall provide by law, a sinking fund, to be applied solely to the payment and extinguishment of the principal of the state debt; which sinking fund shall be continued until the extinguishment of such state debt; and every law hereafter enacted by the general assembly, creating a debt or authorizing a loan, shall provide a sinking fund for the payment of the same.

SEC. 9. The unfunded debt shall not be funded or redeemed at a value exceeding that established by law at the time said debt was contracted, nor shall any discrimination hereafter be made in paying the interest on state bonds, which shall give a higher actual value to bonds held in foreign countries over the same class of bonds held in this country.

SEC. 10. No money shall be paid out of the state treasury except in pursuance of appropriations made by law; and no appropriation shall ever be made for the payment of any debt or obligation created in the name of the state of Virginia, by the usurped and pretended state authorities assembled at Richmond during the late war; and no county, city or corporation shall levy or collect any tax for the payment of any debt created for *the purpose of aiding any rebellion* against the state, or against the United States.

SEC. 11. On the passage of every act which imposes, continues or revives any appropriation of public trust money or property, or releases, discharges or commutes any claim or demand of the state, the vote shall be determined by ayes and noes, and the names of the persons voting for and against the same shall be entered on the journals of the respective houses, and a majority of all the members elected to each house shall be necessary to give it the force of law.

SEC. 12. The credit of the state shall not be granted to, or in aid of, any person, association or corporation.

SEC. 13. No scrip, certificate, or other evidence of state indebtedness, shall be issued, except for the redemption of stock previously issued, or for such debts as are expressly authorized in this constitution.

SEC. 14. The state shall not subscribe to, or become interested in, the stock of any company, association or corporation.

SEC. 15. The state shall not be a party to, or become interested in, any work of internal improvement, nor engage in carrying on any such work, otherwise than in the expenditure of grants to the state of land or other property.

SEC. 16. Every law which imposes, continues or revives a tax, shall distinctly state the tax, and the object to which it is to be applied, and it shall not be sufficient to refer to any other law to fix such tax or object.

SEC. 17. The state shall not assume any indebtedness of the county, borough, nor city, nor lend its credit to the same.

SEC. 18. A full account of the state indebtedness, and an accurate statement of receipts and expenditures of the public money, shall be attached to and published with its laws passed at every regular session of the general assembly.

SEC. 19. The general assembly shall provide by law for adjusting with the state of West Virginia, the proportion of the public debt of Virginia, proper to be borne by the state of Virginia, and West Virginia, and shall provide that such sum as shall be received from West Virginia shall be applied to the payment of the public debt of the state.

SEC. 20. No other or greater amount of tax or revenue shall at any time be levied than may be required for the necessary expenses of the government, or to pay the existing indebtedness of the state.

SEC. 21. The liability to the state of any incorporated company or institution to redeem the principal and pay the interest of any loan heretofore made by the state to such company or institution, shall not be released or commuted.

ARTICLE XI.

MISCELLANEOUS PROVISIONS.

Homestead and other Exemptions.

SEC. 1. Every householder or head of a family shall be entitled, in addition to the articles now exempt from levy or distress for rent, to hold exempt from levy, seizure, garnisheeing, or sale, under any execution, order, or other process, issued on any demand for any debt heretofore or hereafter contracted, his real and personal property, or either, including money and debts due him, whether heretofore or hereafter acquired or contracted, to the value of not exceeding two thousand dollars, to be selected by him: provided, that such exemption shall not extend to any execution, order, or other process issued on any demand in the following cases:

1st. For the purchase price of said property, or any part thereof.

2d. For services rendered by a laboring person or a mechanic.

3d. For liabilities incurred by any public officer, or officer of a court, or any fiduciary, or any attorney at law, for money collected.

4th. For a lawful claim for any taxes, levies, or assessments, accruing after the first day of June, 1866.

5th. For rent hereafter accruing.

6th. For the legal or taxable fees of any public officer, or officers of a court, hereafter accruing.

SEC. 2. The foregoing section shall not be construed as subjecting the property hereby exempted, or any portion thereof, to any lien by reason of any execution levied on property which has been subsequently restored to the defendant, or judgment rendered or docketed, on or after the 17th day of April, 1861, and before the 2d day of March, 1867, for any debt contracted previous to the 4th day of April, 1865, except debts of the character mentioned in either of the above first three exceptions.

SEC. 3. Nothing contained in this article shall be construed to interfere with the sale of property aforesaid, or any portion thereof, by virtue of any mortgage, deed of trust, pledge, or other security thereon.

SEC. 4. The general assembly is hereby prohibited from passing any law staying the collection of debts, commonly known as "stay laws"; but this section shall not be construed as prohibiting any legislation which the general assembly may deem necessary to fully carry out the provisions of this article.

SEC. 5. The general assembly shall, at its first session under this constitution, prescribe in what manner and on what conditions the said householder or head of a family shall thereafter set apart and hold for himself and family, a homestead out of any property hereby exempted, and may, in its discretion, determine in what manner and on what conditions he may thereafter hold, for the benefit of himself and family, such personal property as he may have, and coming within the exemption hereby made. But this section shall not be construed as authorizing the general assembly to defeat or impair the benefits intended to be conferred by the provisions of this article.

SEC. 6. An act of the general assembly, entitled "an act to exempt the homesteads of families from forced sales," passed April 29th, 1877, and an act entitled "an act to stay the collection of debts for a limited period," passed March 2d, 1866, and the acts amendatory thereof, are hereby abrogated.

SEC. 7. The provisions of this article shall be construed liberally to the end that all the intents thereof may be fully and perfectly carried out.

Church Property.

SEC. 8. The rights of ecclesiastical bodies in and to Church property conveyed to them by regular deed of conveyance shall not be affected by the late civil war, nor by any antecedent or subsequent event, nor by any act of the legislature purporting to govern the same, but all such property shall pass to and be held by the parties set forth in the original deeds of conveyance, or the legal assignees of such original parties holding through or by conveyance, and any act or acts of the legislature in opposition thereto shall be null and void.

Heirship of Property.

SEC. 9. The children of parents, one or both of whom were slaves at and during the period of cohabitation, and who were recognized by the father as his children, and whose mother was recognized by such father as his wife, and was cohabited with as such, shall be as capable of inheriting any estate whereof such father may have died seized and possessed as though they had been born in lawful wedlock.

ARTICLE XII.

FUTURE CHANGES IN THE CONSTITUTION.

SEC. 1. Any amendment or amendments to the constitution may be proposed in the Senate and House of Delegates, and if the same shall be agreed to by a majority of the members elected to each of the two houses, such proposed amendment or amendments shall be entered on their journals, with the ayes and noes taken thereon, and referred to the general assembly to be chosen at the next general election of senators and members of the House of Delegates, and shall be published for three months previous to the time of making such choice. And if in the general assembly so next chosen as aforesaid, such proposed amendment or amendments shall be agreed to by a majority of all the members elected to each house, then it shall be the duty of the general assembly to submit such proposed amendment or amendments to the people in such manner and at such times as the general assembly shall prescribe ; and if the people shall approve and ratify such amendment or amendments by a majority of the electors qualified to vote for members of the general assembly voting thereon, such amendment or amendments shall become part of the constitution.

SEC. 2. At the general election to be held in the year 1888, and in each twentieth year thereafter, and also at such times as the general assembly may by law provide, the question, "Shall there be a convention to revise the constitution and amend the same ?" shall be decided by the electors qualified to vote for members of the general assembly; and in case a majority of the electors so qualified voting at such election, shall decide in favor of a convention for such purpose, the general assembly at its next session shall provide by law for the election of delegates to such convention: provided, that no amendment or revision shall be made which shall deny or in any way impair the right of suffrage or any civil or political right as conferred by this constitution, except for causes which apply to all persons and classes without distinction.

SCHEDULE.

That no inconvenience may arise from the changes in the constitution of this state, and in order to carry the same into complete operation, it is hereby declared that—

SEC. 1. The common law and the statute laws now in force, not repugnant to this constitution, shall remain in full force until they expire by their own limitation, or are altered or repealed by the legislature.

SEC. 2. All writs, actions, causes of actions, prosecutions, and rights of individuals and of bodies corporate, and of the state, and all charters of incorporation, shall continue ; and all indictments which shall have been found, or which may hereafter be found, for any crime or offence committed before the adoption of this constitution, may be proceeded upon as if no change had taken place. The several courts, except as herein otherwise provided, shall continue, with the like powers and jurisdiction, both in law and in equity, as if this constitution had not been adopted, and until the organization of the judicial department of this constitution.

SEC. 3. That all fines, penalties, forfeitures, and escheats accruing to the state of Virginia, under the present constitution and laws, shall accrue to the use of the state under this constitution.

SEC. 4. That all recognizances, bonds, obligations, and all other instruments entered into or executed before the adoption of this constitution, to the people of the state of Virginia, to any state, county or township, or any public officer, or public body, or which may be entered into or executed, under existing laws, "to the people of the state of Virginia," to any such officer or public body, before the complete organization of the department of government under this constitution, shall remain binding and valid; and rights and liabilities upon the same shall continue, and may be prosecuted as provided by law. All crimes and misdemeanors, and penal actions, shall be tried, punished and prosecuted, as though no change had taken place, until otherwise provided by law.

PUBLIC FREE SCHOOL LAW.

I.—OF PUBLIC FREE SCHOOLS FOR THE COUNTIES, AND OF THE LITERARY FUND.

Uniform System to be adopted.

1. There shall be established and maintained, in this state, a uniform system of public free schools. 1869-70, c. 259, p. 402, § 1.
Code of 1873, c. 78, p. 678, § 1.

Authorities for Administering It.

2. The public free school system shall be administered by the following authorities, to wit: a Board of Education, a Superintendent of Public Instruction, county and city superintendents of schools, and district school trustees. Id. § 2.

Of the Board of Education; of whom composed; its meetings, records, funds, and duties.

3. The Board of Education shall be a corporation by that name, and shall consist of the Governor, the Superintendent of Public Instruction, and the Attorney-General. It shall have all the rights and powers now or heretofore vested in the board of the literary fund. The Governor shall be the President of the Board, if he is present, and in his absence one of the other members shall be called to preside. Id. § 3.

4. A meeting of the Board may be held at any time upon the call of any member thereof: provided, that due notice of the time of holding such meeting be given to all the members. The place of meeting shall, ordinarily, be the office of the Superintendent of Public Instruction. Id. § 4.

5. A faithful record shall be kept of all the proceedings of the Board, which shall be signed by the member presiding at the sitting when they occurred, and shall be at all times open to inspection. A copy thereof, or any part of the same, certified by the secretary of the Board, shall be evidence in all cases in which the original would be. Id. § 5.

6. Any money which ought to be paid into the public treasury Id. § 6.

to the credit of the literary fund, shall (unless other provision be made therefor) be recoverable, with interest, in the manner prescribed by the first section of the seventy-first chapter of the Code of Virginia, of the year eighteen hundred and sixty, for the recovery of money, to be paid to the credit of the fund for internal improvement. And the second, third, fourth, and fifth sections of that chapter shall apply also to the Board of Education.

The chapter referred to is as follows:

(1). Any forfeiture to the board of public works not under the seventieth chapter, and any money which ought to be paid into the public treasury to the credit of the fund for internal improvement, shall be recoverable, with interest on such money from the time the same ought to be paid, by motion after thirty days' notice, or by action in the *circuit court of the city of Richmond*. The second auditor shall institute and prosecute the proceedings, after an order for such motion or action shall have been made by the board.

(2). The said board may appoint agents for the collection of its debts or claims, and authorize them to secure payment thereof on such terms as it may approve.

(3). When estate of any person taken under execution, or for sale under any decree or deed of trust, for any such debt or claim, will not sell for the amount thereof, such agent may (under the directions of the board as to the price) purchase such estate for the board. He shall immediately report to it every such purchase and the terms thereof.

(4). The board may sell or appoint an agent to sell, any estate so purchased, who shall sell at such time and on such terms as the board may authorize. It shall take bond from such agent if any money is to come into his hands. Any agent selling land under this section shall, when directed so to do by the board, execute a deed (with the resolution giving such direction thereto annexed), conveying to the purchaser all the interest which the board may have in such land.

(5). For the service of any agent under this chapter the board may allow compensation, not exceeding in any case five per centum on the money actually paid into the treasury.

Id. § 7.

The duties of the Board of Education shall be as follows, viz:

7. To make by-laws and regulations for its own government, and for carrying into effect the school laws.

8. To observe the operations of the free school system, and to suggest to the general assembly any improvements deemed advisable therein.

9. To invest all the capital and unappropriated income of the literary fund in certificates of debt of the United States, or certificates of debt of, or guaranteed by this state, or in bonds of railroad companies, secured by first mortgage, whose market value for six months preceding the investment has not been less than ninety cents in the dollar. And the said Board may call in any such investment, or any heretofore made, and re-invest the same as aforesaid, whenever deemed proper for the preservation, security or improvement of the said fund. Whenever, in accordance

with this section, the Board shall invest as aforesaid in original certificates of debt of this state, no premium shall be required or paid on such investment. All securities for money belonging to the literary fund shall be deposited with the second auditor for safe keeping, who shall return, with his annual report, a list thereof, and statement of their value.

10. To appoint and remove county superintendents of schools, subject to confirmation by the senate: provided, that vacancies may be filled on their occurrence, and that any such action taken by the Board in the recess of the general assembly shall continue in force until the expiration of thirty days after the assembling of the next general assembly.

11. To decide appeals from decisions of the Superintendent of Public Instruction: provided, that all the facts and arguments in each case shall be presented in writing.

12. To determine the necessary contingent expenses of the Superintendent's office, including stationery, postage, printing, furniture, and other necessary charges; to examine the accounts thereof, and certify the same for payment, when approved.

13. To audit all claims arising under this act which are to be liquidated out of the state funds, and to allow so much thereof as shall appear to be due: provided, that not more than ten years shall have elapsed from the time when, by law, such claim might have been presented for payment. For any claims so allowed, certified by the secretary and the presiding officer of the Board, the second auditor shall issue his warrant on the treasurer, signed by the said auditor and attested by one of his clerks. All money belonging to the literary fund shall also be received into the treasury on the warrant of the same auditor, who shall also be the accountant of the said fund.

14. To approve of the appointment of a first and second clerk for the office of the Superintendent of Public Instruction, upon the nomination of that officer, and to fix their salaries at a sum not exceeding that allowed by law to other first and second clerks in the other state offices. But the first clerk, who is hereby required to serve also as secretary of the Board of Education, may be allowed for these extra services such reasonable compensation as the Board may deem just and proper, provided that the whole amount received by him for both offices shall not exceed the amount of his present salary as first clerk. 1870–71, c. 298, p. 393. 1874, c. 236, p. 267. 1877–78, c. 261, p. 244. Code of 1873, c. 78, § 7, p. 680.

15. To regulate all matters arising in the practical administration of the school system, which are not otherwise provided for.

PUBLIC FREE SCHOOL LAW.

1871-72, c. 108, p. 85, § 1. Code of 1873, c. 78, § 7, p. 680.
16. To make an annual report to the legislature on or before the first day of December, covering the annual report of the Superintendent of Public Instruction, giving an account of the operations of the Board during the year ending the preceding thirty-first day of July (which shall in all cases be deemed the end of the school year) and especially showing the condition of the literary fund, and making suggestions with regard to the same.

Id. Code of 1873, c. 78, § 7, p. 681.
17. To punish county superintendents for neglect of duty, or for any official misconduct, by reasonable fines, to be deducted from their pay, by suspension from office and pay for a certain time, or by removal, subject in the latter case to confirmation by the senate, as hereinbefore provided.

OF THE SUPERINTENDENT OF PUBLIC INSTRUCTION.

Office for him and the Board of Education; his election, duties, compensation, and Annual Report.

1869-70, c. 259, § 8. Code of 1873, c. 78, § 8, p. 681.
18. A Superintendent of Public Instruction shall be elected by the general assembly, by joint vote, within thirty days after the meeting of eighteen hundred and seventy-three and seventy-four, and every four years thereafter, the term of office to commence on the fifteenth day of the March following his election; any vacancy in the office arising from death, resignation, removal from the commonwealth, permanent disability, or otherwise, to be filled by the Governor temporarily, if the same occur during the recess of the general assembly, the commission to expire at the end of thirty days after the next assembling of that body, whose duty it shall be to elect a successor, who shall enter upon his duties as soon as practicable after his election, and shall continue to serve four years from the fifteenth day of the March following his election.

Id. § 9; and 1870-71, c. 219, § 1, p. 317. Code of 1873, c. 78, § 9, p. 681.
19. The salary of the Superintendent of Public Instruction, after the present year, ending March 15th, 1871, shall be two thousand dollars, payable in monthly instalments. He shall also be allowed his necessary travelling expenses, whilst engaged in the duties of his office, to be approved by the Board of Education, not to exceed, in the aggregate, five hundred dollars in any one year.

1869-70, c. 259, § 10. Code of 1873, c. 78, § 10, p. 681.
20. A convenient office shall be provided for the use of the Superintendent of Public Instruction and the Board of Education.

21. The Superintendent of Public Instruction shall be the chief Id. ? 11. executive of the public free school system, upon whom shall devolve the following duties, to wit:

22. He shall take care that the school laws and regulations be faithfully executed, and shall use all proper means to promote an appreciation and desire of education among the people.

23. It shall be his duty to determine the true intent and meaning of the school laws and regulations, and to explain to the county superintendents and other school officers the several duties enjoined thereby upon them, and his decision shall be final, unless and until reversed by the Board of Education.

24. He shall prepare suitable registers, blank forms and regulations for making all reports and for conducting all necessary business under this act, and by circulars and otherwise, shall give such information and instructions as he shall deem conducive to the proper organization and government of the public free schools and the due execution of their duties by the school officers.

25. He shall require of county superintendents detailed reports annually, and as often besides as he may deem proper; and he may require special reports, at any time, of any officer connected with the school system. He may also appoint persons, at his discretion, to visit or examine all or any of the public free schools in the county wherein such persons reside, and report to him, touching all such matters respecting their condition and management, and the means of improving them, as he may indicate; but no allowance or compensation shall be made to such persons for their services or expenses.

26. It shall be his duty, as often as may be consistent with his other official engagements, to make tours of inspection among the public free schools throughout the state.

27. He shall decide all appeals from decisions of county superintendents of schools, when made in prescribed form; but he may, at his discretion, refer the matter to the Board of Education, whose decision shall always be final. But appeals shall lie in all cases from the decisions of the Superintendent of Public Instruction to the Board of Education.

28. Copies of his decisions and of the decisions of the Board, as well as of all his official papers, shall be kept on file in his office, and be open to the inspection of persons concerned.

29. He shall also preserve, in convenient arrangement in his office, all such school documents from other states and governments, books or pamphlets on educational subjects, school books, apparatus, maps, charts, and the like, as have been or shall be

furnished gratuitously for public use, or purchased for the use of his office.

30. He shall annually, and as often besides as he may deem necessary, prepare a scheme for apportioning the money appropriated by the state for public free school purposes, among the several counties and cities, on the basis of the number of children between the ages of five and twenty-one years, in each school district, as ascertained from the census of the previous year, or in default of that, from the latest and best official authority accessible to him. This scheme shall be accompanied by summaries of the data on which the same is founded, and when approved by the Board of Education, a copy thereof and of the summaries aforesaid, shall be furnished to the second auditor, to each county superintendent of schools, and to each county treasurer.

31. He shall provide for his office a suitable official seal, with which he may authenticate official documents.

<small>1871-72, c. 108, § 11, p. 85. Code of 1873, c. 78, § 11, p. 682. 1874-75, c. 52, § 1, p. 38.</small> 32. He shall annually submit to the Board of Education, on or before the first day of November, a detailed report of his official proceedings for the year ending the thirty-first day of July preceding, exhibiting a plain statistical account of receipts and expenditures for public free schools, and of their condition and progress, showing the number of children, male and female, white and colored, respectively, in the state, and in each county, city and school district, between the ages of five and twenty-one years, the average and total number at school during the year, the average wages paid to teachers of either sex, the amount of each branch of school expenditure severally, the cost of education per scholar, and whatever else may tend to show the degree of success and usefulness of the system. He shall also be at liberty, and it shall be his duty, to offer suggestions to the Board of Education and to the general assembly, concerning matters pertaining to his department, at any time that the public interest seems to him to require it.

33. He shall discharge any other duties which may hereafter be required of him by law.

OF COUNTY AND CITY SUPERINTENDENTS.

Their duties and pay.

<small>1869-70, c. 259, § 12, p. 406. Code of 1873, c. 78, § 12, p. 683. 1876-77, c. 18, p. 13, and</small> 34. There shall be appointed for every county, in the manner provided for, in article eight of the constitution, one superintendent of schools. The regular term of office for such superintendents shall be four years, from the first day of July next succeeding their appointments, and in case of vacancies they

shall discharge the duties of their respective offices from their c. 243, p. 235, first appointment and qualification under the constitution until ₺ 1. their terms begin; and the term of office of superintendents, heretofore appointed and confirmed, shall expire at the expiration of the time for which they were respectively appointed.*

35. The compensation of county superintendents shall be fixed 1876-77, c. 243, ₺ 1. according to the population in their respective counties or districts, to be paid in quarterly instalments out of the state school fund. The said superintendents shall each receive thirty dollars for each thousand population under their respective jurisdictions for the first ten thousand, rejecting fractions less than five hundred; and twenty dollars for each thousand of population in excess of ten thousand, and up to and including thirty thousand, rejecting fractions less than five hundred; and ten dollars for each thousand of population in excess of thirty thousand, rejecting fractions less than five hundred: provided, that the pay of no superintendent shall in any case be less than two hundred dollars.

36. The salaries of county superintendents of schools, so far as 1869-70, c. 259, ₺ 63, p. payable by the state, shall be paid out of the bulk of the state 416. school funds, as distinguished from the appropriations from the same to the several counties.

Duties of Superintendents of Schools.

37. The duties of each county superintendent of schools shall 1869-70, c. 259, ₺ 14. be as follows, viz: Code of 1873, c. 78, ₺ 14, p. 683.

38. To explain the school system upon all suitable occasions, and to promote an appreciation and desire of education among the people by all proper means in his power.

39. To prepare annually, and at such other times as may be 1871-72, c. 370, p. 460. necessary, under directions from the Superintendent of Public In- Code of 1873, struction, a scheme for apportioning the state and county school c 78, ₺ 14, p. 683. funds among the school districts within each county under his supervision; a copy of which scheme shall be furnished to the county treasurer, and to the clerk of each school district, and also to the editor of each newspaper which may be published within the county.

40. To examine persons applying for license to teach in the public free schools, and if satisfied as to their capacity, acquirements, morals, and general fitness, to grant them certificates of

---

* The Act of March 29, 1877, makes the term of office begin January instead of July, but this was evidently owing to inadvertence, inasmuch as it conflicts with the Act of January 11, 1877, which is in accordance with the constitution.

limited duration, subject to revocation; all to be done in accordance with directions from the Superintendent of Public Instruction.

41. To promote the improvement and efficiency of teachers by all suitable and proper methods, under directions from the Superintendent of Public Instruction.

42. To assist in the organization of boards of district school trustees with the privilege of being present at all meetings of such boards, and of participating in the discussions of questions therein, but not of voting.

43. To visit and examine all the schools and school districts under his care as often as practicable, to inquire into all matters relating to their management, the course of study and mode of instruction therein, their text-books and discipline, the condition of the school-houses, sites, out-buildings and appendages; and in general, into whatever concerns the usefulness and perfection of the public free schools under his supervision; to examine the records and official papers of the school districts; to advise with and counsel the school trustees and teachers in relation to their duties, and to call especial attention to any neglect or violations of any laws or regulations pertaining thereto; and when necessary, to take lawful measures to abate nuisances, or to condemn, as unfit to be longer used, any school-houses, the occupancy of which, for any reason, is likely to endanger the health of the pupils.

44. To decide finally all appeals or complaints concerning the acts of any persons connected with the school system within his bounds, unless the matters in question are properly referable to other authorities: provided, that teachers or officers belonging to the system shall have the right of appealing from the decisions of the county superintendent to the Superintendent of Public Instruction.

45. To administer oaths and take testimony in all matters relating to public schools, whenever required, in cases pending or to come before himself or before the Superintendent of Public Instruction, or before the Board of Education; and also to administer the oath of office to district school trustees when called upon so to do.

46. To keep in a bound volume a record of his own official acts, and to file methodically all official papers.

47. To require from clerks of boards of district school trustees detailed reports annually, and oftener, if necessary, of the sta-

tistics touching the public free schools of their respective districts, as the said county superintendent shall prescribe.

48. To observe such directions and regulations as the Superintendent of Public Instruction may from time to time prescribe; to make special reports to that officer whenever required, and on or before the tenth day of September, annually, to make to him a report for the year ending the thirty-first day of July preceding, in such form and containing all such particulars as shall be prescribed and called for; and until such annual report shall have been received at the office of the Superintendent of Public Instruction, the county superintendent shall not draw his last instalment of pay from the state treasury. A brief abstract of the said annual report, unless the Superintendent of Public Instruction shall direct otherwise, shall be furnished to every newspaper published in the county. *1871-72, c. 108, p. 86, ¿ 14. Code of 1873, c. 78, ¿ 14, p. 684.*

DISTRICT SCHOOL TRUSTEES.

Appointed by Trustee Electoral Board composed of County Superintendent, County Judge and Attorney for the Commonwealth; who eligible; their duties and exemptions; how District Boards are organized.

49. On and after the first day of July, eighteen hundred and seventy-seven, vacancies existing or occurring in district boards of school trustees shall be filled by the joint action of the county superintendent of schools, the county judge, and the attorney for the commonwealth in each county, who are hereby created a board for that purpose, to be known as the school trustee electoral board, a majority of whom shall constitute a quorum: provided, that no person who is unable to read and write shall be appointed a trustee; and provided, also, that nothing in this act shall be construed to give any authority or power to said electoral board to interfere in any way with the appointment as heretofore of school trustees by municipal councils, or to disturb in any way the present law bearing on the action of said municipal councils in the premises. *1869-70, c. 259, p. 408, ¿ 15. 1876-7, c. 12, p. 9. Code of 1873, c. 78, ¿ 22, p. 686.*

50. The said school trustee electoral board shall have power, and it shall be its duty to declare vacant, and to proceed to fill the office of any trustee who fails to qualify, and to deliver to the clerk of this board his official oath in the usual form within thirty days after he has been notified of his appointment, which notification shall be promptly given by the clerk. The board shall also

vacate the office of any and every trustee who fails to discharge the duties of his office according to law.

51. The county judge shall be the chairman of said board, and the county superintendent of schools its clerk. Any member may call a meeting by giving due notice to the other two. All proceedings shall be recorded in a bound volume, and such record book, and such stationery and postage as may be required for correspondence with trustees, shall be paid for from the county school fund on the warrant of the said board in the usual form: provided, the cost of the same shall not exceed five dollars in any one year. It shall, furthermore, be the duty of the clerk of said board to furnish the Board of Education with a list of the county trustees and such other information as may be called for.

52. The clerk shall convene the said electoral board promptly when unexpected vacancies occur, and also at least thirty days before the expiration of regular terms of office, so that the district boards may be kept full, and no members be left to hold over unnecessarily. And in case of a failure on the part of the clerk to attend punctually to this or any of the other duties devolving upon him, he shall, for each offence, be fined by the board not less than one nor more than five dollars.

53. It shall be the duty of the county superintendent of schools to report to the said electoral board the failure of the clerk of any district school board to make and deliver his annual report in form and time as required by law, whereupon a fine shall be entered upon the record of the electoral board against such delinquent clerk of five dollars for the original default, and an additional fine of fifty cents a day for every day of continued failure until the report be delivered. The county superintendent of schools, as clerk of the said electoral board, shall immediately notify in writing the chairman of the district board of school trustees of the entering of this fine, and the amount shall be subtracted from the next instalment of the delinquent clerk's pay.

Who eligible as district school trustees; their exemptions; how organized.

1869–70, c. 259, § 16.
Code of 1873, c. 78, § 23, p. 686.

54. No supervisor or county treasurer shall be chosen or be allowed to act as district school trustee.

1869–70, c. 259, § 16.
Code of 1873, c. 78, § 24, p. 687.

55. Every school trustee shall, at the time of his appointment, be a resident of the school district for which he is appointed; and if he shall cease to be a resident thereof, his office shall be deemed vacant, and a successor shall be appointed.

56. Every school trustee shall be exempt from serving on juries, and from militia service in time of peace. _{1869-70, c. 259, § 16. 1875-6. c. 232, p. 290. Id. § 20.}

57. Each board of school trustees shall hold its first meeting at the call of the county superintendent of schools, two members constituting a quorum; and at this meeting, one of the members shall be appointed chairman and another clerk. _{Code of 1873, c. 78, § 27, p. 687.}

Duties of the board of trustees; estimate of funds for the scholastic year; care and control of school property; annual report; visitation of schools.

58. The duties of boards of school trustees shall be in general as follows, subject to be defined more particularly by the Board of Education and in other parts of this act, to wit: _{1869-70, c. 259, § 24, p. 409. Code of 1873, c. 78, § 31, p. 687.}

59. To explain and enforce the school laws and regulations, and themselves to observe the same.

60. To employ teachers, and to dismiss them when delinquent, inefficient, or in any wise unworthy of the position.

61. To suspend or dismiss pupils when the prosperity and efficiency of the schools make it necessary.

62. To decide what children, wishing to enter the schools of the district, are entitled, by reason of the poverty of their parents or guardians, to receive text-books free of charge, and to provide for supplying them accordingly.

63. To see that the census of children, required by section twenty-eight of this act, is taken in the proper time and in proper manner.

64. To hold regular meetings at fixed periods, to be prescribed by the Board of Education, and special meetings, when called by the chairman or by any two members.

65. To call meetings of the people of the district for consultation in regard to the school interests thereof, at which meetings the chairman or some other member of the board shall preside, if present.

66. Within thirty days from the passage of this act, and on or before the 15th day of November* in each year, to prepare and return to the president of the county school board, to be by him laid before said board at its earliest meeting, an estimate of the amount of money which will be needed in the district during the _{1871-72, c. 348, p. 442. Code of 1873, c. 78, § 8, p. 688.}

---

*This is inconsistent with the object of § 74, which requires the county school board to act in this matter before "the first Wednesday in November." The district boards should therefore see that their estimates are returned to the president of the county school board before the meeting of the county board.

next scholastic year, for providing school-houses, school books for indigent children, and other school appliances, and necessary, proper and lawful expenses.

67. To take care of, manage and control the school property of the district.

1871-2, c. 108, § 24, p. 86.
Code of 1873, c. 78, § 31, p. 688.
1874-75, c. 52, § 2, p. 38.
68. To report on any special matter when required by the county superintendent of schools, and to report to him annually, on or before August 15th, down to the first day of that month, on all subjects indicated in the blank forms supplied for the purpose, and until that report shall be delivered, the clerk shall not be allowed to draw his last instalment of pay for his services.

69. To visit the public free schools within the district from time to time, and to take care that they are conducted according to law, and with the utmost efficiency.

Of school districts; to be numbered and incorporated; corporate powers; boundaries; separate districts in town; trustees for towns; how appointed.

1869-70, c. 159, § 25.
Code of 1873, c. 78, § 34, p. 688.
70. School districts shall be numbered, or named, in the several townships, by the county superintendent of schools, and shall be duly reported to the Superintendent of Public Instruction, and recorded in his office and also in that of the clerk of the county court.

Id. § 26.
Code of 1873, c. 78, § 35, p. 689.
71. Each district shall be a body corporate, and shall be designated as school district No.   , in   magisterial district, in the county of   , by which name it may sue and be sued, contract and be contracted with, and take, hold, and convey property.

1870-1, c. 276 p. 367.
1871-2, c. 365 p. 458.
1876-7, c. 86, p. 69.
Code of 1873, c. 78, § 36, p. 689.
72. The districts shall correspond in boundaries with the magisterial districts, except where modified in the creation of sub-districts as provided for in section 77 of this compilation; and excepting further that incorporated towns of more than five hundred and less than five thousand inhabitants shall, if the council of such town so elect, constitute a separate school district; and such council shall have the power to appoint three school trustees, to serve one, two, and three years, respectively; and annually thereafter, it shall appoint a school trustee for said district, to serve for three years.

SCHOOL TRUSTEES AUTHORIZED TO BORROW MONEY·

County treasurer to reserve from township levy amount to pay loan.

1870-1, c. 183   73. The school trustees of any township that has levied a tax

for putting public schools into operation may borrow an amount of money not exceeding fifty per centum of such levy, at a rate of interest not exceeding that allowed by law, and for a period not exceeding six months. p. 202.
Code of 1873,
c. 78, § 32, p. 688.

74. Any board of school trustees who shall borrow money under the provisions of this act, shall notify the county treasurer of their county of the amount of such loan, when due, and the rate of interest, and such treasurer shall reserve from such township levy a sufficient amount to satisfy such loan and pay the same when due.

DUTIES OF THE CLERK OF THE DISTRICT SCHOOL BOARD.

To take school census every five years; to keep a record of his official acts; his pay.

75. It shall be the duty of the clerk of the district school board, during the month of June or July, eighteen hundred and seventy-five, and every five years thereafter, to take a census of all persons residing within the school district between the ages of five and twenty-one years, and to gather statistics relating to the interests of education in the district, according to forms furnished from the office of the Superintendent of Public Instruction. The lists thus prepared shall be submitted for careful revision to the district school board, as soon as may be after their completion, and shall at all times be open to the inspection of any citizen. They shall also be submitted, along with the other papers of the district, to the county board, at its annual meeting, and shall be immediately thereafter delivered to the county or city superintendent of schools. For this service the clerk shall receive out of the district school funds a compensation therefor, at the rate of three dollars per hundred for the children listed by him, subject to abatement or fine by the district board on the discovery before or after the settlement of the account of errors or omissions in the list, as provided in section forty of this act. All errors in the list shall be rectified by the clerk without extra compensation. It shall be the duty of the county superintendent to exercise special care in securing a prompt and accurate discharge of this duty by the district clerks. The duty of taking the census of the school population shall be discharged by no other person. 1869–70, c. 259, § 21.
1874–5, c. 56, p. 40.
1877–8, c. 23, p. 16.
Code of 1873, c. 78, § 28, p. 687.

76. The clerk shall keep in a bound volume a record of the proceedings of the board, and in another book a cash account and a record of his own official acts, and shall keep on file 1869–70, c. 259, § 22.
Code of 1873, c. 78, § 29, p. 687.

vouchers, contracts, and other official papers; all of which shall be open to the inspection of the county superintendent of schools, and of every citizen of the district, and shall be subject to such periodical examinations as shall be prescribed by the Board of Education.

1878-79, c. 78, § 30, p. 362.
77. The clerk shall discharge such other duties in connection with the school business of the district as may be required of him, and for his services he may be allowed, out of the district funds, not exceeding two dollars a day for every day of service rendered: provided, that the whole amount received by him for any one year shall not be greater than at the rate of two dollars for each public free school conducted according to law in his district within that year.

COUNTY SCHOOL BOARDS—THEIR POWERS AND DUTIES.

What property is vested in the board.

1871-2, c. 107 § 1, p. 81.
Code of 1873, c. 78, § 15, p. 684.
78. The county superintendent of schools of each county of the state, or in case there are two in a county, both of such superintendents, together with the district school trustees in each county, including those in cities of the second class, shall, for certain purposes hereinafter specified, constitute a body corporate under the style of "The County School Board of   County," and may, in its corporate capacity, sue and be sued, contract and be contracted with, and take, hold and convey property. This board shall be subject to the higher authorities in like manner as the district boards.

Id. § 2.
79. The county superintendent of schools for each county shall be *ex-officio* president of the county school board, or if there be two superintendents, the one first appointed shall be president, and the other shall be vice-president of the board. Should there be but one superintendent of schools in the county, it shall be the duty of the county school board, at its first meeting, and on the occurrence of a vacancy afterwards, to elect one of its members vice-president.

Id. § 3.
80. It shall be the duty of the president to call meetings of the board whenever, in his judgment, such meetings are needed, and also whenever requested to do so by two chairman of the district boards in his county.

Id. § 4.
81. The county school board shall make and record, in a bound volume, by-laws and regulations for its own government and for

carrying out all duties imposed upon it by law; and it shall keep, in another bound volume, a record of the proceedings of each meeting. It may appoint a clerk at discretion, who shall receive as compensation two dollars per day for each day actually employed; which compensation, together with necessary contingent expenses attending the transaction of business by the board, may be paid out of any funds under the control of the board.

82. The board shall hold a regular annual meeting between the first and fifteenth of August, the exact day to be fixed by the board itself, or in default thereof, by the president. Id. ? 5. 1874–5, c. 52, ? 3, p. 38. Code of 1873, c. 78, ? 19, p. 685.

83. All money, bonds, stocks, debts, funds, effects and other property, real or personal, now held by individuals by virtue of their late office of school commissioner or overseers of the poor of any of the counties of this commonwealth, except the county of Loudoun, under any act heretofore passed by the general assembly of Virginia, acquired by or derived from the sale of Glebe lands, or from any other source, formerly belonging to any of the said counties, and applicable to school purposes; also such real or personal estate in any of the said counties as belonged to the former board of the Literary Fund, together with any other funds or property which was in any manner set apart for school purposes, but which has been practically abandoned or is without trustees; and any funds or property that may be hereafter set apart for public free school purposes, and all donations by will, deed or other conveyance, heretofore or hereafter made for school purposes, shall, on and after the passage of this act, be vested in the said county school board of the said counties respectively, unless inconsistent with the grant or devise, upon such terms and conditions for the security of the same as the court of said county shall prescribe. The said board shall, when not inconsistent with the terms of the grant or devise, invest and manage the same, and apply the profits thereof for the purposes of education, in the same manner and under the same restrictions as the general school fund of the state is applied under the general school law of the state, except that the said boards are authorized to apply such portions of the profits of the funds as in their judgment may be necessary to the erection of school houses in their said counties respectively, or to the purchase of school apparatus for the use of schools; and provided further, that such disposition is not in conflict with the will of the grantor or testator. In cases where funds or other property are held by trustees for purposes of common school education, the county school board shall have power, and it shall be its duty, to examine into the manner in which such
1871–72, c. 107, ? 8. Code of 1873, c. 78, ? 20, p. 685.

trusts are administered; and all such trustees are hereby required to render reports to the county board whenever called on, and to afford every facility wanted by said board in order to obtain a full understanding of all the points connected with such administration; and should such examination reveal any defect or irregularity in the administration of such trust funds or other property, it shall be the duty of the county school board to take immediate measures for carrying the matter before the civil courts. In cases where donations or other funds have been set apart for the education of the poor, the county school board is authorized to receive and apply the same in connection with the public free schools, in obedience to the will of the donor. The county school board of any county may employ counsel and provide for and direct the payment of reasonable attorney's fees, whenever such action may be necessary for effectuating the purposes and objects of this section, or for the protection of the public schools of the county, or of any school district thereof from loss or detriment from any cause: provided, that no such fee shall be paid or allowed by such board unless and until the same shall have been approved by the court in which such litigation was had; and provided further, that nothing in this act contained shall be construed to apply to the twenty-fifth clause of the will of Samuel Miller, deceased, or in any wise to affect or impair any rights or interests whatsoever, either public or private, arising under said clause.

1874-75, c. 52, ¿ 2, p. 38.
84. The county school board shall make an annual report to the Superintendent of Public Instruction on or before the 15th of August in each year, which shall give in detail its official acts for the year ending the 31st day of July preceding.

Duties and Compensation of County Treasurer with Reference to School Board.

1871-72, c. 107, ¿ 7, p. 83.
Code of 1873, c. 78, ¿ 21, p. 686.
85. The county treasurer shall in all cases collect, disburse or invest the funds placed under the control of the county school board by the provisions of this act, in accordance with the direction of said board, and shall receive such compensation as the board may determine, provided that the same shall not be less than one nor more than two per cent. upon the amount received. For the proper application of all such funds, he and his sureties upon his official bond shall be liable.

General Rules for Officers.

1869-70, c. 259, ¿ 28, p.
86. Higher officers may temporarily discharge, or make special

provision for the discharge of, the duties of the lower, in cases of absence, neglect, disability, or unsupplied vacancy.

^{410.} Code of 1873, c. 78, § 37, p. 669.
Id. § 29.

87. No member of the Board of Education, nor any county superintendent of schools, nor school trustee, nor any other school officer, nor any teacher of a public free school, shall have any pecuniary interest, directly or indirectly in supplying books, maps, school furniture, or apparatus to the public free schools of this state, nor shall act as agent for any author, publisher, bookseller, or dealer in any such school furniture or apparatus, or directly or indirectly receive any gift, emolument, reward or promise of reward, for his influence in recommending or procuring the use of any book, map, or school apparatus or furniture of any kind in any public free school of this state. And any school officer or teacher who shall violate this provision, besides being removed from his post, shall be subject to a penalty of not less than ten nor more than five hundred dollars. Exceptions to the requirements of this section may be made by the Board of Education, in the case of a school officer being the author of school books or maps, or the inventor of school furniture or apparatus, in which case the Board of Education may, at its discretion, make specific arrangements whereby such school officer may, if his book or invention be adopted by proper authority, enjoy the benefits of the proceeds thereof without offence: provided, that no unfair advantage be allowed over other competitors in securing the adoption of the book or invention.

88. All school officers going out of office shall deliver to their successors the records and all official papers belonging to the office. In case of the refusal or failure of any officer to do so on demand by his successor, he shall forfeit not less than twenty-five nor more than one hundred dollars therefor, and a like penalty for each month during which he shall persist in withholding the same.

89. Any county superintendent of schools, school trustee, or other school officer, or any teacher in a public free school, who shall, by malfeasance or neglect, offend against the provisions of this act, if no other specific penalty be prescribed, shall be subject to a fine of not less than five nor more than fifty dollars for each offence.

90. All penalties and forfeitures imposed by this act upon a county superintendent of schools, shall be for the benefit of the public free schools of the county, and all penalties imposed upon school trustees, or other district school officers, or upon teachers, shall be for the benefit of the public free schools of the district

where the offence is committed. The suit for such penalties shall be in the name of the commonwealth, and if prosecuted in a court of record, it shall be the duty of the attorney for the commonwealth for the county to conduct the same. It shall also be the duty of the attorney for the commonwealth and any school officer of the county, or of any school district, as the case may be, to set such prosecution on foot: provided, that if a penalty shall be inflicted for any such offence by any of the school authorities in pursuance of this act, the party shall not be a second time subjected to a penalty therefor.

OF TEACHERS; THEIR DUTIES; CERTIFICATE OF COMPETENCY.

Contracts with them; may suspend pupils; their exemptions; meetings of teachers.

1869-70, c. 259, ? 33.
Code of 1873, c. 78, ? 42, p. 690.

91. No teacher of a public free school shall be employed, or shall receive any pay from the public funds, unless he or she shall hold a certificate of qualification in full force, given to him or her by the county superintendent for the county within which he or she is employed. No such payment shall be allowed, if made, and any officer who shall make or sanction it, shall also be subject to a penalty of not less than five nor more than fifty dollars.

Id. ? 34.

92. Every teacher in a public free school shall keep a daily register of facts pertaining to his school, in such form as the school regulations shall require, and shall be responsible for the safekeeping and delivery of the same to the clerk of the school district at the close of the school term, or of the period of his service, whichever shall first happen.

Id. ? 35.

93. Written contracts shall be made with all public free school teachers, in a form to be prescribed by the school regulations, before they enter upon their duties. Such contracts shall be signed in duplicate, each party holding a copy.

Id. ? 36.

94. A teacher of a public free school may, for sufficient cause, suspend pupils from attendance on the school until the case is decided by the board of school trustees, which shall be with as little delay as possible.

Id. ? 37.

95. A teacher of a public free school, whilst acting as such, during vacation as well as during the school term, shall enjoy the same exemptions which are granted to school trustees.

Id. ? 38.

96. The board of education shall have power, at its discretion, to invite and encourage meetings of teachers at convenient places, and to procure addresses to be made before such meetings, touching the processes of school organization, discipline, and instruc-

tion: provided, that no public money shall be expended for the purposes of this section.

OF SCHOOLS AND SCHOOL PROPERTY.

97. School houses, school furniture, school apparatus, and all other school property pertaining to each school district, shall be vested in such district, and held by it as a corporation, in pursuance of section seventy-five preceding. Id. § 39.

PROPERTY DONATED TO PUBLIC SCHOOLS VESTED IN COUNTY SCHOOL BOARD.

Donated to school districts vested in trustees of district.

98. When real or personal property is, or has been, donated to any county for the benefit of public free schools within its limits, the same shall be vested in the county school board of the county, and the same shall be managed and applied by the said county school board; and when given to a school district, shall be vested in the trustees of the said school district as a corporate body, and shall be managed and applied by the said school trustees of such district according to the wishes of the donor, under regulations prescribed by the county school board; and in case of any change in the limits of the district, the county school board shall make provision for the continued fulfilment of the purposes of such donors as far as practicable. Id. § 40. 1871–72, c. 107, § 8, p. 83.

TO AUTHORIZE SCHOOL TRUSTEES TO PERMIT UNUSED AND UNOCCUPIED PUBLIC FREE SCHOOL-HOUSES

To be occupied by teachers other than those employed by school trustees.

99. That where in any school district the school-house belonging to the public free school of said district is unoccupied and unused for public free school purposes, because of want of school funds to employ a teacher therefor, it shall be lawful for the school trustees for the district in which said school-house is situated to permit the same, under such regulations and rules as to them may seem proper, to be occupied and used for school purposes by any teacher, though not employed by said school board: provided, that such arrangement shall not in anywise interfere with or prevent said school-house being occupied and used at any time by said trustees for public free school purposes. 1878–79, c. 200, § 1, p. 173.

SCHOOL-HOUSES AND FURNITURE, HOW PROVIDED.

Appeal to board of reference from action of district board in fixing location of school-house; appeals in other cases to the board from action of district boards.

1871-72, c
370, § 41, p.
461.
1874-75, c.
310, p. 392.
1876-77, c.
79, p. 65.
Code 1873, c.
78, § 53, p.
892.

100. The board of school trustees shall provide suitable school-houses with proper furniture and appliances in every school district; and to that end may hire, purchase, or build such houses according to the exigencies of the district and the means at their disposal: provided, that any five heads of families belonging to the district, who may feel aggrieved by the action of the district board in fixing the location of a school-house on a particular spot, or in discontinuing a school, which they may have established by employing and paying a teacher in any house they may have purchased, hired, or occupied free of rent for the purposes of said school, shall be allowed to appeal from such action to a special board of reference, to be composed of the county superintendent as president, and any two trustees whom he may associate with him from any other district in the county, except the one concerned; and on the written request of heads of families aforesaid, addressed to the county superintendent, it shall be the duty of that officer, without unnecessary delay, to call a meeting of the board of reference at or near the disputed place or places, giving due notice to all parties concerned. And if, at the time and place appointed, the board of reference be present, the said board shall proceed to hear both sides of the case, to examine in person all competing locations, and to decide where the school-house in question shall stand; or, as the case may be, whether the school in question shall be continued as a public free school; which decision shall be final. This board shall have jurisdiction over all questions which shall be presented to its consideration by similar appeal concerning the action of the district board in respect to any subject on which the district board now has final power. Any action taken by this board of reference shall be duly recorded in the record book of the district board whose action is reviewed, and also in the book of the county superintendent of schools.

CONDEMNATION OF LAND FOR SCHOOL-HOUSES.

1869-70, c.
259, § 42, p.
412.
1874, c. 302,
p. 447.
Code 1873, c.
78, § 54, p.
693.

101. If in the judgment of such school trustees the public interests demand that a school-house be located on a particula spot, and no equitable arrangement for its purchase prove to be practicable, the board of trustees shall be authorized, and it shall

be its duty, to cause the desired parcel of land to be surveyed by the county or other competent surveyor, and a plat of the same to be filed together with a general statement of the case, with the clerk of the county court, and thereupon shall ensue the same proceedings as are prescribed to enable a company, county or town to take land without the owner's consent in section six to twenty-one inclusive, of chapter fifty-six of the Code of eighteen hundred and seventy-three, or in any amendment of the same or other law providing for the condemnation of lands for such purposes: provided, that no parcel of land thus condemned shall exceed forty square poles in a city, eighty square poles in an incorporated town, or five acres in the country; and provided also that no dwelling, yard, garden, or orchard, shall be invaded, nor in an unincorporated village any space within one hundred feet of a dwelling, nor in the country any space within four hundred yards of a mansion house without the consent of the owner; and provided further, that if the land condemned, lying in a county outside of a city or incorporated town, shall cease to be used for the purpose aforesaid for five years continuously, the title thereto shall revert to the original owner, his heirs or assigns.

STYLE AND EXPENSE OF STRUCTURE OF SCHOOL HOUSES.

102. In erecting or providing school-houses for public free schools, the utmost economy shall be observed consistent with health and decency, and no house shall be erected without first consulting with the county superintendent concerning the style of the structure and the arrangements about the buildings and grounds. No public school shall be allowed in any building which is not in such condition and provided with such conveniences as are required by a due regard to decency and health; and when a school house shall appear to the county superintendent of schools to be thus unfit for occupancy, it shall be his duty to condemn the same, and immediately to give notice thereof in writing to the chairman of the board of district school trustees, and thenceforth no public free school shall be held therein, nor shall any part of the state or county fund be applied to support any school in such house until the county superintendent shall certify in writing to the board of district school trustees that he is satisfied with the condition of such building and with the appliances pertaining thereto.

[1869-70, c. 259, § 43, p. 413. Code 1873, c. 78, § 55, p. 693.]

SCHOOL DISTRICT NOT ENTITLED TO FUNDS UNTIL PROVISION IS MADE FOR SCHOOL HOUSES, &c.

Id. ₴ 56.

103. No school district shall receive any part of the funds unless it has made provision for school houses, furniture, apparatus, text-books for indigent children, and all other means and appliances needful for the successful operation of the schools.

When state funds to be paid for school purposes.

Id. ₴ 57.

104. No state money shall be paid for a public free school in any school district, until there is filed with the county superintendent a written statement, signed by the chairman and clerk of the board of district school trustees, testifying that the school has been kept in operation for five months during the current school year, or that arrangements have been made which will secure the keeping it in operation that length of time: provided, that in case of the unavoidable discontinuance of a school before the expiration of the time required, the Board of Education shall be allowed to relax the requirements of this section, and to decide the case on its merits.

WHO ADMITTED TO PUBLIC SCHOOLS; PUPILS FROM CONTIGUOUS STATES.

Pupils from adjoining districts; white and colored to be separate; who excluded.

1869-70, c. 259, ₴ 43, p. 413.
Id. ₴ 47.
1871-72, c. 370. p. 461.
1876-77, c. 38, p. 28.
1877-78, c. 14, p. 10.
1881-82, c. 40, p. 36.

105. The public free schools shall be free to all persons between the ages of five and twenty-one years, residing within the school district; and the school board of any district bordering on another state: provided said state grants the same privilege to the state of Virginia, may, in its discretion, admit into the schools, free of tuition, persons of school age residing outside of the limits of the state, and near thereunto, if their parents or guardians pay taxes in the said school districts; and the Board of Education shall have power, and it shall be its duty, to make regulations whereby the children of one district may attend the schools in an adjoining district, either in or out of the county: provided that no school has been located and opened in the district in which the said children reside, and sufficiently near to attend the same, or if located and opened, that some unavoidable hindrance prevents their attendance; and the cost of their tuition be drawn from the funds pertaining to the district wherein they reside: provided that

white and colored persons shall not be taught in the same school, but in separate schools, under the same general regulations as to management, usefulness, and efficiency; and any violation of these regulations which will impair the efficiency of the schools, or any discrimination in the pay of teachers in the same grade of schools in any school district, shall be deemed sufficient cause for the removal of the county school superintendent by the Board of Education. It shall be lawful for boards of district school trustees, in their discretion, to admit as pupils into the public free schools of their respective districts, persons between the ages of twenty-one and twenty-five years, on the prepayment of tuition fees, under regulations to be made by the Board of Education: provided such admission of pupils over twenty-one years, does not, in the opinion of the district school trustees, impair the usefulness and efficiency of such school.

Who to send children to any public free school in any town or county school district.

106. It shall be lawful for any person who is a tax-payer and citizen of Virginia, owning real estate in any city, town, or county school district of the commonwealth, to send his children to any public free school in said city, town, county, or school district, subject to the laws regulating public free schools in said city, town, county, or school district, as though said tax-payer resided in said city, town, county, or school district. And any guardian who is a tax-payer for his ward or wards, as aforesaid, shall be entitled to the privileges above named for his ward or wards, if citizens of Virginia. 1881-82, c. 218, § 1, p. 232.

NUMBER OF PUPILS REQUIRED TO FORM A SCHOOL.

Regulations against contagious diseases; vaccination.

107. A minimum number of pupils, under regulations to be prescribed by the Board of Education, shall be required in order to form a public free school, and special provisions shall be made whereby minorities in a district, who might, under the general law, be deprived of the benefits of free school education, may enjoy a proportionate share of the school funds. 1869-70, c. 259, § 48, p. 414. Code 1873, c. 78, § 59, p. 694.

108. Persons suffering with contagious diseases shall be excluded from the public free schools while in that condition, and the teachers shall require of the pupils cleanliness of person, and good behavior during their attendance at the school and on the way thither and back to their homes; and no pupils shall be 1871-72, c. 105, § 1, p. 86. Code 1873, c. 78, sec. 6?, p. 694.

admitted unless they have been vaccinated: provided that the operation of this clause concerning vaccination may be suspended in whole or in part by the school board of any city or county.

WHAT TO BE TAUGHT IN SCHOOLS; TEXT-BOOKS AND FURNITURE.

1869-70, c. 59, p. 414, § 50.
Code 1873, c. 78, § 61, p. 695.

109. In every public free school shall be taught orthography, reading, writing, arithmetic, grammar and geography, and no other branches shall be introduced except as allowed by special regulations to be devised by the Board of Education.

How the higher branches are introduced.

1874-75, c. 226, p. 269.

110. *For the purpose of encouraging an intermediate grade of instruction between that of the common school and that of the college, it shall be lawful for any district school board of Rockbridge county (or of any other county, the county school board of which may elect to avail themselves of the provisions of this act), to admit into any one of the public schools in their district instruction in any branches necessary to qualify pupils to become teachers in the public schools, or to enter with advantage any of the colleges or higher institutions of the state; and for instruction in any other branches than those provided for in the first clause of this section, the said board of trustees may require a fee to be paid, monthly or quarterly in advance, not exceeding two dollars and fifty cents per month for each pupil: provided,

111. That the introduction of such higher branches in any school shall be first sanctioned by the county school board, and shall be discontinued whenever said board shall think advisable.

112. That they shall not be allowed to interfere with regular and efficient instruction in the elementary English branches, and to secure this end in schools having but one teacher, not less than five hours each day shall be given exclusively to instruction in said elementary branches.

113. That in schools having not less than forty pupils enrolled, with an average attendance of thirty, at least two teachers shall be employed, the whole time of one of whom shall be devoted to instruction in the elementary branches.

1869-70, c. 59, p. 414, § 51.

114. Uniformity of text-books, and the furnishing of school houses with such apparatus and library as may be necessary, shall

---

*The date in the margin shows that this act was subsequent to the act included in the preceding section. The two acts are inconsistent on their face, and must be construed so as to carry out the intent of the later act.

be provided for on some gradual system by the Board of Education. _{Code 1873, c. 78, § 62, p. 695.}

PREFERENCE TO BE GIVEN TO GRADED SCHOOLS.

115. In all localities where the number of children is sufficient, preference shall be given, under suitable regulations, to graded schools; that is to say, to schools in which the pupils are taught in different rooms and by different teachers, according to advancement—the studies being the same as in the schools which have but one teacher. _{1871-72, c. 108, § 62, p. 86. Code 1873, c. 78, § 63, p. 695.}

REGULATIONS AS TO NUMBER OF SCHOOLS IN STATE.

116. The number of schools in the state shall be according to the funds available for the purpose, and they shall be distributed, under the direction of the Board of Education, amongst the counties and cities, in proportion to the number of children between the ages of five and twenty-one years, resident in such counties and cities. _{1869-70, c. 259, § 53, p. 414. Code 1873, c. 78, § 64, p. 695.}

117. It shall be the duty of the Board of Education to guard, by regulation, against so great a multiplication of schools, in proportion to the funds provided, as will tend to occasion a low grade of instruction in the public free schools. _{1869-70, c. 259, § 55, p. 414.}

SCHOOL FUNDS; LITERARY FUND; OF WHAT TO CONSIST.

Board of Education to manage it; auditor annually to set apart amount for school fund.

118. There shall be and are hereby set apart as a permanent and perpetual literary fund, the present literary funds of the state, the proceeds of all public lands donated by congress for public school purposes, of all escheated property, of all waste and unappropriated lands, of all property accruing to the state by forfeiture, and all fines collected for offences committed against the state, donations made for the purpose, and such other sums as the general assembly may appropriate. The same shall be known by the name of The Literary Fund, and shall be invested and managed by the Board of Education, as prescribed in clause three of section seven of this act. The principal of the said fund shall always remain unimpaired and entire, and the annual income arising therefrom shall be and hereby is dedicated exclusively to the support and maintenance of public free schools in this state. It shall be _{Id. § 56.}

56   PUBLIC FREE SCHOOL LAW.

<small>1872-3, c.
275, p. 253.
Code 1873, c.
78, § 66, p.
696.</small> the duty of the auditor of public accounts, annually, to pay over, in money, according to the usual forms and general provisions of law, all that portion of the annual revenue of the state which is set apart for public free school purposes.

OF WHAT THE FUNDS FOR PUBLIC FREE SCHOOLS TO CONSIST.

<small>1869-70, c.
259, § 57.
Code 1873, c.
78, § 67, p.
696.</small> 119. The funds applicable annually to the establishment, support and maintenance of public free schools in this state, shall consist of—

120. State funds, embracing the annual interest on the literary fund, a capitation tax of not exceeding one dollar per annum on every male citizen who has attained the age of twenty-one years, and such tax on property, not less than one mill nor more than five mills on the dollar, as the general assembly shall from time to time order to be levied.

<small>1871-72, c.
348, p. 442.
Code 1873, c.
78, § 67, p.
696.</small> 121. County funds, embracing such tax as shall be levied by the board of supervisors in pursuance of section 74 of this act, fines and penalties imposed in pursuance of section 41 of the same, and donations, or the income arising therefrom in pursuance of section 49 hereof.

<small>1871-72, c.
348, p. 442.
Code 1873, c.
78, § 67, p.
696.</small> 122. District funds, embracing such tax as shall be levied by the board of supervisors of the county for the purposes of the school district, in pursuance of section 74 and clause eight of section 31 of this act, fines and penalties imposed by section 41 of the same, and donations, or the income arising therefrom, in pursuance of

<small>1875-76, c.
145, p. 149.</small> section 49 thereof; provided that no tax levied by any county for public free school purposes therein shall in any case exceed ten cents in the hundred dollars upon the assessed value of the taxable property of any county, and no tax to be levied by any school district for public free school purposes therein shall exceed ten cents upon the assessed value of the taxable property therein: provided, however, that it shall be lawful for the board of trustees of any school district, or the county school board of the county, to include in their annual estimates for such school districts, and for the board of supervisors of the county to include <small>1872-73, c. 341, p. 333. Code 1873, c. 78, § 67, p. 696.</small> in their levy for public free school purposes in said district, any amount, which, together with any county tax levied in such district for the purposes of the public free schools of the county, shall not exceed twenty cents in the hundred dollars upon the taxable value of the property in said school district: provided, however, that in the county of Alexandria, if three-fourths of those voting on the question vote affirmatively, any school

district may impose on itself a tax not exceeding fifty cents on the hundred dollars. Any excess of such levy for district school purposes, over five cents upon the hundred dollars of the taxable value of the property of such district, may be applied by the board of trustees thereof to the payment of the salaries of teachers therein.

ESTIMATES OF AMOUNTS NEEDED FOR SCHOOL PURPOSES, HOW AND WHEN TO BE MADE.

To be submitted to board of supervisors; board of supervisors to revise estimates and levy tax necessary.

123. It shall be the duty of the county school board of each county, on or before the first Wednesday in November in each year, to prepare and file with the president of such board, to be by him submitted to the board of supervisors (of such county) at their earliest meeting, an estimate of the aggregate amount of money, not in excess of the maximum prescribed in the third clause of section sixty-seven (as amended by an act of assembly entitled an act to amend and reënact section sixty-seven, chapter seventy-eight, Code of eighteen hundred and seventy-three, approved March seventeenth, eighteen hundred and seventy-six), which will be needed during the next scholastic year for the support of the public free school system of the county.

1869-70, c. 259, § 64.
1870-71, c. 264, p. 359.
1871-2, c. 348, p. 444.
Code 1873, c. 78, § 74, p. 699.
1876-77, c. 243, p. 235.

124. The county school board of each county shall, on or before the first Wednesday in November in each year, after carefully revising the said estimates of the district boards of trustees, submitted to such county board in accordance with the provisions of the eighth clause of the thirty-first section, prepare and file with the president thereof, to be by him laid before the board of supervisors of the county, separate estimates of the probable, proper, necessary and legal expenses of the public free schools in each school district of the county for the next scholastic year.

125. It shall be the duty of the board of supervisors of each county, at a meeting which they are required to hold within ten days after they shall have been requested so to do by the president of the county school board, in such year, or at their first meeting after the said estimates shall have been submitted to said board of supervisors, to examine and revise the said estimates: provided, no money arising from such tax shall in any case be applied to the salaries of county superintendents of schools; except that in Nelson county the salary of the superintendent may be increased, and paid out of the county or district free school

funds, to an extent that may be deemed just and proper for extra duties imposed upon him on account of the Dawson school fund, if there be no power to pay for such extra duties out of the said Dawson school fund donated to said county.

126. It shall be the duty of the said board of supervisors, after carefully considering said estimates, to levy a tax upon the property of the county, not exceeding the maximum prescribed in the third clause of section sixty-seven (as amended by an act entitled an act to amend and reënact section sixty-seven, chapter seventy-eight, Code of eighteen hundred and seventy-three, approved March seventeenth, eighteen hundred and seventy-six), sufficient to realize the amount recommended by the county school board in their estimates for county school purposes, or so much thereof as the board of supervisors may allow; and to levy a tax upon the property of each school district for which an estimate shall have been furnished, not exceeding the rate aforesaid, sufficient to realize the amount recommended by the county school board for public free school purposes in such school district, or so much thereof as the board of supervisors may allow.

1879-80, c.
106, p. 82.
1881-82, c.
221, p. 233.

127. It shall be lawful, and authority is hereby given to the supervisors of a county, to levy a tax on the roadway and track, depots, depot grounds and lots, station buildings, and other real estate of a railroad company, and its telegraph lines, whose line or lines pass through such county. Such tax shall be equal to the tax imposed upon other property for county and school purposes, and based upon the assessment per mile of the roadway and track made by the state for its purposes.

SCHOOL TAXES; HOW ASSESSED AND COLLECTED.

Duty of commissioners of revenue and auditor.

1869-70, c.
256, § 58, p.
415.
1871-2, c.
348, § 58, p.
443.

128. All taxes imposed for public free school purposes, whether by the state, or by or for any county, or by or for any school district, shall be assessed at the same time, and in the same manner, as are state and county taxes for ordinary purposes; and in any county or district where such tax has been levied by the board of supervisors of the county, it shall be the duty of the commissioners of the revenue therein to assess and enter such tax in the copies of their land and property books which they return to the treasurer of the county.

1876-77, c.
133, p. 125.

129. Where two or more school districts are included in the same commissioner's district, it shall be the duty of the commissioners of the revenue, when they assess and enter the school tax

in their land and property books, to keep separate the tax for each school district, indicating by name or number the district wherein the property is taxed. It shall be the duty of the auditor of public accounts to have the land and property books of the commissioners of the revenue prepared with three columns, one for entering the county school levies, one for entering the district school levies, and the third for entering the name or number of school district wherein the property is taxed.

SCHOOL MONEYS; HOW RECEIVED AND DISBURSED.

County treasurer to collect taxes; his duties and compensation.

130. All school moneys to be disbursed in any county shall be received, kept and disbursed by the county treasurer thereof, subject to similar responsibility as in case of other funds by law committed to him It shall be his duty also to receive and collect all taxes levied or ordered by the board of supervisors of his county for public free school purposes therein, at the same time and in the same manner, and subject to the same provisions, regulations, restrictions and penalties, as are or may be prescribed by law for the receipt or collection of county taxes and levies for other and ordinary purposes. He shall keep the district funds in separate accounts from those of the State and county; but his books shall show whence and on what accounts the moneys were severally derived, and by what order, on what account, and to whom the disbursements were made. He shall make disbursements only in pursuance of an order or warrant, in writing, from the proper authority, in manner and form as in this act prescribed. For receiving, collecting and disbursing taxes or levies imposed for and by counties or school districts, he shall be entitled to the same commissions and compensation allowed him by law for receiving, collecting and disbursing county taxes or levies, and for other ordinary purposes. His compensation for disbursing moneys apportioned to the county from the state funds, for public free school purposes, shall be a commission of not exceeding two per centum upon the amount thereof, to be fixed by the county school board.

1871-72, c. 348, § 59, p. 443.

To pay to the public free schools the money set apart by the constitution and laws for their benefit.

131. The auditor of public accounts, immediately upon receipt of the land and property books of the several commissioners of the

1877-78.
1878-79.
1881-82.

PUBLIC FREE SCHOOL LAW.

revenue of the commonwealth, to make a calculation of the gross sum of all the funds applicable to public free school purposes for the ensuing year, of which amount he shall report ninety per centum thereof to the Superintendent of Public Instruction as an approximate basis for distribution, whereupon said Superintendent of 'Public Instruction shall at once make out and furnish to the auditor of public accounts a distributive statement of the amounts due the several counties and corporations in the state upon this approximate basis. Upon receipt of such statement, the auditor of public accounts shall issue his warrant upon the treasurer of the state in favor of the superintendent of each county or corporation, for the amount which each county or corporation is entitled to receive under said statement, which warrant, when endorsed by said county or corporation superintendent to the treasurer of his county or corporation, as hereinafter provided by the second section of this act, shall be paid by the treasurer of the state, or shall be accepted from such county or corporation treasurer as cash in all settlements for public revenue made by him with the auditor of public accounts, so far as paid by the warrants hereinafter provided for.

132. The superintendent of schools of each county or corporation shall, upon the receipt of such warrant, endorse the same to and deposit it with the treasurer of his county or corporation, taking his receipt therefor, who shall enter the same upon his books as a credit to said superintendent of schools.

133. All warrants drawn by district school boards of trustees upon the public school fund of the state, as now provided by law, shall, if approved by the county or corporation superintendent, be taken up by him, and his own warrants issued therefor, which shall be paid by the treasurer of the county or corporation out of any state funds collected by him. The county or corporation superintendent may issue his warrants in such sums, not less than five dollars, in which case the warrant shall be for the amount due as will best suit the convenience of the payee; but in no case shall he issue his warrants for an aggregate amount greater than the warrant received by him from the auditor of public accounts, nor shall the county or corporation treasurer pay any' warrant upon the state fund unless issued by the superintendent of his county or corporation, nor an aggregate amount greater than the said superintendent has credit for. Any superintendent who shall issue warrants to an aggregate amount greater than is provided by this section, and any treasurer who shall pay any warrant upon the state fund aforesaid in violation of this act, shall be

guilty of a misdemeanor, and be fined not less than five hundred nor more than one thousand dollars.

134. At the annual meeting in August in each year, the county school board shall compare the warrants issued by each district board with those issued by the county or corporation superintendent and report the result to the state superintendent of schools;

135. The auditor of public accounts shall furnish to the several superintendents of schools blank warrants, as follows:

Warrant No. ——.	No. ——.
Issued to ———————	Payable out of state funds.
For services rendered as Teacher	County of ——, ——, 188—.
———— in ————	The treasurer of —— county
district, public free school No.—,	will pay to ———— or order
for —— ——.	—— dollars, services as teacher
	—— in —— district school
	No. ——, for which this shall be your voucher.

This certificate shall be paid by the county treasurer on whom drawn, at its face value, in preference to other warrants, when

Signed by

———— ————,

Superintendent of public free schools —— county.

136. Should there be found, upon the collection of taxes, an amount greater than the approximate amount hereinbefore provided, due to the public free schools of the state for any one year, then the excess due the schools shall be distributed as now provided by law, and nothing in this act shall be construed to interfere with the same.

137. The auditor of public accounts is hereby directed and required, on the first day of April, eighteen hundred and eighty-two, and each three months thereafter, to turn over to the second auditor the sum of twenty-five thousand dollars in currency out of the proceeds of the license taxes, and continue to make these quarterly payments without further order, demand, or requisition, until full payment shall have been made of all arrearages due from capitation and property taxes, and all other sources, by mandate of the constitution and laws made in pursuance thereof, for the support of the public free school system for the years eighteen hundred and seventy-one, eighteen hundred and seventy-two, eighteen hundred and seventy-three, eighteen hundred and seventy-four, eighteen hundred and seventy-five, eighteen hundred and seventy-six, eighteen hundred and seventy-seven, eigh-

teen hundred and seventy-eight, eighteen hundred and seventy-nine, and eighteen hundred and eighty (with legal interest thereon computed from the end of each year without compounding), which when paid in as herein provided, shall be annually appropriated amongst the several cities, counties and towns of the commonwealth as other school funds are appropriated and supplied.

138. Chapter two hundred and forty-eight of the acts of assembly of eighteen hundred and seventy-seven-eight, and chapter one hundred and seventy-seven of the acts of assembly of eighteen hundred and seventy-eight–nine, be and the same are hereby repealed.

To return to the public free schools a portion of the moneys diverted therefrom

1881–82, c. 255, p. 262.

139. Whereas the Board of Public Works of Virginia, by contract dated February tenth, eighteen hundred and eighty-one, sold to U. L. Boyce and F. J. Kimball, acting for themselves and their associates, all the rights, title, and interest of the state of Virginia in, or to, or against the Atlantic, Mississippi and Ohio railroad company, by virtue of the covenant or mortgage executed by said company, dated December twenty-second, eighteen hundred and seventy, for the sum of five hundred thousand dollars, upon certain terms as to payment, and subject to the ratification of the general assembly; and whereas afterwards, to-wit, on the tenth day of February, eighteen hundred and eighty-one, Clarence H. Clark, on behalf of himself and his associates, including said Boyce and Kimball, became the purchasers of the said Atlantic, Mississippi and Ohio railroad at a foreclosure sale thereof, made under decree of the ninth day of May, eighteen hundred and seventy-nine, in the United States circuit court for the eastern district of Virginia, in the cause of Frances Skiddy and others, trustees, *vs.* The Atlantic, Mississippi and Ohio railroad company and others, therein pending, and said parties proceeded to reorganize said railroad company under the name of the Norfolk and Western railroad company, whereby and by virtue of sundry assignments, the benefits of said contract of February tenth, eighteen hundred and eighty-one, now enure and belong to said Norfolk and Western railroad company; and whereas by an act passed ——— day of ———, eighteen hundred and eighty-two, the general assembly of Virginia has ratified and confirmed said contract, and allowed the Norfolk and Western railroad company until the first day of March,

eighteen hundred and eighty-two, to complete the payment of said five hundred thousand dollars to the Board of Public Works of Virginia; and whereas out of the revenues assessed for the years eighteen hundred and seventy to eighteen hundred and seventy-nine, inclusive, a sum amounting to one million five hundred and four thousand two hundred and forty-five dollars and seventy-seven cents, and dedicated by sections seven and eight of article eight of the constitution of Virginia, to the public free school fund, was diverted to other purposes prior to the year eighteen hundred and eighty, as appears by reference to Senate document number twelve, Senate Journal, and so forth, eighteen hundred and seventy-nine–eighty, whereof up to the present time the sum of two hundred and twenty-five thousand dollars due to the public free school fund, has been restored to said funds; and whereas the general assembly conceives it to be its paramount duty, under the constitution, to restore to said public free school fund as speedily as possible, the amount so as aforesaid from it diverted; therefore,

140. Be it enacted by the general assembly, That whenever the said Norfolk and Western railroad company shall pay unto said Board of Public Works the sum of five hundred thousand dollars aforesaid, or any part thereof, it shall be the duty of the Board of Public Works to pay the sum of four hundred thousand dollars, part thereof into the treasury to the credit of the public free school fund, and subject to the draft of the State Board of Education, at the rate of one hundred thousand dollars per annum, to be expended by said Board for purposes of public education, and apportioned ratably among the school districts of this state as current revenues for similar purposes are apportioned.

141. The remaining one hundred thousand dollars, of the sum so paid, shall be paid into the treasury on special deposit subject to the future action of the general assembly, the same being intended for the erection and maintenance of a normal school for colored teachers, to be hereafter established.

HOW STATE FUNDS OTHER THAN THOSE PROVIDED FOR IN THE ACT APPROVED MARCH 6, 1882, ARE PLACED IN COUNTY TREASURY.

Treasurer to notify county superintendent thereof.

142. At the proper time each county superintendent of schools shall notify the county treasurer, in writing, that the state money apportioned to the county is ready for distribution, whereupon

1869-70, c. 259, § 60, p. 416.
Code 1873, c. 78, § 70, p. 698

the county treasurer shall forthwith make requisition in due form upon the second auditor of the state for the amount specified; and as soon as the money has been received into the county treasury, it shall be the duty of the treasurer to inform the county superintendent, in writing, of the fact.

HOW MONEY FOR SCHOOL PURPOSES

Other than those provided for in the act approved March 6, 1882, is drawn from county treasury.

143. The methods of drawing school moneys from county treasurers shall be as follows:

Code 1873, c. 78, § 71*, p. 698.

144. For the pay and allowances of the county superintendent of schools, so far as the same is to come out of the county funds, a warrant therefor in writing shall be drawn, signed by the county superintendent himself, stating on its face the ground on which such pay or allowance is claimed, and verified by his own affidavit; but if the county treasurer has reason to doubt the validity of the claim, or any part of it, it shall be his duty to withhold payment, and to state the ground of his doubts on the back of the warrant, and transmit the same to the Superintendent of Public Instruction, and finally to be governed by his instructions. But if the warrant be manifestly in accordance with the provisions of law the treasurer shall pay it.

145. For the pay of public free school teachers, of the clerks of boards of district school trustees, the cost of providing school houses, and the appurtenances thereto, and the repairs thereof, school furniture and appliances, necessary text-books for children attending the public free schools, in cases where the parent or guardian is unable by reason of poverty to furnish them, and any other expense attending the public free school system, so far as the same is under the control or at the charge of the school district or its officers, it shall be necessary first to obtain from the board of school trustees of the district concerned an order approving the claim, and directing it to be paid, which shall be duly recorded in the proceedings of the said board; whereupon a warrant in writing shall be drawn, signed by the chairman of the said board, and countersigned by the clerk thereof, payable to the order of the person entitled to receive such money, and stating on its face the purpose or service for which it is to be paid, and that such warrant is drawn in pursuance of an order of the board.

---

* Virtually repealed by the third clause of section 74 of ch. 243, Acts 1876-77.—S. P. I.

TREASURER'S ACCOUNTS, HOW RENDERED AND EXAMINED.

146. The treasurer of each county shall once a year, or oftener if required, render to the county superintendent an account of all receipts and disbursements of school moneys which have passed through his hands during the year, and exhibit his vouchers for disbursements; and the county superintendent, having examined the said accounts and vouchers, shall transmit the account to the Superintendent of Public Instruction, and report whether the vouchers are satisfactory. Code 1873, c. 78, § 72, p. 698.

REPORT OF THE COUNTY TREASURER, WHEN TO BE MADE, WHAT TO CONTAIN.

Reports of clerks of district boards; delinquencies of officers, how noted.

147. It shall be the duty of the treasurer of the county to furnish for the use of the county board, at its annual meeting August 1-15 of each year, a full report, together with his vouchers and other official papers, which contain all accounts, evidences of payments, and other transactions pertaining to the receipt and disbursement of funds for public free school purposes during the year next preceding; and in like manner it shall be the duty of the clerks of all the district boards to lay before the county board at the annual meeting their official record and account books, vouchers, contracts, deeds, and all other official books and papers pertaining to the school business of the year just closed. Upon the examination of these records, accounts and other papers, should there appear to have been any delinquency or irregularity in the acts of any treasurer, district board of trustees, or of any officer or member thereof, it shall be the duty of the county school board to make a minute of the facts upon its records, and to take such other action as the case or cases may require. 1869-70, c. 259, § 40, p. 412. Code 1873, c. 78, § 49, p. 691. 1871-72, c. 107, § 8, p. 83.

FINES FOR NEGLECT OF DUTY BY THESE OFFICERS; DUTY OF COUNTY SUPERINTENDENT.

Who may remit fines.

148. Should any county treasurer, or clerk of any district school board, fail to produce and lay before the county board his books and papers, as required in the preceding section, it shall be the duty of the clerk of the county board to enter upon the minutes 1871-72, c. 107, § 10, p. 84. Code 1873, c. 78, § 51, p. 691.

of that meeting a fine of five dollars against every such delinquent treasurer or clerk, which amount shall be deducted from the pay or percentage of such officer. Moreover, it shall be the duty of the county superintendent, before sending his annual report to the Superintendent of Public Instruction, to visit and examine the books and papers of every such delinquent officer, and to make a special report thereon in connection with his annual report. It is hereby provided that the county board shall have power to remit the fine of five dollars on the presentation of good and sufficient reasons for so doing.

SETTLEMENT OF OFFICERS' ACCOUNTS; LEGAL PROCEEDINGS AGAINST THEM.

Code 1873, c. 78, § 52, p. 092.

149. The county school board shall have power, and it is hereby expressly made the duty of said board, in the event of any delinquency or irregularity in the acts of any treasurer, district board of trustees, or of any officer or member thereof, to take such steps and institute such legal proceedings as may be necessary and proper in order to secure a complete settlement of the accounts of such treasurer, board of trustees, or officer or member thereof, and a full and clear exhibit of the transactions of said officer or board in connection with the receipts and disbursements of any funds for public school purposes, and to compel the payment over of any balance that may be in the hands of such treasurer, board of trustees, or officer or member thereof. The county school board shall have power, and it shall be the duty of said board to take such steps and institute such legal proceedings as may be necessary and proper to secure a complete settlement of the accounts of any trustees to whom any funds or other property for the purposes of common school education shall have been entrusted, and to secure a full and proper administration of the said trusts; and to this end they may apply to the courts for the removal, for good cause shown, of the old trustees, and for the appointment of new trustees, either in place of those so removed, or to fill vacancies, and to institute such suits or action as may be necessary to compel the payment over of any balances in the hands of the old trustees so removed, or to correct any defect or irregularity whatever in the administration of such trust fund or other property. It is hereby made the duty of the attorney for the commonwealth to act as attorney for the said county school board, and to institute such legal proceedings as the said board may think proper and necessary.

UNEXPENDED SCHOOL FUNDS, HOW DISPOSED OF.

150. All sums of money derived from state funds, which are unexpended in any year in any public free school district, shall go into the general school fund of the state for redivision the next year; and all sums derived from county or district funds, unexpended in any year, shall remain a part of the county or district funds respectively, for use the next year. But no sums derived from county or district funds shall be subject to redivision outside of the county or district respectively. 1869-70, c. 259, § 64, p. 417. Code 1873, c. 78, § 75, p. 700.

Of sub-districts; embrace the area assigned to each school-house; may include portions of two districts; how formed; what pupils admitted to school; three school directors to be elected, and mode of their election; provision for expenses of school; census to be taken of any territory added to old district; apportionment of money to conform thereto; school directors to choose the teacher; other duties of directors; these provisions not to interfere with authority and duties of county superintendent; Board of Education to give effect to this law; which shall not apply in counties where disapproved by county school board; act of February 5, 1875, repealed.

151. In due time before the opening of schools in the next school year, it shall be the duty of each district school board to determine by specified boundaries what shall be the area to be attached to each school-house for whites, and to each school-house for blacks. These areas shall be called sub-districts, and their boundaries may be changed, from time to time, at the discretion of the district board. The sub-districts for the whites shall be numbered with cardinal numbers, and the sub-districts for the blacks shall be lettered with capital letters. A full record of the sub-districting shall be made in the record book of the district. 1877-78, c. 161, p. 144.

152. Whenever it is found necessary for the convenience of the people, a sub-district may be made to include portions of two or more districts, or portions of two or more counties. Every sub-district thus formed shall be under the school board, on whose territory the school-house is situated. When it is desired to form a sub-district from parts of two or more districts in the same county, the matter shall be considered by the district school boards immediately concerned, and on their mutual agreement the boundary lines shall be established. But in case these boards fail to agree, either one of the parties may appeal to the board of reference provided in the act approved February 13th, 1877, and

entitled an act to amend and reënact an act entitled an act to provide for appeals from the action of district school boards in certain cases, approved March 30th, 1875. In like manner, when it is desired to form a sub-district from districts belonging to different counties, the boundary lines may be established by the mutual agreement of the school boards immediately concerned. But in case these boards fail to agree, either party may appeal to a board of reference, to be composed of the two county superintendents, together with the chairman of some district school board not concerned, to be selected by these superintendents, and the decision of this special board shall be final as to the first establishment of the boundary lines, or as to any subsequent changes therein. Any doubtful question as to the location of the school-houses in such sub-districts, as are contemplated in this section, shall be decided in the same manner as the question of boundary lines.

153. No children from beyond the limits of a sub-district shall be received into the school therein, except such as are included in some general order of the district board, or such as bring a special written permit issued by order of the district board, and signed by one of its officers. The district board may grant such permits not only to children residing in its own district, but to children from other districts, whose tuition is provided for by agreement with the school boards, from whose territory they come, and to any children from outside of the sub-district, whose tuition is paid for privately to the board: provided, that the privileges of children residing within the sub-district shall in no wise be interfered with injuriously by the admittance of other children.

154. As soon as practicable after the laying off of the sub-districts, and annually thereafter, the district board shall, with due notice, appoint a meeting of all resident tax-payers and heads of families at some convenient place in each sub-district for the election of school directors, and for other purposes. Should any district school trustee be present at the meeting, he shall preside; or, if more than one be present, the one holding an office, or the higher office in the board, shall preside. If no school officer be present, a chairman shall be chosen by a vote of the meeting in the ordinary way. The chairman shall appoint a secretary. It shall be the duty of the clerk of the district school board to furnish the meeting in question with a copy of this act (the same to be furnished to him by the Superintendent of Public Instruction), and such act shall either be read to the meeting, or the substance thereof explained to the same, by any district trustee who may be present. This being done, the secretary shall make a list of all

persons present who are entitled to vote. If it be ascertained that less than a majority of the persons entitled to vote are present, the meeting shall adjourn from time to time until at least *one-fourth* of the voters are in attendance. When it has been ascertained that the meeting is a lawful one, it shall then proceed to elect three persons residing in the district to serve as school directors, one of whom is to serve one year, one to serve for two years, and one for three years from the date of the meeting at which they are elected: provided, that at subsequent annual meetings, expiring terms shall be renewed by elections for three years. Vacancies occurring between meetings may be filled by the remaining directors, and appointments thus made shall be valid until the next public meeting. It shall be the duty of the secretary of the meeting to make report to the district board of the names and terms of office of persons chosen as school directors, and also such other action as may be taken by the meeting. No compensation shall be allowed to any officer provided for in this act. No one shall be chosen a director who is unable to read and write. Should the people, in any case, fail to appoint directors, the district school board shall make the appointments.

155. At the same meeting, or at an adjourned meeting, provision shall be made by such method as may be agreed upon for the current contingent expenses of the contemplated school, including repairs, fuel, and such like, but not including teacher's salary, furniture and apparatus; but no pupil shall be excluded from attendance upon the school by reason of the failure of his parent or guardian to contribute to these current expenses: provided, that this section shall not prohibit the district school board from making contribution in whole or part for the supply of these wants, when for good reasons, and especially in cases of general poverty among the people, it seems proper to do so. Special meetings of the people may be called at any time by the chairman or secretary on the application of any five citizens residing in the district.

156. In cases where sub-districts have been made to include territory which before belonged to other districts, either in or out of the county, it shall be the duty of the clerk of the board of district school trustees, as soon as may be after the sub-districting shall have been completed, and before any apportionment of school money shall have been made, to take a census, in the usual form, of the school population in any such addition of territory. One copy of such census shall be furnished to the board of trustees of the district to which the territory has been added, and another to the board of trustees of the district from which the

territory has been taken; and after the correctness of the census shall have been established, due report thereof shall be made to the county superintendent, or superintendents, concerned, and also to the Superintendent of Public Instruction in cases where the school population of counties is affected; and thereafter, all apportionments of school money shall be made in accordance with the results thus obtained.

157. The teacher for each *school district** shall be chosen by the school directors of that sub-district from among those licensed by the county superintendent, and when chosen, information thereof shall be communicated to the board of district school trustees, which shall in due time enter into contract with this teacher. The compensation of the teacher, so far as drawn from public funds, and also the time of opening and closing the school, shall remain under the control of the board of district school trustees: provided that this board shall, when practicable, adopt the system of opening every alternate school during the first five months, and the remaining schools during the second five months of the school year.

158. The school directors shall collect and apply the contributions provided for in the fifth clause of this section; shall attend promptly to any repairs needed on or about the school-house; shall make known to the district boards the wants of the school in respect to furniture, apparatus, and other appliances, and shall do all in their power to protect and improve the school property, and to render it comfortable, decent and attractive. They shall also support and counsel the teacher, and do what they can to secure justice and harmony among all concerned. They shall also do what they can to secure the enrolment and regular attendance of children at school, and to promote the appreciation and desire of education among the people.

159. Should any violations of the school laws and regulations come to their knowledge, or any practical difficulties occur which they are unable to control, it shall be the duty of the directors to report the facts promptly to the district board of trustees, which board shall continue to have ultimate power and authority in all matters pertaining to the schools. Moreover, if the teacher or any parties residing in the sub-district shall feel aggrieved respecting the acts of the directors, or any one of them, or by reason of the neglect of duty or improper conduct of any director, such teacher, or other party concerned, shall be allowed to lodge formal complaint before the district board against such director

---

* Evidently this means *sub-district*.—S. P. I.

or directors, and if the district board shall deem the complaint of sufficient importance, it shall give due notice to both or all parties affected, and decide the complaint upon its merits, either by dismissing it, or requiring some change of action, or, if it seem proper, by declaring vacant the office of the director or directors complained of: provided that to either party is hereby reserved the right of appeal from the action of the district board to the board of reference referred to in second clause of this section.

160. This act shall not interfere with the duties and authority of the county superintendent in respect to teachers and schools as heretofore provided by law. Nor shall this act be considered as applicable to cities or towns set off as separate school districts, except that such separate town districts are hereby empowered to extend their lines beyond the corporate limits so as to embrace the children in the suburbs, when the school boards of the two districts affected shall agree upon the same, and in case of disagreement the matter shall be determined by appealing as hereinbefore provided; and where new lines have been thus established, the apportionment of school money to the said districts shall be made to conform to such change.

161. It shall be the duty of the Board of Education to make any regulations which may be needed for carrying out the provisions of this act.

162. Except in the counties of Fairfax and Loudoun, this act shall not apply to counties in which the county school board shall, after due consideration, adjudge its provisions to be unsuited to its county, and as calculated to impair the successful working of the public school system therein: provided further, that after trial of one year of the operation of this law in the said counties of Fairfax and Loudoun, the county school board of either county, or any twenty-five heads of families whose children have attended the public schools may, if in their judgment the operations of this law be deemed injurious to the interests of education, apply to the State Board of Education for relief, whereupon it shall be the duty of the State Board of Education to make all needful inquiry as to the facts in the case, and it shall have power, and it shall be its duty either to confirm the law in its operation, or to suspend its action in those counties, according as the said Board may deem best for the interests of the public education therein. [1878-79, c. 199, p. 193.]

163. The act approved February 5th, 1875, entitled an act authorizing the division of school districts into sub-districts, and to provide for the management of the public schools therein, is hereby repealed.

UNIVERSITY OF VIRGINIA.*

University† continued; visitors, when and how appointed.

Code 1873, c. 80, p. 705.
1 R. C., p. 90, c. 34, §§ 2, 8, 9.

164. The University of Virginia shall be continued, and the visitors thereof shall be and remain a corporation, under the style of The Rector and Visitors of the University of Virginia. They shall be at all times subject to the control of the legislature.

1881-82, c. 46 p. 370.

165. Be it enacted by the general assembly of Virginia, That the board of visitors of the University of Virginia shall consist of nine members. The term of office of said visitors shall be for four years, commencing the first day of May, eighteen hundred and eighty-two.

166. That the offices of all the visitors of the University of Virginia be and the same are hereby declared vacant.

167. That the governor, by and with the consent of the senate, shall, immediately upon the passage of this act, appoint a new board of visitors for the University of Virginia; three of whom shall be selected from the division of the state in which the institution is situated, and two from each of the other grand divisions of the state. If a vacancy happen in the office of visitor, the senate not being in session, the governor shall fill the same for the unexpired term.

---

*In 1817-18 (p. 11 to 15) an act was passed providing for a university as soon as a site should be fixed; it appropriated $15,000 a year for defraying the expenses of procuring the land and erecting buildings, and for its permanent endowment. There was also passed on the 25th January, 1819, an act for establishing an university.—Acts 1818-19, c. 19, p. 15; 1 R. C., p. 90, c. 34. Temporary laws relative to it, since the first edition, are acts authorizing the rector and visitors to borrow $25,000 to erect a new building, (Acts 1852, p. 28, c. 31); $25,000 appropriated to repair buildings and furnish a supply of water, (1853-4, p. 26, c. 36); and the acts since the edition of 1860 are referred to in the margin, or in the notes to this chapter in the present edition. By Acts 1872-3, c. 64, p. 42 to 45, the society of the alumni of the University was incorporated.

† By act of April 25, 1867, Acts 1866-7, c. 93, p. 898, $500 were appropriated for completing the work of raising and placing in position the statue of Thomas Jefferson. By act of March 29th, 1873, Acts 1872-3, c. 285, p. 260, the balance remaining on hand of the appropriation for the erection of the statue of Jefferson is appropriated to the publication of the address of Hugh Blair Grigsby, delivered on the occasion of the inauguration of the statue at the University.

168. The said board of visitors shall meet at the University at least once a year, and at such other times as they shall determine; the days of meeting to be fixed by the board. Special meetings may be called by the rector or any three members of the board. Notice of the time of meeting shall be given by the secretary to every member of the board. Five members shall constitute a quorum for the transaction of business.

How office of visitor vacated and vacancy filled.

169. If any visitor fail to perform the duties of his office for one year, without sufficient cause shown to the board, the said board shall, at their next meeting after the end of such year, cause the fact of such failure to be recorded in the minutes of their proceedings, and certify the same to the governor, and the office of such visitor shall be thereupon vacant. If so many of such visitors fail to perform their duties that a quorum thereof do not attend for a year, upon a certificate thereof being made to the governor by the rector, or any member of the board, or by the chairman of the faculty, the offices of all the visitors so failing to attend shall be vacant. 1852, p. 29, c. 32. 1822-3, p. 14, c. 10, § 2.

Rector and other officers; when and where board to meet.

170. The board of visitors shall appoint from their own body a rector, or in his absence, a president pro tempore, who shall preside at their meetings. They shall also appoint a secretary to the board. 1 R. C., p. 90, § 3. 1827-8, p. 14, c. 18.

Duties of the board; expenses of visitors paid.

171. The said board shall be charged with the care and preservation of all the property belonging to the University. They shall appoint as many professors as they deem proper, and, with the assent of two-thirds of the whole number of the visitors, may remove any professor. They may prescribe the duties of each professor, and the course and mode of instruction. They may appoint a bursar and proctor, and employ any other agents or servants, regulate the government and discipline of the students, and the renting of the hotels and dormitories, and generally, in respect to the government and management of the University, make such regulations as they may deem expedient, not being contrary to law. To enable the rector and visitors of the University to procure a supply of water for the University, they shall have authority to acquire such springs, lands and rights of way 1 R. C., p. 91-2, § 6, 8, 9, 10 1855-6, p. 80, c. 92. 1857-8, p. 116 c. 164.

UNIVERSITY OF VIRGINIA.

as may be necessary, according to the provisions of chapter fifty-six.*

Id.   172. They shall examine into the progress of the students in each year, and shall give to those who excel in any branch of learning such honorary testimonials of approbation as they deem proper.

173. Such reasonable expenses as the visitors·may incur in the discharge of their duties shall be paid out of the funds of the University.

When annual report to be made, and what to contain.

1822-3, p. 12, c. 10, § 2.
1855-6, p. 81, c. 91, § 1.
Code 1873, c. 57, § 44-5.

174. They shall, before the first of October annually, deliver to the second auditor a report to the general assembly, of the progress of the University, and its receipts and disbursements during the year ending on the first day of July preceding, with the amount of salary received by each professor, including fees received from the students.

Code 1873, c. 80, § 10.
1875-76, c. 120, p. 126.
1876-77, c. 82, p. 68.

175. Each professor shall receive a stated salary, and also such additional compensation out of the fees of tuition and other revenues of the University as the visitors may from time to time direct. He shall also have assigned to him by the board, one of the pavilions at the University, or other suitable residence (or commutation therefor), and such other accommodations as the said board may prescribe.

WHAT BRANCHES OF LEARNING TO BE TAUGHT.

1 R. C., p. 19.   176. The following branches of learning shall be taught at the University—that is to say: the Latin, Greek, Hebrew, French, Spanish, Italian, German, and Anglo-Saxon languages; the different branches of mathematics, pure ănd physical; natural philosophy, chemistry, mineralogy, including geology; the principles of agriculture; botany, anatomy, surgery and medicine; zoology, history, idiology; general grammar, ethics, rhetoric, and belles lettres; civil government, political economy, the law of nature and nations, and municipal law.

Board of visitors authorized to issue bonds to discharge their floating debt and maturing obligations; security therefor.

1874-75, c. 234, p. 176.

177. The rector and board of visitors of the University of Virginia are hereby authorized, at any meeting at which a majority

---

* See Code of 1873, c. 56, from § 6 to 22 inclusive.

of said visitors shall be present, to issue bonds of the said corporation, either registered or with coupons, for interest, or in part of the one class and in part of the other, convertible from one class into the other at the pleasure of the holder, in sums of one hundred dollars, or any multiple thereof, to run not more than thirty years, bearing interest at a rate not exceeding eight per centum per annum, such interest to be payable at such place as the board of visitors shall designate.

178. The amount of the loan hereby contemplated shall not exceed the sum of ninety-five thousand dollars, and the proceeds thereof shall be applied exclusively to the redemption of the existing debt of the University.

179. For the purpose of securing the payment of the said bonds the rector and board of visitors of the University are hereby authorized to convey, by deed of trust, all the real estate belonging to or held for the said University, and also by said deed to pledge the annual appropriations made to the University, subject to any previous pledge of said appropriation which has been heretofore made.

Annuity to University payable out of Treasury.

180. There shall be paid annually out of the public treasury thirty thousand dollars for the support of the University of Virginia, which shall be payable out of any money in the treasury not otherwise appropriated; but this annuity is on condition that the said institution during its continuance, shall educate all students of the state of Virginia, over the age of eighteen; who shall be matriculated under rules and regulations prescribed by the board of visitors, without charge for tuition in the academic department, consisting of the following schools, to wit: the schools of Greek, Latin, history and literature, moral philosophy, modern languages, natural philosophy, natural history and agriculture, general and industrial chemistry, and pure mathematics: provided, that no person shall be admitted as a student, free of charge for tuition fees under the provisions of this act, unless the faculty shall be satisfied by actual examination of the applicant, or by a certificate of some college or preparatory school, that he has made such proficiency in the branches of study which he proposes to pursue as will enable him to avail himself of the advantages afforded by this University. [1875-76, c. 102, p. 110.]

181. Out of the said appropriation of thirty thousand dollars, all necessary repairs, and the interest on the existing debt, shall first

be paid, and a sinking fund of one thousand dollars per annum shall be established and placed under the control of the board of visitors, to be annually applied to the liquidation of the principal.

Bequests to the University legalized; how to be invested and applied.

1872-3, c. 121
p. 101, § 1.

182. Any person may deposit in the treasury of this state, or bequeath money, stocks or public bonds of any kind to be so deposited, or grant, devise or bequeath property, real or personal, to be sold and the proceeds to be so deposited, in sums not less than one hundred dollars, which shall be invested in certificates of debt of the state of Virginia, or the United States, or any other state thereof, for the benefit of the University of Virginia; and in such case the interest or dividends accruing on such stocks, certificates of debt or bonds, shall be paid to the rector and visitors of the University, to be by them appropriated to the general purposes thereof, unless some particular appropriation shall have been designated by the donor or testator, as hereinafter provided.

Id. § 2.

183. If any particular purpose or object connected with the University be specified by the donor at the time of such deposit, by writing filed in the treasurer's office (which may also be recorded in the clerk's office of the county court of Albemarle county, as a deed for land is recorded), or in the will of such testator, then the interest, income and profits of such fund shall be appropriated to such purpose and object, and none other; or, if the donor or testator shall so direct in such writing or will, the interest accruing on such fund shall be reinvested by the treasurer of the commonwealth every six months, in the manner prescribed in the first section of this act, and the interest thereon be, from time to time, reinvested in like manner for such period as such writing or will shall prescribe, not exceeding thirty years; and at the expiration of the time so prescribed, or of thirty years, whichever shall happen first, the fund, with its accumulations, shall be paid over to the rector and visitors of the University, or the interest, income and profits thereafter accruing upon the aggregate fund shall be paid to them as the same shall accrue, according as the one or the other disposition shall be directed by such writing or will, and in either case the same shall be appropriated and employed according to the provisions of such writing or will, and not otherwise; and the rector and visitors of the University shall annually render to the general assembly an account of the disbursement of any funds so derived.

184. Such donations shall be irrevocable by the donor or his representatives; but if the authorities of the University, within one year after being notified thereof (which it shall be the duty of the treasurer to do immediately upon the making of such deposit with him), shall give notice in writing to the treasurer that they decline to receive the benefit of such deposit, the same, with whatever interest and profits may have accrued thereon, shall thereupon be held subject to the order of such donor or his legal representatives; and if at any time the object for which such donation or deposit is intended, by the legal destruction of the University, or by any other means, shall fail, so that the purpose of the gift, bequest or devise shall be permanently frustrated, the whole fund, principal and interest, then unexpended, as it shall then be, shall revert to and be vested in the said donor or his legal representatives. Id. § 3.

185. If the donor shall, in such writing filed as aforesaid, reserve to himself or to any other person the power to nominate to any professorship, scholarship or other place or appointment in the University, or to do any other act connected therewith, and he or such other person shall fail at any time for six months to make such nomination in writing, or to do such other act, the board of visitors may proceed to make such appointment or to do such act at their discretion. Id. § 4.

186. The state of Virginia is hereby constituted the trustee for the safe keeping and due application of all funds which may be deposited in the treasury in pursuance of this act. The treasurer and the sureties in his official bond shall be liable for the money or other funds deposited as herein provided, and separate accounts of each such deposit shall be kept by the accounting officers of the state in the same manner as of other public funds. Id. § 5.

Colleges and academies; visitors or trustees to make reports.

187. The visitors, trustees, or other body having the government of any college or academy established in this state, shall annually, before the first day of October, make a report to the second auditor, showing the condition of such college or academy, the state of its funds, the amount of its revenue, and the sources whence derived, its accommodations for and the number of its teachers and pupils, its fees of tuition, and the branches of learning taught in the institution.* 1829–30, p. 38
c. 48, § 13.
1832–3, p. 13,
c. 11, § 2.
1834–5, p. 254
No. 10.
1835-6, p. 7,
c. 4.
1846-7, p. 24,
c. 18, § 9.

---

* By act passed February 25, 1854, the Medical College of Virginia at Richmond was incorporated. After the first board of visitors, when vacancies occur, the governor supplies the same, selecting the visitors from each of the grand divisions of the state. The

Id.

Code 1873, c. 57, § 45.

188. If no such report is made from any college or academy which receives any portion of the revenue of the literary fund, or to which any loan has been made out of the said fund, the second auditor shall withhold (until the report is made) the payment of such portion of the literary fund, or proceed to enforce payment of the said loan.

Payment of interest on state stock to colleges and seminaries of learning.

189. The second auditor is hereby authorized and directed to draw upon the public treasury, in favor of the proper authorities of any incorporated college or other institution or seminary of learning, academies or manual labor school in this state, or the trustees may hold obligations of this state for any such college, or other institution or seminary of learning, academies, or manual labor school, or any department thereof, for all interest which has accrued, or which may hereafter accrue, and as the same may fall due, upon all obligations of the commonwealth, or the James River and Kanawha company guaranteed by the commonwealth, held by or for said college or other institution or seminary of learning, academies, or manual labor school, or to which they may have been entitled on the first day of January, eighteen hundred and eighty-two, so long as they may continue to hold the same: provided no interest shall be paid upon any bonds, the payment of which is forbidden by the constitution.

---

visitors and the faculty are required to make an annual report to the second auditor, such as is required by this section. Acts 1853–4, p. 26, c. 37. All such reports are required to be made on or before the 1st of October annually. See Code 1873, c. 57, § 44, 45. The word "October" in this section has been substituted for the word "November." The act of 1859–60 appropriates $30,000 for the purpose of enlarging the hospital or infirmary, for extending the college buildings, and for improvement and extension of the college museum; but the appropriation is not to take effect until the college shall convey all its property to the literary fund, by deed to be prepared by the attorney-general and approved by the governor. Acts 1859–60, p. 104. By act passed February 26, 1866, (Acts 1865–6, c. 331, p. 438), the sum of fifteen hundred dollars was appropriated for repairs and insurance of the public buildings belonging to the college, and for replacing apparatus destroyed by the troops of the United States.

By act of 1865–6, c. 130, p. 224, amended by act of 1871–2, c. 69, p. 48, the land scrip donated by congress to the state was directed to be sold and the proceeds, by a subsequent act, (1871–2, c. 234, p. 312), were appropriated in the proportion of one-third to the Hampton Normal and Agricultural Institute, in the county of Elizabeth City, and the remaining two-thirds to the Virginia Agricultural and Mechanical College at Blacksburg, in the county of Montgomery. These acts are inserted in chapter 77, Code of 1873.

In 1871–2 an act was passed to incorporate Jefferson College, in the county of Giles; required to report its condition to the Board of Education. Acts 1871–2, c. 180, p. 240. See also act to incorporate Norwood College. Acts 1871–2, c. 208, p. 270.

190. The provisions of this act shall apply to the obligations of the state known as the Dawson fund, held by the literary fund in trust for educational purposes; and also to the dividends on the stock of the old James River company, due and payable, or which may hereafter become due and payable by the commonwealth to such college, or other institution or seminary of learning, and held as set forth in the first section.

Scholarships; how established.

191. The board of visitors of the Virginia Military Institute,* and the visitors or trustees of the University of Virginia, and the colleges of William and Mary,† Hampden Sydney,‡ Washington,§ Randolph Macon,‖ Henry and Emory, and Richmond, may respectively establish scholarships in such institute, university and colleges, under such regulations as they may prescribe.¶

1847-8, p. 19, c. 17, § 2.

---

* The laws relating to this institution are to be found in Code 1873, c. 31. Those relating to the University of Virginia, in chapter 80, § 1 to 14 inclusive. By an act passed April 16, 1870, (Acts 1869-70, c. 51, p. 62,) the annuity to the institute for the year 1870 was made payable in advance. A similar act was passed in 1871 (Acts 1870-71, c. 300, p. 394).

† In 1660-61 it was directed that land be obtained for a college (Hen. Stat., vol. 1, p. 25, c. 20), and that a petition be drawn up to the king for letters patent—to gather the charity of people in England—(Id., p. 30, c. 35). The governor, council of state, and burgesses severally subscribed considerable sums of money and quantities of tobacco; and it was ordered that the commissioners of the county courts subscribe, and that they and the vestries of the parishes take the subscriptions of others.—Id., 37. Under a charter, bearing date the 8th of February, in the fourth year of the reign of William and Mary, the college was established by this name, near the church then standing in Middle plantation old fields.—3 Hen. Stat., 122, c. 3. Other acts were afterwards passed for the better support of the college.—Id., p. 123, c. 4; vol. 4, p.74, c. 3; p. 148, c. 1, § 20; p. 432-3, c. 15, §§ 9, 10; vol. 5, p. 236, c. 9; p. 317, c. 1, § 18; vol. 6, p. 91, c. 35; vol. 7, p. 285, c. 13, § 2; vol. 8, p. 335, c. 6. Under its charter, the college had a representative in the general assembly.—Id., vol. 7, p. 529, c. 1, § 27; vol. 8, p. 317, c. 1, § 24. It was deprived of this in 1776 by the operation of the constitution.—Id., vol. 9, p. 55, c. 4, § 4; note, p. 114, art. 5. After the revolution there was vested in it the land adjoining Williamsburg, called the palace lands, and some other property not required for public uses, (Id., vol. 11, p. 406, c. 34, § 3); and for some time there was appropriated to it a sixth part of the surveyor's fees (Id., p. 310 c. 4, § 1). The reservation to the college of a part of the surveyor's fees, as well as that of certain counties in favor of Randolph Academy, was struck out at the revisal of 1819; see 1 R. C., p. 324, note recited. The charter of the college is recited in the case of Bracken v. The College, 3 Call, 573, 1 Call, 161; a case involving the power of the visitors to change the schools and put down professorships.

‡ The college of Hampden Sydney was incorporated by an act of May, 1783. See 11 Hen. Stat., 272, c. 28, and 1 Munf. 324.

§ By an act approved February 4, 1871, (Acts 1870-71, c. 64, p. 60 to 62,) the charter of Washington College was modified, and the name thereof changed to Washington and Lee University. See also Acts 1865-6, c. 323, p. 433 to 435.

Funds therefor to be invested; donations irrevocable; donor's right to nominate pupils.

1847-8, p. 10, c. 17, § 2.

192. Whenever any persons shall deposit in the treasury of the state, or bequeath money to be so deposited, or devise or bequeath property to be sold, and the proceeds so deposited, for the benefit of such institute, university, colleges and academy, to such an amount that the interest thereof will be sufficient to educate and maintain thereat one or more cadets or students, the said fund shall be invested in state stock in the name and for the benefit of

Id. §§ 2, 3.

such institution. Such donation shall be irrevocable, but the donor or his heirs, or their guardian, if they be under twenty-one years of age, shall have the right to nominate and place in such institution one or more cadets or students, according to the regulations aforesaid.

Provision, if donor fail to nominate.

193. If such donor or his heirs, or such guardian, shall fail for one year to nominate as aforesaid, the said board of visitors or trustees may appropriate the income of the said fund to the education and maintenance of indigent cadets or students, to be selected by them from the state at large.

How society of alumni may provide a scholarship.

Id. § 4.

194. The society of alumni of any institution aforesaid may provide for and maintain a scholarship therein, by annual contributions, under such regulations as may be prescribed as aforesaid.

‖ By act approved March 29, 1871, (Acts 1870-71, c. 224, p. 326,) the sum of $110.16 was refunded to Randolph Macon College for taxes illegally assessed upon the college property.

¶ The words "Bethany and Rector, and the Northwestern Academy in Harrison county," are omitted. These institutions are now located in West Virginia.

VIRGINIA MILITARY INSTITUTE.*

Name of school; its annuity for support.

195. The military school established in the county of Rockbridge, near the town of Lexington, shall be continued under the

Code of 1873, c. 31, p. 270.
1815-16, p. 32, c. 16.
1825-6, p. 7,
c. 4.

* An act of the 8th of February, 1816 (Acts 1815-16, p. 32, c. 16), required the executive to select and purchase three proper situations for arsenals; one on the western side of the Alleghany, and two on the eastern side thereof, above the city of Richmond, and to have buildings erected for the preservation of the arms and fortifications for the defence of the arsenals. The executive had a discretion as to which should be built first; and that first erected was to be supplied with certain arms and guards before another was commenced. See act in Code of 1819, p. 93, c. 35, for regulating the militia, contained in ?103 to 113, and the act of February, 1816. Under those acts the Lexington arsenal was established. Further provision on the subject was made by the acts of 1823-4, p. 34, c. 31, ? 1, 2, 4; 1826-7, p. 10, c. 6, ? 1, 6; 1827-8, p. 10, c. 9; and 1834-5, p. 21, c. 21, ? 1 to 4. By the act of 1828, so much of the previous acts as provided for erecting any arsenal, not heretofore erected, was repealed.

1829, p. 17, c. 20
1841-2, p. 21, c. 24, ? 1.
1846-7, p. 18, c. 17.
1847-8, p. 15, c. 18.
1869-70, c. 259, ? 67, p. 417.
1870-71, c. 307, p. 403.
1871-2, c. 386 p. 487.

On the 22d of March, 1836, an act was passed (Sess. Acts 1835-6, p. 12, c. 12) for re-organizing the Lexington arsenal and establishing a military school in connection with Washington College. This act was amended by that of 1836-7, p. 20, c. 22. And the two acts were amended and reduced into one by that of 1839, p. 17, c. 20; which has since been amended by the acts of 1840-41, p. 55, c. 28; 1841-2, p. 21, c. 24; Id., p. 22, c. 26; 1844-5, p. 17, c. 19, ? 1.

On the 8th of March, 1850 (see Acts 1849-50, p. 16, c. 19), an appropriation was made for the erection of a new barracks for the cadets; and by act of 29th May, 1852, this act was repealed, and $30,000 was appropriated for this purpose. An additional appropriation was made for the same purpose on the 1st March, 1854; Acts 1853-4, p. 31, c. 42; and by act of March 31, 1858 (see Acts 1857-8, p. 115, c. 162), $25,00 more were appropriated to complete these buildings, enclose the grounds, and procure a supply of water for the institute.

The act of 1859-60, p. 103, c. 7, contains a preamble, reciting "that the present buildings at the said institute are insufficient for the purposes of the school as a military organization, and that additional appropriations are absolutely required to provide additional accommodations for cadets and for the support of the school, and that the corps of cadets in the course of their regular military education may readily be employed to prepare such munitions of war as may be demanded by the wants of the state;" and appropriates $20,000 "for the erection of such additional buildings as may in the judgment of the board of visitors be demanded for giving effect to the purposes of the act; the amount to be drawn in two annual payments: one-half in 1860, and the other half in 1861, upon the order of the board of visitors." The act took effect on the 28th of March, 1860.

By joint resolution adopted on the 8th of March, 1856, the governor was authorized to

name of "The Virginia Military Institute," and for the support of the said school the sum of fifteen thousand dollars shall be annually paid out of the public treasury." *

Board of visitors; their meetings; vacancies supplied; their pay.

1881-82, c. 201, p. 211.

196. The board of visitors of the Virginia Military Institute is hereby declared vacant. And the governor, by and with the consent of the senate, immediately upon the passage of this act, shall appoint a new board of visitors for the institute, which shall consist of nine members, three of whom shall be selected from the division of the state in which the institute is situated, and two from each of the other three grand divisions of the state. The term of office for the board of visitors shall be four years, commencing March first, eighteen hundred and eighty-two. Five members of said board shall constitute a quorum. They shall be and are hereby declared to be a corporation, and as such may sue and be sued for any cause or matter which has heretofore arisen, as well as for any cause or matter which may hereafter arise.

197. The board of visitors appointed under this act shall meet at the institute on the twenty-fifth day of June, eighteen hundred and eighty-two, or as soon thereafter as practicable, and proceed to reorganize said institute as the board may deem right and

---

contract with Wm. J. Hubard for a bronze cast of Houdon's statue of Washington, to be placed at the institute, and ten thousand dollars was appropriated therefor. This statue has been erected. 1855-6, p. 291, Res No. 12.

In 1861, Acts 1861, c. 36, p. 58, an act was passed appropriating the sum of one thousand dollars, or so much thereof as may be necessary, to be applied, under the direction of the governor, for the removal of the remains of General Harry Lee from the cemetery of P. M. Nightingale, Esq., in the Island of Cumberland, Georgia, to the public grounds of the Lexington Military Institute, and for erecting over them a suitable monument.

* This section has been altered It read in the edition of 1860, "the sum of seven thousand seven hundred and ten dollars shall be annually paid out of the public treasury, and in addition thereto fifteen hundred dollars shall be annually paid out of the surplus revenue of the literary fund, as directed by the fourth section of the seventy-ninth chapter," and by the 13th section the additional sum of five thousand seven hundred and ninety dollars is appropriated annually, which makes the sum of fifteen thousand dollars. That latter amount is omitted in the 13th section. By act of 1869-70, c. 259, ¿ 67, p. 417, the 79th chapter is repealed, and consequently the appropriation of the fifteen hundred dollars, contained in the fourth section, is also repealed. In consequence of this, an appropriation of fifteen thousand dollars has been regularly inserted into the annual appropriation law, which thus restores the amount now inserted into the section. See Acts 1870-71, c. 307, p. 403; 1871-2, c 386, p. 487. There have been several acts passed providing for the advance payment of the annuity to the institute for several years, but these laws are omitted as temporary. Acts 1869-70, c. 51, p. 62; 1870-71, c. 300, p. 394.

proper. They shall fix the salaries of the professors and officers, and may remove at will any officer who shall be appointed under this act for good and sufficient cause; but no order to remove a professor shall be made without the concurrence therein of a majority of the whole number of visitors; and the board shall forthwith communicate to the governor a full statement of the reasons on which the removal was made.

198. The board, after the first meeting under this act, shall meet at the institution, or other places than the institute, when in their opinion it shall be necessary to do so. A meeting shall be held annually at such time as may be designated for their annual meeting in their last resolution on the subject. A meeting may also be called at any time by the adjutant-general or superintendent of the institute, when either may deem it advisable. And the board may adjourn from time to time.

199. Any vacancy in the board of visitors shall be communicated by the adjutant-general to the governor, who shall forthwith supply the same.

200. Such reasonable expenses as the visitors may incur in the discharge of their duties shall be allowed by the governor and paid by warrant on the treasury.

Power to make by-laws.

201. The board may make by-laws and regulations, not inconsistent with the laws of the state, for their own government and the management of the affairs of the institution, and may, for the purpose of transacting such business as in its opinion can be properly transacted by a less number than the majority, authorize not less than four members to constitute a quorum.

The arsenal and its grounds vested in institute.

202. The arsenal and all its grounds and buildings shall be considered as belonging to the institution, and the board shall cause the same, and all the arms and other property therein, or belonging thereto, to be guarded and preserved.

Power to borrow money and secure its payment.

203. Whereas the library, apparatus, and most of the buildings of the Virginia Military Institute were destroyed by fire in the year eighteen hundred and sixty-four; and whereas, the authorities of said institute, for the purpose of restoring said loss, have contracted a debt which will soon become payable; and whereas,

1869–70, c. 152, p. 192. 1874–75, c. 9, p. 9.

it is desirable, so as not to impede the operations of the said institute, that the payment of the said debt should be deferred, therefore the said Virginia Military Institute, by its board of visitors, is hereby authorized to borrow a sum not exceeding sixty thousand dollars, and issue certificates of indebtedness therefor; said certificates being in sums of one hundred dollars, or any multiple thereof, payable to bearer, redeemable in twenty years, or in not less than five years, at the pleasure of the board of visitors, and bearing interest not exceeding eight per centum per annum: provided, that the amount realized from said bonds be used and appropriated solely to the reduction of the existing debt, which has been contracted in pursuance of law, of the Virginia Military Institute

For the relief of the Virginia Military Institute.

1875-76, c. 139, p. 146.

204. The treasurer of the commonwealth of Virginia shall pay to the superintendent of the Virginia Military Institute the sum of ten thousand dollars, annually, on or before the first day of July of each year, for the period of six years from the passage of this act, out of any moneys in the treasury not otherwise appropriated: provided, however, that upon the payment of each of the said several sums, the superintendent of the Virginia Military Institute shall deliver to the commissioners of the sinking fund the bonds of the Virginia Military Institute, for said several sums as they may be paid to him, bearing six per centum interest payable annually, and secured by mortgage upon the lands and buildings of the Virginia Military Institute, and made payable twenty-five years from their respective dates—the said bonds to be placed to the credit of the sinking fund, and the annual interest, as paid, to be invested by the said commissioners as they are now required by law to invest receipts on account of said fund: provided, further, that if the claim now before the congress of the United States for compensation for damages by the federal army in the year 1864, be allowed, the money now asked for shall be returned with interest.

205. The title to all property now held by the commonwealth, for the purposes of the said Virginia Military Institute, shall be and is hereby vested in the corporation known as the Virginia Military Institute for the purposes only of this act.

1874-75, c. 9, p. 9.

206. For the purpose of securing the payment óf the bonds herein authorized to be issued, it shall be lawful for the said Virginia Military Institute to convey, by trust deed, mortgage, or in

such other manner as the board of visitors may prescribe, all the real estate held by or vested in said corporations.

Amount to be expended annually for repairs.

207. They may expend, annually, a sum not exceeding five hundred dollars, in erecting, altering or repairing buildings, so as to have such as may be suitable, and proper for the military school.

Treasurer of the institute; his annual report.

208. The board shall, annually, appoint a treasurer, who shall give bond, with sufficient sureties, in the penalty of fifteen thousand dollars, payable to the commonwealth, conditioned for the performance of the duties of his office, which bond being approved by the board and entered at large on its journal, shall be transmitted to the auditor of public accounts, and remained filed in his office. 1839, p. 18, c. 20, § 2.
1840-41, p. 55 c. 28, § 3.

209. The treasurer shall, annually, on or before the first day of October in each year, make a detailed report of his accounts to the Board of Education, to be by them reported to the general assembly. The board of visitors shall cause a careful examination of his accounts, and a full settlement thereof to be made at least once a year.*

How professors are appointed and removed; their salaries.

210. The board of visitors shall appoint professors to give instruction in military science, and in such other branches of knowledge as they may deem proper. 1839, p. 18, c. 20, § 2.

GOVERNOR TO COMMISSION THE OFFICERS OF THE VIRGINIA MILITARY INSTITUTE.

211. The officers of the Virginia Military Institute shall constitute a part of the military organization of the state, subject to orders of the governor; and the governor is authorized and directed to issue commissions to the professors, assistant professors, and other officers, according to the rank prescribed by the regulations of the Virginia Military Institute. Such commissions shall confer no rank in the militia, nor entitle any person holding the same to any pay or emolument by reason thereof. 1876-77, c. 143, p. 129.

---

* The word "education" has been inserted in lieu of the words "literary fund," because the board of the literary fund has been abolished by the repeal of the 79th chapter of the Code of 1860, and the Board of Education has been invested with its powers and rights.—Acts 1869-70, c, 259, § 67, p. 417, and same chapter, § 1, p. 402.

ADMISSION OF PAY AND STATE CADETS; THEIR NUMBER, INSTRUCTION, AND SERVICE.

Id.
1870-71, c.
96, p. 151.
1872-3, c. 132
p. 108.

212. They shall prescribe the terms upon which cadets may be admitted, their number, the course of their instruction, the nature of their service, and the duration thereof, which shall not be less than two nor more than five years. All so admitted shall make full compensation, except such as are provided for in the following section.

1859-60, p.
103, c. 7, § 2.
1839, p. 18, c.
20, § 2.
1859-60, p.
103, c. 7, § 2.

213. The board of visitors shall admit as state cadets, free of charge for board and tuition, upon evidence of fair moral character, not less than fifty young men, in lieu of the number now required, who shall be not less than sixteen nor more than twenty-five years of age; one of whom shall be selected from each of the senatorial districts as at present constituted. Whenever a vacancy has occurred, or is likely to occur, due notice of the time and place of making the appointment to supply the vacancy shall be given. If, after such notice, no suitable person shall apply from any district, the vacancy may be supplied from the state at large.†

Power to make arrangement with Washington and Lee University.

1839, p. 18, c.
20, § 5.
1870-71, c.
64, p. 61.

214. The board may enter into arrangement with the trustees of Washington and Lee University, by which the cadets at the military school and the students at the University may respectively be admitted to the advantages of instruction provided at either place.‡

How commissioned officer of the militia may become a student.

Id. § 4.

215. Any commissioned officer of the militia of this state may become a student at the institute for a period of time not exceeding ten months, and receive instruction in any or all the departments of military science taught therein, without being required to pay any fee or charge for tuition.

---

† The words "and for the purpose of providing a fund for the support of the state cadets herein required to be admitted, the additional sum of five thousand seven hundred and ninety dollars is hereby appropriated annually; and the auditor of public accounts is hereby authorized and required to issue his warrant or warrants on the treasury for the same, in the manner that other warrants to the said institute have been heretofore issued," have been omitted for the reason given in the note to section 195. See note to § 195.

‡ The words "Washington and Lee University" have been substituted for "Washington College," the name of the college having been changed.—Acts 1870-71, c. 64, p. 61.

Cadets to be guards of institute.

216. The cadets shall be a military corps under the command Id. ₤ 2. of the superintendent, and constitute the guard of the institution.

Duty of superintendent as to arms; annual report to adjutant-general.

217. The superintendent shall from time to time inspect the Id. arms at the arsenal; cause the same to be kept safe and clean; give receipt for such arms as may be brought there to be deposited, and obey such orders for the delivery of arms therefrom as he may receive from the governor, as directed by the twenty-fifth chapter.

218. The superintendent shall annually, by the first day of October, make a return to the adjutant-general, showing the names and number of the officers and cadets at the institute, distinguishing those between the ages of eighteen and forty-five, and showing also the public arms, ordnance, equipments and accoutrements at the arsenal, and under the charge of the said corps. 1844-5, p. 17, c. 19, ₤ 1.

How degree of graduate is conferred.

219. The governor of the state and the board of visitors and faculty of the institute may confer the degree of graduate upon any cadet found qualified to receive it, after examination upon all the branches of the arts and sciences and of literature taught at the institute. 1841-2, p. 22, c. 26.

OBLIGATION OF CADET TO ACT AS TEACHER.

220. Every cadet who, since the eighth day of March, eighteen hundred and forty-two, has been or hereafter shall be received on state account, and shall have remained in the institution during the period of two years or more, shall act in the capacity of teacher in some school within this state for two years after leaving the institution, unless excused by the board of visitors; but this section shall not be construed so as to deprive such cadet of any of the compensation which he may be able to obtain for teaching. Id. p. 21, c. 24, ₤ 2.

Annual inspection and report of visitors.

221. The board of visitors shall annually inspect the public arms and other property at the arsenal, and make a report of their condition, and of the condition of the school, to the governor, to be by him laid before the general assembly. 1839, p. 18, c. 20, ₤ 2.

*How musicians are enlisted and paid.**

222. The superintendent may enlist musicians for service on that post, to be paid out of the annual appropriation heretofore provided.

Power to condemn lands and springs.

Id. p. 499, c. 291.   223. To enable the Virginia Military Institute to procure a supply of water for the institute, it shall have the authority to acquire such springs, lands and rights of way as may be necessary, according to the provisions of chapter fifty-six of this edition of the Code.

---

* The 22d and 23d sections of this chapter, Code of 1860, have been omitted because the 22d section is repealed by Acts 1866-7, p. 795, c. 27. It provided for bestowing military commissions upon the officers of the Institute. And the 23d section, relative to the enlistment in the public guard of a sergeant to serve as ordnance and quartermaster-sergeant at the institute, and to be allowed the same pay as other soldiers of the guard are paid, cannot be executed because the public guard has been abolished.

THE INSTITUTION FOR THE DEAF AND DUMB AND THE BLIND.*

Institution incorporated; its powers.

224. The asylum established "for the education of the deaf and dumb, and of the blind," by the act of the thirty-first day of March, one thousand eight hundred and thirty-eight, shall be continued, and the visitors thereof shall be a corporation by the name of The Institution for the Deaf and Dumb and the Blind, and be invested with all the rights and powers now vested in the corporation created by the said act, and be subject to the control of the general assembly.

Code of 1873,
c. 81, p. 711.
1838, p. 31, c.
19, §§ 1, 6, 7.
1839, p. 205,
No. 4.

Appointment of visitors; their term of office; president of board.

225. The governor shall annually apoint seven persons as visitors of said institution, who shall be a board for the government thereof. Their term of service shall commence on the first Monday in January in each year, and may continue until their successors shall be appointed. If any vacancy happen in the office of visitor, the governor shall fill it.

1838, p. 31, c. 19, § 1.

226. The board shall appoint one of the visitors as their president, and in case of his absence a president pro tempore. They shall also appoint a secretary.

Id. § 2.

Duties of board; removal of a professor.

227. The board shall be charged with the erection, preservation and repair of the buildings of the institution, and the care of its property, and shall direct and do, or cause to be done by officers, professors and agents appointed by them, all things necessary or expedient for promoting the objects of the institution, not inconsistent with law. But for the removal of any professor the assent of two-thirds of all the visitors shall be necessary.

Id. § 4.

---

* In Acts 1870-71, c. 198, p. 288, a joint resolution was adopted, asking congress to aid by an appropriation in the establishment of the American printing house for the blind and the American University for the blind.

Annual and special meetings.

Id. § 5. 228. The board shall have one annual meeting, and such intermediate meetings as they shall prescribe; the time and place of meeting to be fixed by them. A special meeting may be called at any time by the president or any three members of the board, notice of the time and place of such meeting being given to the other members.

Fiscal year; annual report to second auditor.

1846–7, p. 17, c. 15, § 6, p. 241, resolution No. 19. See § 18, c. 19, Code 1873.
229. Each fiscal year of said institution shall end on the thirtieth day of September, to which time the accounts of the institution shall be made up, and the said board shall annually, before the first day of October, deliver to the second auditor a report to the general assembly, showing the condition of the institution and its receipts and disbursements for the said year.

Schools for deaf and for blind; how pupils selected.

1828, p. 31, § 3.
1878–79, c. 244, p. 203.
230. There shall be in said institution one school for education of deaf mutes, and another for the education of the blind. The pupils of each shall be selected as the visitors shall prescribe, among such persons as are unable to pay for their maintenance and support, to the extent of the means of the institution, and also from other persons, residents of this state, on such terms for their maintenance and support as may be agreed upon. But hereafter there shall be no charge for the education of pupils.

Arbitrators authorized.

1878–79, c. 61, p. 833.
231. If the president and directors of a company incorporated for work of internal improvement, the court of a county, or the council of a town, the directors of the Deaf and Dumb and Blind Institution, of the Western Lunatic Asylum, of the Eastern Lunatic Asylum, and Central Lunatic Asylum, cannot agree on the terms of purchase with those entitled to lands wanted for the purposes of the company, county, town, institution, or asylums aforesaid, five disinterested freeholders shall be appointed by the court of the county or corporation in which the land, or the greater part thereof, shall lie (any three of whom may act), for the purpose of ascertaining a just compensation for such lands.

DEAF AND DUMB AND BLIND INSTITUTE.

Annual appropriation for the institution.

232. There is hereby appropriated* out of the public treasury, annually, thirty-five thousand dollars for the support of said institution, to be paid quarterly, on the orders of the board of visitors thereof, attested by their secretary and countersigned by the president.

_{1869–70, c. 425, p. 574.}

---

*Additional temporary appropriations have been made at different times: To pay for furniture and for arrears in support account, $6,000.—Acts 1849–50, p. 4, c. 1, § 1. To complete buildings, $2,500.—Acts 1850–51, p. 5, c. 2, § 1. To purchase a library, philosophical apparatus and organ, $2,000.—Acts 1852, p. 29, c. 35. Annuity increased from $15,000 to $20,000—for heating, lighting, &c., the same, $10,000—Acts 1852–53, p. 25, c. 9, § 1. Same amount of $10,000 for the next year, for same purposes and for an additional building.—Id, p. 126, c. 145, § 2. For supplying institution with water, $10,000.—Acts 1853–54, p. 30, c. 41. Addition of $2,000 for heating and lighting.—Acts 1853–54, p. 9, c. 3, § 1. To complete heating the buildings by steam and to meet deficiency in support fund $5,580.06, to purchase fire engine and erect engine house $1,000, for organ $1,500, for fencing the grounds $1,000, to supply deficiency on account of chapel, steam and gas fund $2,841.—Acts 1855–56, p. 80, c. 93. Annuity increased $5,000 for the years 1857, 1858 and 1859, out of the first years appropriation, $1,500 to be applied to purchase musical instruments for the blind department —Acts 1857–58, p. 118, c. 169, 170. Annuity permanently increased, making it $25,000.—Acts 1859–60, c. 12 and c. 5, p. 84, § 1, and for the erection of a shop building to warm and light the same with steam and gas $7,000.—Acts 1859–60, c. 12, p. 106. The payments to the institution for support are to be made one-fourth in advance on the first of October, one-half on the first of January, (if the visitors or directors so require), and the remaining one-fourth on the first day of April.—Acts 1859–60, p. 86, c. 5, § 3. In 1866–67, c. 105, p. 560, an appropriation was made of $15,000 for restoring, repairing and refitting the institution; and in 1869–70, c. 68, p. 73, an appropriation of an additional $15,000 to supply deficiency in previous appropriation.

VIRGINIA AGRICULTURAL AND MECHANICAL COLLEGE.

Donation of public lands made by the government of the United States to this state, accepted.

1863–64, (Alexandria), c. 21, p. 24.
Code of 1873, c. 77, p. 672.

233. Whereas, it is provided by an act of congress, approved July second, eighteen hundred and sixty-two, that certain donations of public lands (to be appropriated to the endowment, support and maintenance of colleges for the benefit of agriculture and mechanic arts) shall be made to such states and territories as shall signify their acceptance of their proportions, respectively, of said donations, and of the conditions and provisions of said act: therefore, the donation of public lands proffered to the commonwealth of Virginia by the act of congress of July second, eighteen hundred and sixty-two, with the conditions and provisions therein prescribed, the same is hereby accepted; and the auditor of public accounts, under the direction of the governor, is hereby directed and empowered to apply for and receive from the government of the United States the land scrip to which the State of Virginia will be entitled under the said act of congress, and that he hold the same subject to further order of the general assembly.

1869–70, c. 25 p. 28.

BOARD OF EDUCATION AUTHORIZED TO SELL THE LAND SCRIP.

1865–6, c. 130 p. 224–5.
1871–2, c. 69, p. 48.
1872–3, c. 193 p. 179..

234. The Board of Education is hereby authorized to sell, in the manner that shall seem to them most advantageous, the land scrip donated to the State of Virginia, by act of congress of the United States, approved July second, eighteen hundred and sixty-two, and the acts amendatory thereof; and with the proceeds of such sale, which have not been heretofore invested, the said Board shall purchase bonds of the State of Virginia, issued since July the first, eighteen hundred and seventy-one, or bonds of the United States, or any other safe bonds or stocks, not bearing less than five per centum interest, and shall set the same apart, and constitute them into an educational fund, for the endowment, support and maintenance of one or more schools, in accordance with the provisions of said act of congress.

Interest on proceeds of land scrip, how appropriated.

235. The annual interest accruing from the proceeds of the land scrip donated to the state of Virginia, by act of congress of July second, eighteen hundred and sixty-two, and the acts amendatory thereof, shall be appropriated as follows, and on the conditions hereinafter named; that is say, one-third thereof to the Hampton Normal and Agricultural Institute, in the county of Elizabeth City, and two-thirds thereof to the *Preston and Olin Institute, in the county of Montgomery. † 1871-2, c. 234 p. 312, § 1.

Conditions upon the grant of the annuity to the Preston and Olin Institute; name changed to the Virginia Agricultural and Mechanical College.

236. The said annuity to the Preston and Olin Institute shall be on these express conditions: Id. § 2.

237. The name of the said institute shall be changed to the Virginia Agricultural and Mechanical College.

238. The trustees of the said institute shall transfer, by deed or other proper conveyance, the land, buildings, and other property of said institute, to the Virginia Agricultural and Mechanical College.

239. The county of Montgomery shall appropriate twenty thousand dollars, to be expended in the erection of additional buildings, or in the purchase of a farm for the use of the said college.

240. A number of students equal to twice the number of members of the House of Delegates, to be apportioned in the same manner, shall have the privilege of attending said college without charge for tuition, use of laboratories, or public buildings, to be selected by the school trustees of the respective counties, cities, and election districts for said delegates, with reference to the highest proficiency and good character, from the white male students to the free schools of their respective counties, cities, and election districts, or, in their discretion, from others than those attending said free schools. 1877-78, c. 250, p. 238.

241. If at any time the said annuity should be withdrawn from the said Virginia Agricultural and Mechanical College, located at

---

*Name changed in section 237.

† By joint resolution, it is provided that the interest on state bonds held by the Board of Education, purchased with the proceeds of the congressional land scrip, shall be paid as the same is paid to other colleges—see Acts 1872-3, c. 50, p. 31—not exceeding one year's interest.

Blacksburg, in the county of Montgomery, the property, real and personal, conveyed and appropriated to its use and benefit by the trustees of the Preston and Olin Institute, and by the county of Montgomery, shall revert to the said trustees and to the said county, respectively, from which it was conveyed and appropriated.

What to be taught at college.

1871-2, c. 234, p. 312, § 3.

242. The curriculum of the Virginia Agricultural and Mechanical College shall embrace such branches of learning as relate to agriculture and the mechanic arts, without excluding other scientific and classical studies, and including military tactics.

Students, how to be selected; and their term at college.

Id. § 4.

243. The said students, privileged to attend said college without charge for tuition, use of laboratories, or public buildings, shall be selected as soon as may be after the establishment of the said school, and each second year thereafter: provided, that on the recommendation of the faculty of the said college for more than ordinary diligence and proficiency, any student may be returned by the said trustees for a longer period.

Visitors, how and when appointed; their term of office.

1871-2, c. 234 p. 312, § 1.
1872-3, c. 60,
§ 5, p. 88-9.
Code 1873, c.
77, p. 673-79.
1874, c. 106,
p. 94.
1875-76, c.
185, p. 221.
1879-80, c.
241, p. 236.

244. All the offices of all the members of the present board of visitors of the Virginia Agricultural and Mechanical College at Blacksburg, shall be vacated on the fourth day of June, eighteen hundred and eighty, and their successors shall be appointed in the manner hereinafter provided. It shall be the duty of the governor, as soon as practicable after the passage of this act and prior to the close of the present session of the general assembly, by and with the advice and consent of the senate, to appoint a new board of visitors, whose terms of office shall commence on the fourth day of June, eighteen hundred and eighty, and to consist of eight persons, four of whom to be designated as the first class, shall continue in office until the first day of January, eighteen hundred and eighty-two; four to be designated as the second class, shall continue in office until the first day of January, eighteen hundred and eighty-four, and on the first day of January, eighteen hundred and eighty-two, or as soon thereafter as practicable, and biennially thereafter to appoint four persons to fill the vacancies in said board, who shall continue in office four years, or until the appointment and acceptance of their successors. If a vacancy shall at any time occur in the office of visitor, the governor shall fill the same for the unex-

pired term thereof subject to the ratification of the Senate at the next session thereof. The Superintendent of Public Instruction shall be ex-officio member of the board of visitors of the Virginia Agricultural and Mechanical College, and of the board of curators of the Hampton Normal and Agricultural Institute; and the persons so appointed shall be distributed as nearly equally as practicable between the four grand divisions of the state.

Office of visitor, how vacated and refilled.

245. If any visitor fail to perform the duties of his office for one year, without good cause shown to the board, the said board shall, at the next meeting after the end of such year, cause the fact of such failure to be recorded in the minutes of their proceedings, and certify the same to the governor, and the office of such visitor shall thereupon be vacant. If so many of such visitors fail to perform their duties that a quorum thereof do not attend for a year, upon a certificate thereof being made to the governor by the rector or any member of the board, or by the chairman of the faculty, the offices of all the visitors failing to attend shall be vacant. [1872–3, c. 60, § 6.]

Rector, president pro tempore, and clerk of board.

246. The board of visitors shall appoint from their own body a rector, who (or, in his absence, a president pro tempore) shall preside at their meetings. They shall also appoint a clerk to the board. [Id. § 7.]

Meetings of board.

247. The said board shall meet at Blacksburg, in the county of Montgomery, at least once a year, and at such other times or place as they shall determine, the days of meeting to be fixed by them. Special meetings of the board may be called by the governor, the rector, or any three members. In either of said cases, notice of the time and place of meeting shall be given to every other member. [Id. § 8.]

Duties of board; president and professors of college; agents and servants; pay of visitors.

248. The board shall be charged with the care and preservation of the property of the college. They shall appoint as many professors as they may deem proper, and with the assent of two-thirds of their members, may at any time remove any professor or other officer of the college. It shall be the duty of said board, [1879–80, c. 244, p. 236.]

at a special meeting thereof to be held on the seventh day of June, eighteen hundred and eighty, or as soon thereafter as practicable, to remove from office such of the officers of the college as they may deem proper, said removals to take effect on the twelfth day of August, eighteen hundred and eighty, and said board shall proceed at once or as soon as practicable, to reorganize the Virginia Agricultural and Mechanical College by filling the several and various vacancies so made, or as many of them as they may deem proper; said appointments to take effect on the twelfth day of August, eighteen hundred and eighty. They shall prescribe the duties of each professor, and the course and the mode of instruction; they shall appoint a president of the college, and may employ such agents or servants as may be necessary; shall regulate the government and discipline of the students, and generally, in respect to the government of the college, may make such regulations as they may deem expedient, not contrary to law. Such reasonable expenses as the visitors may incur in the discharge of their duties shall be paid out of the funds of the college.

PAY AND FEES OF PROFESSORS.

1872-3, c. 60, § 10.

249. Each professor shall receive a stated salary, to be fixed by the boards of visitors; and the board shall fix the fees to be charged for tuition of students other than those allowed under this act to attend the college free of tuition, which shall be a credit to the fund of the college.

Property to be valued and transferred to visitors.

Id. § 11.

250. The trustees of said college shall transfer to the said board of visitors, the real estate and buildings, and such other property as they design to be used under this act, with an estimated valuation thereof; and if, in the opinion of the visitors, such valuation should be unjust, appraisers shall be selected and agreed upon by the visitors and the trustees, who shall fix such valuation.

Lands for experimental farms.

Id. § 12.

251. A portion of said fund, not exceeding ten per centum of the proportion assigned to the Agricultural and Mechanical College, and the Hampton Normal and Agricultural Institute, may be expended, in the discretion of the boards of visitors of the said respective schools, for the purchase of lands for experimental farms for each of them; and a portion of the accruing interest may be, from time to time, expended by the respective boards of

visitors in the purchase of laboratories suitable and appropriate for the said schools.

College incorporated; general powers.

252. The board of visitors of the Virginia Agricultural and Mechanical College, shall remain, and are hereby declared to be, a corporation, under the name and style of the board of visitors of the Virginia Agricultural and Mechanical College; and they shall have the right to sue, and be liable to be sued, by that name. They may have a common seal, and shall at all times be under the control of the legislature. 1872–3, c. 195 § 1, p. 180.

Pay of rector; bond of treasurer.

253. The said board may allow and authorize such pay to the rector or other officer of said college, as they deem reasonable; and they shall require the treasurer, or officer in whose hands the funds of the college may be placed, to give bond in double the amount of the annual income of said college, to the said board, conditioned for the faithful performance of the duties of his office. Id. § 2.

Funds to be turned over to visitors by board of education; interest on state debt held by the college, to be paid.

254. The Board of Education are authorized, and hereby directed, to pay and turn over to the said board of visitors, or to their order, all funds received by them for the use and benefit of said college; and the second auditor is hereby authorized and directed to draw on the public treasury in favor of the said board, from time to time, until otherwise ordered, for the same rate of interest as may be paid by act of the legislature to other incorporated colleges or seminaries of learning in the state, on all bonds of the commonwealth, or guaranteed by the commonwealth, held by or for such Virginia Agricultural and Mechanical College. Id. § 3.

HAMPTON NORMAL AND AGRICULTURAL INSTITUTE.

255. The said appropriation to the Hampton Normal and Agricultural Institute shall be on the following conditions, namely: that the trustees of the same shall, out of the annual interest accruing, as soon as practicable, institute, support, and maintain therein one or more schools or departments, wherein the leading object shall be instruction in such branches of learning as relates Code of 1873, c. 77, p. 676. 1876–77, c. 62, p. 50.

especially to agriculture and the mechanic arts, and military tactics; and the governor, as soon after the passage of this act as may be, and on the first day of January, eighteen hundred and seventy-three, and on the same day in every fourth year thereafter, shall appoint six persons, three of whom shall be of African descent, citizens of the commonwealth, to be curators of the fund hereby set apart for the use of the said institute, and without the personal presence of a majority of said curators, after a reasonable notice to all of them to be present, and without the sanction of a majority of such as are present, recorded in the minutes of the said board of trustees, no action of said board taken under and by virtue of this act shall be valid and lawful.

STUDENTS, HOW SELECTED; THEIR PRIVILEGE.

256. And the trustees of said college may select not less than one hundred students, with reference to their character and proficiency, from the colored free schools of the state, who shall have the privilege of attending the said institute on the same terms that state students are allowed to attend the Agricultural and Mechanical College, under the eighteenth section of this chapter.

Treasurer for Hampton Normal and Agricultural Institute; his bond.

257. The curators of the Hampton Normal and Agricultural Institute shall appoint a treasurer, who may be allowed a reasonable compensation, and who shall be required to enter into bond to the commonwealth, in a penalty at least double the amount of the annual income which may arise from the proceeds of the land scrip apportioned to said institute, conditioned for the faithful performance of the duties of his office.

Funds to be turned over to institute; interest on state debt held by curators, to be paid.

258. The Board of Education are authorized and are hereby directed to pay and turn over to the said treasurer, for the said institute, all funds received by them for the use and benefit of said institute; and the second auditor is hereby authorized and directed to draw on the public treasury in favor of the said treasurer of the said institute, from time to time, until otherwise ordered, for the same rate of interest as may be paid by act of the legislature to other incorporated colleges or seminaries of learning in this state, on all bonds of the commonwealth, or guar-

anteed by the commonwealth, held by or for such Hampton Normal and Agricultural Institute

Reports of colleges.

259. An annual report shall be made by the proper authorities of each of said institutions, after the close of each collegiate year, of the condition of the institute, and its receipts and disbursements during the preceding year, with the amount of salary paid to each professor, and the amount received in tuition fees from pay students; recording any improvements and experiments made, with their costs and results; and such other matters, including state, industrial and economical statistics, as may be supposed useful, copies of which shall be delivered to the state Superintendent of Public Instruction, to be laid before the general assembly. 1871-2, c. 234 p. 312, § 14.

Reservation of control by legislature.

260. The general assembly expressly reserves to itself the right and power at any time to repeal or alter this act, and to withdraw from either of said institutions the whole or any part of the appropriations herein granted. Id. § 15.

Board of visitors may accept subscriptions by counties and individuals to the Virginia Agricultural and Mechanical College; how to be held, and when to revert to subscribers.

261. It shall be lawful for the board of visitors of the said Virginia Agricultural and Mechanical College to accept and receive the subscription of any county made under an act to authorize subscriptions in aid of the Virginia Agricultural and Mechanical College at Blacksburg, Virginia, approved March twenty-one, eighteen hundred and seventy-two, and also of any individual, in aid of the purposes and objects of said college; and such donations and subscriptions when made shall be held by said board in trust for the benefit of said college, on condition that the same shall revert to the several donors or subscribers, *pari passu*, if at any time the state of Virginia should withdraw from the use of the said college, the interest accruing on the proceeds of the land scrip, as provided in this chapter. 1871-2, c. 257 § 6, p. 339.

Prohibiting the sale of liquor to students.

262. Any person who shall hereafter sell either directly, or knowingly indirectly, to any student of the Hampton Normal and 1879-80, c. 135, p. 119.

Agricultural Institute alcoholic or malt liquor, shall be guilty of a misdemeanor, and upon conviction thereof shall be fined not less than twenty nor more than fifty dollars.

263. It shall be the duty of the county court, from which the party convicted under the first section of this act obtained his license, forthwith to revoke the same, and no other license to sell liquor shall be granted to such party within two years from the date of said conviction.

MILLER MANUAL LABOR SCHOOL OF ALBEMARLE.

264. Be it enacted by the general assembly of Virginia, That in order to give complete legal capacity to the Miller Manual Labor School, in the county of Albemarle, the same be and is hereby created a corporation, under the following charter, to wit:

265. The members of the Board of Education and their successors in office, and the second auditor and his successor in office, shall be a corporation by the name of The Miller Manual Labor School of Albemarle, and shall have perpetual succession and a common seal, which it may alter and renew at pleasure; and may sue and be sued; implead and be impleaded; contract and be contracted with; purchase and take by grant, devise, or bequest; and hold estate, real and personal, for the uses and purposes of the said manual labor school. *1874, c. 61, p. 53; 1876-77, p. 293.*

266. It shall not be necessary for the persons designated in clause one to accept this charter, but they shall be deemed *virtute officii* to have accepted the same, nor shall it be necessary for them to hold any meeting for organization, but if they deem it proper to hold any meeting the governor shall preside, and the second auditor shall act as secretary. Such meetings shall be held, if at all, at such times and places as shall be designated by the governor, as president.

267. In such case any of the public offices, the incumbents of which are constituted corporators of the said Manual Labor School, shall hereafter be abolished or changed, the general assembly will designate what person or persons shall be constituted corporators in lieu of such. And it shall, at all times, be competent for the general assembly, at its discretion, to change the organization of the said corporation and the agencies by which the said charity shall be administered, more effectually to carry out the objects and purposes of said testator for the establishment and perpetual support of the school in the said twenty-fifth clause of said will mentioned, from which objects and purposes the Miller Fund shall not be diverted.

1876-77, p. 293.

268. The corporation created by clause one shall hold the legal title to all the property dedicated by the will of Samuel Miller, and by the compromise aforesaid, to the said manual labor school, and all other property hereby acquired by it, for the use and benefit of said school. The Board of Education shall discharge, in respect to the said fund, all the duties devolved, and shall exercise all the powers conferred by said twenty-fifth clause of said will upon the board of the literary fund. The second auditor shall discharge all the duties devolved by the said clause upon him, and is hereby authorized to receive the compensation thereby provided. The county court of Albemarle county is authorized and required, sitting in term, to discharge, by orders entered in a record book, to be kept by the clerk of said court specially for that purpose, all the duties devolved, and exercise all the powers conferred by said twenty-fifth clause upon the county court of said county. The charges and expenses attending the establishment and support of the said school, including the purchase of land (should any be purchased), the erection of the buildings, the feeding, clothing, and education of the pupils, the charges for medical attendance upon them, and everything incident to and connected with the school, shall, when examined, allowed and certified by the said county court of Albemarle, and approved by the Board of Education, be paid by the said Board of Education out of the income and profits of the trust fund created by the twenty-fifth clause of said will. The record book aforesaid shall be provided from the fund, and the clerk of said court shall receive for keeping the same, the same fees allowed by law for orders in the order book of said court, to be paid out of the fund as other claims are provided to be paid. And the district school trustees of the respective school districts of said county shall select and designate, subject to approval by the county court, as provided for in the said twenty-fifth clause of said will, as pupils of said school, those described in the said clause, and required by the testator to be so selected.

269. The funds, stocks, securities and investments belonging to the Miller Fund, shall be kept and preserved by the Board of Education in the same manner with those belonging to the literary fund of the commonwealth, but shall be kept scrupulously separate from all other funds, and be sacredly and forever devoted to the uses and purposes of the said Manual Labor School; and the accounting officers of the commonwealth in whose custody the same, or any part thereof may be, and the sureties in their

official bonds, shall be liable for the safe preservation thereof, in like manner as for the property of the literary fund.

270. The same rate of interest shall be paid on the bonds held by the Miller Manual Labor School of Albemarle as is provided shall be paid on bonds held by other incorporated colleges, under section twenty-two, chapter eighty of the Code of eighteen hundred and seventy-three. 1874-75, c. 284, p. 374.

271. The Board of Education is hereby authorized and required, in pursuance of the said agreement of compromise, by deed duly executed, to release to the said Robert W. Davidson, James M. Davidson, John Davidson, Samuel Miller Davidson, and Bennett Marion Davidson, respectively the reversions to the estate of Samuel Miller, limited upon the respective bequests and devises to them in the eighth, ninth, tenth, eleventh and twelfth clauses of said will; and authority is hereby given to Henry E. Smith, the guardian of Samuel Miller Davidson and Bennett Marion Davidson (or to his successor as such guardian) for them and in their behalf, to execute and deliver a proper deed, surrendering, releasing, transferring, granting and conveying to the Manual Labor School, created by section one of this act, for the uses and purposes prescribed by the testator in the said twenty-fifth clause of his will, all right, title, interest and claim, present and prospective, beyond what they shall receive under the said compromise, to the residuum of the said estate of Samuel Miller, deceased; and authority is given to Robert W. Davidson, James M. Davidson and John Davidson, by such deed, to release, surrender, transfer, grant and convey to said Manual Labor School, for the uses and purposes prescribed by the testator in the said twenty-fifth clause of his will, all their like respective rights, title, interest and claim, present and prospective, beyond what they shall receive under said compromise; and such deed, when so executed and delivered, shall have the effect conclusively to bar all future rights, title, interest or claim, however the same may arise, by or on behalf of the said Davidsons, or any or either of them, or any person claiming by, through or under them, or either of them, to any part of, or interest in the fund which, under the said compromise, shall pass to the said Manual Labor School. The executor of Samuel Miller, shall cause the deed, or deeds, executed in pursuance of this section, to be recorded in the clerk's offices of the counties of Albemarle and Rockbridge, and of the chancery court of the city of Richmond.

272. Nothing in this act contained shall be construed in any manner to affect the rights of the heir, or heirs at law, of Samuel Miller, deceased, if any such rights there be.

273. In the event the said compromise shall fail, from any cause whatever, then all the parties to the said appeals, in the preamble of this act mentioned, shall be immediately remitted to all their legal and equitable rights, and shall stand, in relation thereto, precisely as if no plan of compromise had been proposed or adopted, or any application for the ratification thereof made to the circuit court of Richmond, or any decree made thereon, and as if no petition had been presented to the general assembly for any act upon the subject, and as if no action had been had thereon, or any act done in pursuance thereof; but each and all of the said parties shall stand in all respects to each other, to the subject of litigation and to the questions involved, as if no plan of settlement and compromise had been set on foot or anything done in reference thereto.

VIRGINIA NORMAL AND COLLEGIATE INSTITUTE.

274. The governor of Virginia shall, on or before the first day of March, eighteen hundred and eighty-two, appoint a commission of five persons, who shall forthwith proceed to select a suitable site on the south side of the James river for the establishment of an institution of learning, to be used exclusively for the education of colored persons, under and in pursuance of the conditions and regulations hereinafter prescribed.

1881-82, c. 266, p. 283.

275. The said commission shall proceed, as soon as practicable, to select such a site, and report said selection to the Board of Education, composed of the governor, attorney-general, and Superintendent of Public Instruction, for its approval, so that the same may be approved and purchased by said board before the fifteenth day of March, eighteen hundred and eighty-two.

276. After purchase of said site by the said Board of Education, the board of visitors hereinafter provided for, shall proceed at once to construct or repair, upon said site, a suitable building or buildings, on plans admitting of enlargement, to be used for the purposes aforesaid. In the construction or repair of said building or buildings, the said board of visitors shall exercise their best discretion, and have full power to act in the premises, without further authority, so that the sum of money expended in the purchase of said site, and in the construction or repair of said building or buildings, and in fitting up and putting in order the same for opening the school, shall not exceed the sum of one hundred thousand dollars.

277. The said school shall be known as The Virginia Normal and Collegiate Institute. It shall be under the government and control of seven visitors, six of whom shall be well-qualified colored men, who shall be appointed by the governor, with the consent of the senate: provided, that the provisions of section two of chapter eleven, Code of eighteen hundred and seventy-three, shall not apply to the visitors appointed to this institution. The governor shall fix a day for the first meeting of said visitors,

and notify them thereof, and thereafter said visitors shall have two stated meetings in each year at the institution aforesaid, to-wit: on the first Tuesday in June and November, and occasional meetings at such other times as they shall appoint, or on a special call by the chairman of said board of visitors, which meetings shall be at the institute.

278. A majority of the members of the aforesaid board of visitors shall constitute a quorum for the transaction of business, and on the death or resignation of a member, or failure to act for one year, or on his removal out of this state, the Board of Education of the state, with the consent of the senate, shall appoint a successor.

279. The said visitors, or so many of them as being a majority, shall appoint a rector, of their own body, to preside at their meetings, in the absence of the Superintendent of Public Instruction, and a secretary to record, attest, and preserve their proceedings. They shall, annually, examine into the state of the property, real and personal; shall make and keep an inventory of the same, specifying every item whereof it consists; shall make annual report to the Board of Education, to be laid before the general assembly, with such suggestions or recommendations as, in their judgment, would be promotive of the objects of the institute. In said report they shall also embrace a full account of all disbursements, all funds on hand, and a general statement of the condition of said institute.

280. In the said institute there shall be a normal department, in which shall be taught such branches as are usually taught in the best normal schools in the country; said branches to be prescribed by the visitors to said institute: provided, that such normal course of instruction shall not be longer than three years.

281. There shall be connected with said institute, a college, and such professional departments as the board of visitors may think expedient and proper, for the higher education of colored persons. In the college department shall be taught the classics, the higher branches of mathematics, and such other branches as are usually taught in colleges, which branches shall be prescribed by the board of visitors to said institute.

282. The Superintendent of Public Instruction for this state shall be a member of said board of visitors, and ex-officio chairman. The said visitors shall be charged with the repair of the buildings, and care of the grounds and appurtenances, and with the interest of the schools generally. They shall appoint and remove professors and other necessary agents, two-thirds of the

whole number voting for appointment or removal; shall prescribe their duties in conformity with the law; shall establish rules for the government and discipline of students, not contrary to the laws of this state; shall regulate tuition fees; shall prescribe the duties and control the proceedings of all officers and employés, with respect to buildings, lands, appurtenances, and other property and interests of the institute; shall draw such money as may be appropriated, or otherwise contributed. for the support of the same, and disburse it through their chosen disbursing agent; and, in general, shall direct and do all things, which not being inconsistent with the laws of this state, shall to them seem most promotive of the purposes of said institute, which several functions they shall be free to exercise in the form of by-laws, rules, resolutions, orders, instructions, or otherwise, as they shall deem proper.

283. The said Superintendent of Public Instruction, and the visitors of said school shall be a body corporate, under the name and style of the board of visitors of the Virginia Normal and Collegiate Institute, with the right as such to use a common seal. They may plead and be impleaded in all courts of justice in all cases concerning the institute, which may be subject of legal cognizance and jurisdiction, which pleas shall not abate by the termination of their office, but shall stand revived in the name of their successors; and they shall be capable in law and in trust, for the institute, of receiving subscriptions and donations, real and personal, as well as from bodies coporate, or persons associated, as from individuals.

284. The said visitors shall, at all times, conform to such laws as the legislature may, from time to time, think proper to enact for their government; and the said institute shall, in all things, and at all times, be subject to the control of the legislature. The visitors above provided for shall be appointed on or before the first day of April, eighteen hundred and eighty-two, and every fourth year thereafter.

285. The number of professors or teachers in the institute, all of whom shall be colored, shall be fixed by the visitors; the salary of no one of them shall exceed the sum of fifteen hundred dollars per annum, except by consent of the said Board of Education, given in writing to the visitors.

286. The board of visitors shall designate one of their number to be treasurer, and shall fix the amount of his bond at not less than fifteen thousand dollars. The said bond shall be made payable to the commonwealth of Virginia, shall have good and

sufficient sureties, conditioned for the proper accounting and paying over of all money and other things committed to his custody, which bond being approved by the state Board of Education, and entered on the journal of the board of visitors, shall be transmitted to the auditor of public accounts, and remain on file in his office. The pay of the treasurer shall in no case exceed one hundred and fifty dollars a year for the first three years.

287. The board of visitors shall prescribe the terms upon which students, other than state students, may be admitted; the nature of their services, and the duration thereof, which shall not be less, in any case, than two years, and in the case of state students, more than four years. They shall admit as state students, free of charge, for tuition, as soon as practicable, upon evidence of good moral character, fifty young men, who shall be not less than sixteen nor more than twenty-five years of age, one of whom shall be selected from each senatorial district, and ten from the state at large, all to be chosen by the board of visitors; and when a vacancy has occurred, or is likely to occur, due notice of the time and place of making the appointment shall be given by the secretary of the board of visitors. If, after such notice, no suitable person shall apply from any district, the vacancy may be supplied from the state at large: provided that the students so admitted free of charge shall first enter into a written contract and agreement with the board of visitors to teach or engage in educational work for two years. This shall apply only to state students, and should any student fail to fill the terms of his contract, he may be relieved from the same by the payment of one-half of his tuition fee while at the institute.

288. And be it enacted, That out of the funds due the commonwealth of Virginia from the sale of the Atlantic, Mississippi and Ohio railroad, as ratified and confirmed by senate bill number fifty-six, of session eighteen hundred and eighty-one-two, the sum of one hundred thousand dollars shall be retained by the treasurer of the commonwealth to the credit of the state Board of Education, to be paid out by said treasurer on the orders or warrants of said board of visitors in the execution of this act; and within six months after the board of visitors shall have declared the institution ready to receive students, and annually thereafter, there shall be paid by the auditor of public accounts, on the order of the said state Board of Education, to the treasurer elected by the board of visitors, the sum of twenty thousand dollars, as annuities to the other state institutions of learning are now paid.

289. The board of visitors shall examine into progress of stu-

dents in each year, and shall give to those who excel in any branch of learning such honorary testimonials of approbation as they may deem proper. Such reasonable expenses as the visitors may incur in the discharge of their duties shall be paid out of the funds of the institute: provided the sum paid to any one visitor in any one year shall not exceed fifty dollars.

290. Any person may deposit in the treasury of the state, or bequeath money, stocks or bonds to be deposited, or grant, devise, or bequeath property, real or personal, to be sold, and the proceeds so deposited, which shall be invested as the donor may indicate, or the board of visitors may see proper for the benefit of the institute; and in such case the interest or dividend accruing on such deposits shall be paid to the treasurer of the institute on the order of the state Board of Education, to be used for the purpose thereof, unless some particular appropriation shall have been designated by the donor or testator, in which case such particular use or appropriation shall be respected.

TO PROTECT THE INSTITUTIONS OF THE STATE, PUBLIC TRUSTS AND FUNDS.

291. Be it enacted by the general assembly of Virginia, That no person who is a member of any board of visitors of any state institution, or an employé or agent thereof, or a trustee of any public trust or fund, or a salaried officer of any such state institution, or of any such public trust or fund, shall contract or be interested in any contract with such institution, or with the governing authority of such public trust or fund in any manner or form for furnishing supplies or for performing any work for said institution, or for said governing authority of said trust or fund; and any person violating the provisions of this act shall be guilty of a misdemeanor, and on conviction thereof shall be fined not exceeding five hundred dollars.

1878-79, c. 182, p. 162.

WAR DEPARTMENT.

INFORMATION RELATIVE TO THE APPOINTMENT AND ADMISSION OF CADETS.*

Appointments.

How made. 292. Each congressional district and territory—also the District of Columbia—is entitled to have one cadet at the academy. Ten are also appointed *at large*. The appointments (excepting those *at large*) are made by the secretary of war, at the request of the representative or delegate in congress, from the district or territory; and the person appointed must be an actual resident of the district or territory from which the appointment is made. The appointments *at large*—limited to ten in all—are specially conferred by the president of the United States.

Manner of making applications. 293. Applications can at any time be made by letter to the secretary of war to have the name of the applicant placed upon the register, that it may be furnished to the proper representative or delegate when a vacancy occurs. The application must exhibit the full name, exact age, and permanent abode of the applicant, with the number of the congressional district in which his residence is situated.

Date of appointment. 294. Appointments are required by law to be made one year in advance of the date of admission, except in cases where, by reason of death or other cause, a vacancy occurs, which cannot be provided for by such appointment in advance. These vacancies are filled in time for the next annual examination.

Alternates.

Alternates. 295. Any representative or delegate in congress who does *not* select his candidate by *competitive examination*, and who has reason to doubt his ability to pass the preliminary examination for admission to the Military Academy, can nominate a legally qualified *alternate*. The alternate will be examined with the regular

---

* Any further information can be obtained by addressing the secretary of war.

nominee, and admitted in the event of his success and the latter's failure to pass the prescribed preliminary examinations.

Like the nominee, the alternate should be designated as nearly one year in advance of date of admission as practicable.

Examination of Candidates.

296. Cadet candidates and alternates are ordered to report in person to the Superintendent of the Military Academy between the 10th and 20th of June annually, and are examined immediately after the annual examination of the cadets. *Preliminary examinat'ns*

No candidate will be examined at any other time unless prevented from reporting himself by sickness, or some other unavoidable cause, in which case he may be authorized by the secretary of war to be examined during the last three days in August.

Any candidate found deficient in his examination will not be allowed a reëxamination except upon the recommendation of the academic board.

Qualifications.

297. The age for the admission of cadets to the academy is between seventeen and twenty-two years. Candidates must be at least five feet in height, and free from any infectious or moral disorder, and generally from any deformity, disease or infirmity, which may render them unfit for military service. They must be well versed in reading, in writing, including orthography, and in arithmetic, and have a knowledge of the elements of English grammar, of descriptive geography, particularly of our own country and of the history of the United States.

298. A sound body and constitution, suitable preparation, good natural capacity, an aptitude for study, industrious habits, perseverance, an obedient and orderly disposition, and a correct moral deportment, are such essential qualifications, that candidates, knowingly deficient in any of these respects, should not, as many do, subject themselves and their friends to the chances of future mortification and disappointment by accepting appointments at the academy, and entering upon a career which they cannot successfully pursue.

299. Each cadet upon his *admission* shall take the oath of office prescribed by act of congress of July 2, 1862, and *before receiving his warrant* shall, in the presence of the superintendent, or some officer deputed by him, subscribe to an engagement in the following form:

United States Military Academy.

300. I, ———— ————, of the state of ——— ———, aged ——— years ——— month—, having been selected for appointment as a cadet in the Military Academy of the United States, do hereby engage, with the consent of my (parent or guardian), in the event of my receiving such appointment, that I will serve in the army of the United States for eight years, unless sooner discharged by competent authority. And I, ———— ————, *do solemnly swear* that I will support the constitution of the United States and bear true allegiance to the national government; that I will maintain and defend the sovereignty of the United States paramount to any and all allegiance, sovereignty or fealty I may owe to any state, county, or country whatsoever; and that I will at all times obey the legal orders of my superior officers and the rules and articles governing the armies of the United States.

———— ————.

Sworn and subscribed to at ———, this ——— day of ———, eighteen hundred and ———, before

———— ————.

REGULATIONS
GOVERNING THE ADMISSION OF CANDIDATES INTO THE NAVAL ACADEMY AS NAVAL CADETS.

Nomination.

301. The number of naval cadets allowed at the academy is one for every member and delegate of the house of representatives; one for the district of Columbia, and ten appointed at large. According to the act of congress approved June 17, 1878, "there shall not be at any time more in said academy appointed at large than ten."

302. The nomination of candidates for admission from the district of Columbia and at large is made by the president. The nomination of a candidate from any congressional district or territory is made on the recommendation of the member or delegate from actual residents of his district or territory.

303. Each year, as soon after the 5th of March as possible, members and delegates will be notified in writing of vacancies that may exist in their districts. If such members or delegates neglect to recommend candidates by the 1st of July in that year, the secretary of the navy is required by law to fill the vacancies existing in districts actually represented in congress.

304. The nomination of candidates is made annually between the 5th of March and the 1st of July. Candidates who are nominated in time to enable them to reach the academy on the 15th of May will receive permission to present themselves at that time to the superintendent of the naval academy for examination as to their qualifications for admission. Those who are nominated prior to July 1, but not in time to attend the May examination, will be examined on the 1st of September following; and should any candidate fail to report, or be found physically or mentally disqualified for admission in May, the member or delegate from whose district he was nominated will be notified to recommend another candidate, who shall be examined on the 22d of September following. When any of the dates assigned for examinations fall on Sunday, the examination will take place on the following Monday.

305. A sound body and healthy constitution, good mental abilities, a natural aptitude for study and habits of application, persistent effort, an obedient and orderly disposition and correct moral principles and deportment are so necessary to success in pursuing the course at the academy, that persons conscious of any deficiency in these respects are earnestly recommended not to subject themselves or their friends to the mortification and disappointment consequent upon failure, by accepting nominations and attempting to enter a service for which they are not fitted.

306. Students from the empire of Japan are received for instruction under a resolution of the senate and house of representatives of the United States, approved July 27, 1868.

Examination.

307. Each candidate for appointment as naval cadet must present to the academic board satisfactory testimonials of good moral character, and must certify *on honor* to his precise age, which must be over fourteen and less than eighteen years at the time of the examination. No candidate will be examined whose age does not fall within the prescribed limits.

308. Candidates must be physically sound, well formed, and of robust constitution; they will be required to pass a satisfactory examination before a medical board composed of the surgeon of the naval academy and two other medical officers to be designated by the secretary of the navy.

309. Any *one* of the following conditions will be sufficient to cause the rejection of a candidate:

Feeble constitution, inherited or acquired;
Greatly retarded development;
Permanently impaired general health;
Decided cachexia, diathesis, or predisposition;
All chronic diseases or results of injuries that would permanently impair efficiency, viz:

Weak or disordered intellect;
Cutaneous and communicable diseases;
Unnatural curvature of spine, torticollis, or other deformity;
Permanent inefficiency of either of the extremities or articulations from any cause;
Epilepsy or other convulsions within five years;
Impaired vision, chronic disease of the organs of vision, imperfect color sense;
Great hardness of hearing or chronic disease of the ears;

Chronic nasal catarrh, ozæna, polypi, or great enlargement of the tonsils;

Impediments of speech to such an extent as to impair efficiency in the performance of duty;

Chronic diseases of heart or lungs or decided indications of liability to cardiac or pulmonary affections;

Hernia or retention of testes in inguinal cavity;

Sarcocele, hydrocele, stricture, fistula, or hæmorrhoids;

Large varicose veins of lower limbs, scrotum, or cord;

Chronic ulcers.

Attention will also be paid to the stature of the candidate, and no one *manifestly* under size for his age will be received at the academy. In the case of doubt about the physical condition of the candidate, any marked deviation from the usual standard of height will add materially to the consideration for rejection. Five feet will be the minimum height for the candidate.

The board will exercise a proper discretion in the application of the above conditions to each case, rejecting no candidate who is likely to be efficient in the service, and admitting no one who is likely to prove physically inefficient. No candidate rejected by the board will be allowed a re-examination, and when rejected, the department will not reverse the action of the board.

310. The candidate must pass a satisfactory examination before the academic board in reading, writing, spelling, arithmetic, geography, English grammar, history, and algebra.

311. All the examinations, except in reading, will be written. Candidates who fall below the standard will receive a second and final examination in the subjects in which they fail. Deficiency in any one of the subjects at the second examination will be sufficient to insure rejection.

312. Candidates rejected at such examinations shall not have the privilege of another examination for admission to the same class unless recommended by the board of examiners."—(*Rev. Stat.*, § 1515.

Any further information can be obtained by addressing the secretary of the navy.

UNIVERSITY AT NASHVILLE.
STATE NORMAL COLLEGE FOR TRAINING WHITE TEACHERS.

313. This institution has for its object the training of professional teachers; and its connection with the public school system of Virginia is best explained by the following extracts from the letter of the Hon. J. L. M. Curry, agent of the Peabody Education Fund, dated May, 1882, and published in the June number of the *Educational Journal.* He says:

314. "In view of the want of well established normal schools of a high order in the South, and to build up an institution which would stand as a permanent memorial of Mr. Peabody's magnificent gift for education in the South, the trustees of the Peabody Fund for several years have been contributing liberally to the maintenance of the Normal College in Nashville. In connection with this college a number of scholarships, $200 each, have been established for the encouragement and aid of students who purpose to make teaching their vocation. These scholarships are apportioned among the states included in the Peabody benefaction, somewhat in proportion to the school population. Virginia, during the next session, October, 1882–May, 1883, will be entitled to nine additional scholarships.

315. This aid is furnished, not longer than two years, to students whose capacities, abilities, general culture and health, give special promise of usefulness as teachers. The college is professional, and its aim is to magnify the office of teaching, to instruct the students in the improved processes of teaching and management, and generally, to furnish the best facilities for the complete and thorough preparation of those who are to make teaching a life work. Not being a mere literary institution, nor designed to give the instruction which may be obtained in primary and grammar schools and in academies, it is necessary that applicants pass a preliminary examination before receiving appointment to scholarships. If this examination can be made rigid and competitive, the honor of the appointment will be enhanced, a better class of students will be obtained, and the mortification of failing to enter

after reaching Nashville, or of being discharged for incompetency, will be avoided.

316. The trustees, in the administration of the fund, act in coöperation with the state educational authorities. All appointments to scholarships are made by the state Superintendents of Public Instruction.

317. Receiving free tuition and an additional bonus of $200 a year, the students are presumed in good faith, to have chosen teaching as a profession. Each one pledges himself, or herself, to teach, after graduation, at least two years in the public schools, if opportunity be offered."

318. The college is under direct control óf President Eben S. Stearns, a gentleman who understands thoroughly the *art* of making good teachers.

319. Virginia, at present, is entitled to fourteen scholarships. The number, of course, is determined by the representative of the Peabody Fund. The vacancies each year depend upon the number who graduate or quit. These scholarships are free to any man or woman in the state, between the ages of seventeen and thirty, who desires to compete, and who is willing to pledge himself, or herself, to teach, at least two years, after graduation, in some of the free schools of Virginia.

320. Full information as to how and when to apply, can be obtained by addressing the Superintendent of Public Instruction at Richmond, Virginia.

OF PUBLIC FREE SCHOOLS
IN THE CITIES AND TOWNS OF THE COMMONWEALTH.

How established and governed.

1870-71, c. 308, p. 405, § 1.
Code of 1873, c. 79, § 1, p. 700.

321. Public free schools shall be established in all the cities and towns of the commonwealth, which are not embraced in whole or in part within the bounds of a magisterial district; and the provisions of an act entitled "an act to establish and maintain a uniform system of public free schools," approved July eleventh, eighteen hundred and seventy, save as hereinafter provided, shall be applicable to such cities and towns in like manner as to the counties of the commonwealth.

Cities and towns classified according to population.

Id. § 2.

322. Cities and towns, such as are described in section three hundred and twenty-one, which have a population of ten thousand and upwards, shall, for school purposes, be known as cities of the first class, whilst cities and towns, such as described in said section, and which have less than ten thousand, shall be known as cities of the second class; but the provisions of the law concerning cities shall be applicable to both classes alike, unless the one or the other class be specifically referred to.

Number and bounds of school districts.

Id. § 3.

323. The school boards of the respective cities shall have power, subject to the approval of the common councils, to prescribe the number and boundaries of the school districts, and the number of trustees (not exceeding three from each district); but until such provision is made, every such city which is not divided into wards shall constitute a single school district; and in every city which is divided into wards, each ward shall be a school district. The number and boundaries of districts shall be duly reported to the Superintendent of Public Instruction, and recorded in his office, and also in that of the clerk of the corporation court.

School board of city; its officers, powers and duties.

Id. § 4.

324. All the school trustees in a city or town shall constitute a

single corporation, under the style of "The school board of the city (or town) of ————," which shall have the same officers, powers and duties as ordinary boards of district school trustees, except as otherwise provided; and the trustees of the several districts shall have no organization or duties except such as may be assigned to them by the consolidated body.

Limits of its authority; quorum; clerk, and his pay.

325. The official care and authority of the school board shall Id. ? 5. cover all the territory included in the corporate limits of the city. A majority of its members shall constitute a quorum. It may at discretion appoint a clerk, who need not be a member of the board; it may add to the pay of the clerk from any funds at its disposal other than those of the state, and may make by-laws and regulations for its own government and for the management of its official business, so far as they do not conflict with the provisions of this act.

Who ineligible as superintendent of schools.

326. No mayor, member of council, or treasurer of a city, shall Id. ? 6. be allowed to act as superintendent of schools therein; nor shall the number of members of the council in the school board of any city or town exceed one-third of the entire number of the school board.

School trustees; how appointed.

327. School trustees already in office in cities by appointment Id. ? 7. of the Board of Education, and members of any city board of education created by the municipal authorities thereof, shall constitute the city school board, so far as the number and locality of these officers respectively meet the conditions prescribed in this act; and any deficiencies which may exist in the beginning, and all vacancies which may afterwards occur in the school board, may be supplied at any time within sixty days after their occurrence, by appointment made by the city council: provided, however, that as soon as may be after the passage of this act, the city council of such cities shall designate which of the trustees then in office shall go out of office at the end of one year, which at the end of two, and which at the end of three years. Should the city council in any case fail to act within the time prescribed, it shall be the duty of the Board of Education to fill the vacancy or vacancies without further delay.

Tax for public schools, how levied.

Id. § 8. 328. The municipal authorities of any such town or city as described in section three hundred and twenty-one, may, in their discretion, raise from time to time, by tax on property, as by law provided for the defraying of the expenses of the municipal government, such sum or sums as they may deem requisite for the support of the public schools therein: provided, that no tax thus levied on property for school purposes shall exceed three mills on a dollar in any one year, and that no annual capitation tax shall exceed fifty cents for all purposes; and still further provided, that no municipal or school authorities shall have power to raise or appropriate funds for the benefit of any school which does not form an integral part of the public free school system of either the city or the state, as by law established.

Estimates of necessary funds for city schools; council to make appropriations.

Id. § 9. 329. It shall be the duty of the school board of every city once in each year, and oftener, if deemed necessary to submit to the city or town council, in writing, a classified estimate of what funds will be needed for the proper maintenance and growth of the public schools of the city, and to request the council to make appropriations accordingly.

How state funds to be apportioned to cities, and who to be treasurer.

Id. § 10. 330. The state school funds shall be apportioned (separately from their counties) to such cities as are contemplated by sections three hundred and twenty-one and three hundred and twenty-two; and all funds designed for the benefit of public free schools therein shall be deposited with the treasurer of such cities (for the safety of which due security shall be given), and shall be kept by such treasurer in separate accounts, and shall be disbursed only on orders from the city school boards respectively.

City superintendent of schools.

Id. § 11. 331. There shall be a city superintendent of schools in cities of the first class, and whenever the population of any county, in which a city of the second class, or the greater part thereof is located, exceeds fifteen thousand without including the population of said city, such city may have a superintendent of schools separate from so much of the said county as lies without the city limits: provided, the public school interests in the city and county would, in the opinion of the Board of Education, be promoted thereby; and such separate city superintendent of schools shall be appointed by the Board of Education.

His compensation.

332. A city superintendent shall receive pay from the state in Id. § 12. like proportion as county superintendents of schools; but nothing in this act contained shall be construed to limit the amount of additional remuneration which he may receive from the council of the city within which he acts.

His powers, privileges and duties.

333. A city superintendent may teach in a public school *ex* Id. §§ 13, 14, *officio* when requested to do so by the city school board. 15, 16.

334. A city superintendent may suspend or dismiss pupils from the public schools: provided, that the city school board shall have power to reverse his action in the premises.

335. A city superintendent shall have the privilege of being present at all meetings of the school board, of making motions, and participating in the discussions therein, but not of voting.

336. City school boards and superintendents shall be required to perform the same duties, and shall be subject to the same rules and limitations as the district boards and county superintendents respectively, except so far as may by this act be otherwise provided.

How to be appointed and removed.

337. City superintendents of schools shall be appointed and Id. § 17. removed by the Board of Education, subject to confirmation by the senate.

Powers of school board of trustees.

338. The school board of trustees in every city of the first class Id. § 18. shall have power, and it shall be its duty to establish and maintain therein a general system of public free schools in accordance with the requirements of the constitution and the general educational policy of the commonwealth; and it is empowered specially to make and carry out regulations for the management of public school property and funds in the city; the location, renting, enlarging, repairing, erection and furnishing of school houses, and the proper care of the same; the attendance of pupils upon the schools; the providing of indigent children with text-books; the

determining of studies; the methods of teaching and government employed in the schools; the employment, remuneration and dismissal of teachers, and the length of the school terms. It shall also have power to establish high and normal schools as well as those of lower grade. All city school boards shall have the same powers and duties as are granted and imposed upon county school boards under section 20 of chapter 78 of the Code of 1873. (See page 44 of this compilation.)

1874-75. c. 354, p. 439.

Text-books for schools.

Id. § 19.

339. The text-books for use in the schools of the city shall be prescribed by the city school board of a city of either class, except that for the primary schools they shall be chosen from lists prescribed for the State at large by the Board of Education. But the Board of Education may, for reasons satisfactory to themselves, allow other text-books for primary schools in the cities of Richmond, Petersburg and Norfolk, in which public schools have already been established.

Duty of city council to make appropriations for school purposes; tax therefor limited.

Id. § 20.
1871-72, c. 366, p. 469.
1877-78, c. 223, p. 215.

340. It shall be the duty of the city or town council, and of every incorporated town of over five hundred inhabitants, which has been erected into a separate school district, to provide in due time, and it shall have no power to withhold, the sum or sums reported by the city or town school boards and declared to be necessary for the proper maintenance and growth of the public schools of the city or town, except the city of Richmond, the council of which said city shall have the discretion of the board of county supervisors in similar cases: provided that the council shall not be required to appropriate a sum greater than double the amount received from school funds of the state during the same scholastic year; but the council may, in its discretion, appropriate a larger sum, but it shall not have power to impose a tax on property for school purposes exceeding three mills on a dollar in any one year.

REGULATIONS OF THE BOARD OF EDUCATION.

Qualification of school officers—Oaths they are required to take.

341. School officers are required to take and subscribe the following oaths:

I, ——, do declare myself a citizen of the Commonwealth of Virginia, and a resident of the county of ——, and do solemnly swear (or affirm) that I will support and maintain the constitution and laws of the United States and the constitution and laws of the State of Virginia; that I recognize and accept the civil and political equality of all men before the law, and that I will faithfully perform the duties of county superintendent of schools to the best of my ability. So help me God. Constitution, Art 3, § 5, p. 7.

I swear (or affirm) that I have not, since the first day of May, 1882, fought in a duel, the issue of which was or might have been the death of either party; nor have I been knowingly the bearer of any challenge or acceptance to fight a duel actually fought; nor have I been otherwise engaged or concerned, directly or indirectly, in a duel actually fought since said time; nor will I, during my continuance in office, be so engaged, directly or indirectly. So help me God. Acts 1881-82, c. 69, p. 404.

This is to certify that —— this day personally appeared before me, a —— of the county of ——, and took and subscribed the above oaths.

Witness my hand this —— day of ——, 188—.

342. School superintendents must file the said oaths, when taken by them, with the Superintendent of Public Instruction; and district school trustees must file their oaths with the clerk of the school trustee electoral board within thirty days after being notified of their appointment. § 50, p. 39.

United States officers cannot be school officers.

Code 1873, c. 11, §2 p. 174.   343. No one holding an office of profit, trust, or emolument under the United States Government can act as superintendent of schools or as district school trustee.

School Officers prohibited from teaching in public schools.

344. County superintendents of schools and district school trustees are not allowed to teach in the public schools.

Age prescribed.

345. All applicants for examination to obtain a license to teach in the public schools must be at least eighteen years old.

County Superintendents; some of their duties more specifically defined.

346. It shall be the duty of county and city superintendents of schools to see that all school laws and regulations are literally and strictly carried out.

Superintendents' monthly reports.

347. Superintendents of schools shall make a monthly report to the Superintendent of Public Instruction in form to be prescribed by him, which report shall be due at the office of the Superintendent of Public Instruction on or before the fifteenth day of the month next succeeding, and every superintendent whose report fails to arrive by the aforesaid date shall be subject to a fine of five dollars for the first day of delay, and one dollar additional for each day's delay thereafter: provided the whole amount of the fine shall not exceed one-twelfth part of his salary; and the secretary of the board is hereby instructed to call upon each delinquent superintendent to show cause within thirty days why the fine should not be entered against him.

Examination of teachers.

348. The county or city superintendent shall hold examinations for those who desire to teach school in his county or city for the current school year, at such times and places as he may deem proper, after giving due notice of the same; and he shall not examine any applicant for a teacher's license except at such duly appointed examinations, unless he is satisfied that it was not in the power of the applicant to be at any of said examinations. He

may admit the public under such restrictions and regulations as he may deem necessary to secure a fair, rigid and impartial examination.

Basis of Examination—Of what to consist.

349. Examinations shall be held on orthography, reading, writing, arithmetic, grammar, geography and history, and, if the applicant desires to take charge of a school in which the higher branches have been introduced, he must be examined on all such higher branches. The examination shall be both oral and written, and the same or similar questions shall be propounded to all applicants for the same grade of certificate, under such regulations as the superintendent may prescribe. The superintendent, for sufficient reasons, such as the applicant being under the age prescribed by regulations, immorality, drunkenness, unfitness, or other cause that would render it improper for the applicant to teach a public school, may refuse to examine such applicant: provided that all such cases, other than those under age shall be reported to the Board of Education with the reason for refusing such examination.

List of questions to be made out and a copy to be furnished to the Superintendent Public Instruction.

350. Prior to the examination of teachers each year, the superintendent shall make up a list of all the questions upon which applicants will be examined by him, and shall designate which of them require oral, and which written answers. He shall also state on said list his method of grading teachers, the per cent. he requires applicants to make to entitle them to the several grades of certificates, and shall forward a copy of said questions, in due form, to the Superintendent of Public Instruction.

Examination papers.

351. At the close of each examination the superintendent shall endorse on the papers of the applicants their names, sex, color, place of nativity, addresses, where educated, previous occupations, whether or not they have ever taught a public school in this State, and if so, how long, and whose certificates they held; and having duly examined said papers, shall plainly mark on the same the per cent. of questions answered correctly on each branch, and the grade of certificate given, or, if no certificate was granted, the reason for refusing the same; and any other information that will show a fair record of each case.

The said examination papers shall be filed by the superintendent and kept during the current school year, and any applicant or other party interested, who feels aggrieved by the action of the superintendent shall be entitled to a certified copy of said papers, upon a written application to said superintendent, respectfully setting forth his reasons for desiring the same, duly signed by himself. This right shall not exist after the year for which the examination was held.

Superintendents' duty in regard to school funds.

352. School revenue now consists of four distinct classes:

1st. All money apportioned under the act approved March sixth, eighteen hundred and eighty-two, known as the Grandstaff act.

2d. All cash balances provided for by the sixth section of said act, together with all money paid on account of arrearages, interest on literary fund, and so forth.

3d. The county school tax levied by the different counties under the one hundred and twenty-first and one hundred and twenty-third sections.

4th. The district school tax levied by the different counties under the one hundred and twenty-second and one hundred and twenty-fourth sections.

353. The net proceeds of the first three funds *must be used exclusively* for the pay of *teachers*, and cannot be used for any other purpose.

354. The amount apportioned under the Grandstaff act is paid out by the treasurer upon warrants drawn by the superintendent, as provided for by the act.

355. All other State money is apportioned to the several districts by the Superintendent, as directed by law, and paid out on the warrant of the district board, exclusively for the pay of teachers. See section 145.

356. County school taxes should be apportioned to the several districts as fast as the treasurer reports them collected, and cannot be used for any purpose *except the pay of teachers.*

357. District school tax is levied and collected for the exclusive benefit of the respective districts. It is under the direct control of the district board, and is used to build and furnish schoolhouses and to meet contingent expenses of the schools in the district: provided that no account shall be considered by the Board unless duly itemized.

358. Any excess of levy for district school purposes over five cents upon the one hundred dollars of the taxable value of pro-

perty of such district may be applied, by the board of trustees thereof, to the payment of the salaries of the teachers therein.

359. It shall be the duty of the superintendent to see that the books of the district clerks are correctly kept, that these funds are properly applied, and that the money appropriated exclusively for the pay of teachers shall not be used for any other purpose whatever.

Superintendents to require county treasurers to make stated reports under section 146, page 65.

360. School superintendents shall require county treasurers to report to them on or before the first day of September of each year and thereafter at intervals of two months, until their final settlement at the end of the fiscal year, which report shall show the amount of State money received on current revenue or from the second auditor: the number and amount of warrants on the respective State funds presented for payment: the number and amount paid by the treasurer: the balance of State funds on hand, if any and to what districts due: the amount of county school funds received and apportioned to the districts by the school superintendent: the number and amount of warrants on the county fund presented: the number and amount paid by the treasurer: the balance of county funds on hand, if any, and to what districts due: the amount of district taxes collected for the respective districts up to the expiration of the said two months: with the number and amount of the warrants on the several districts presented and paid: and the balance, if any, due the districts: also the amount of county school tax collected, which has not been apportioned to the several districts by the superintendent.

361. The superintendent shall require the treasurer on or before the first day of December in each year to make a statement showing the amount of all county and district school money collected on current revenue by him up to said date, the amount on hand at that time due the county school fund and the several districts.

362. Whenever the treasurer reports county school money on hand, or the superintendent knows that it should be, he shall immediately apportion said fund to the several districts as provided by law for the pay of teachers, and shall notify the district clerks, in writing, of the amount apportioned their respective districts as well as the amount of district tax in the hands of the treasurer, belonging to their districts.

To enter reports, &c.

363. County and city superintendents in the records required to be kept, shall enter in full the reports of the county treasurer ordered to be made by them, also the scheme of each apportionment of state and county school funds made to the several districts in their respective counties, showing the amount and date of said apportionments.

To keep a register of applicants for teacher's certificate.

364. County and city superintendents shall keep a register of all who apply to them for examination for teacher's certificates, and shall enter therein the name of teacher, age, color, sex, place of nativity, where educated (if in public schools of Virginia so state); whether or not they hold a diploma of any institution; grade of free-school certificate held, name of district, number of school; total number of months contracted for the current year, total length of time taught, total length of time taught in a public free school; in what counties employed, where last employed, salary per month for current year, post-office address; whether or not the applicant expects to make teaching a profession; number licensed, white and colored separately; number employed, white and colored separately.

County school boards.

Page 45, § 82. 365. County school boards are required under the law to hold two meetings each year—one between the 1st and 15th of August, the exact date to be fixed by the board itself, or in default thereof, by the president; the other on or before the first Wednesday in November. (See the law for full instructions.)

Page 57, §§ 123 and 124

Boards of school trustees; when to meet.

(For *duties of board* see page 41, sections 58 to 69, inclusive.)

Page 41, § 64. 366. Boards of school trustees shall hold two regular meetings in each school year, one on the first Wednesday in August and the other on the last Wednesday in October.

Page 42, § 69. 367. At the August meeting the several boards shall prepare a detailed report embracing a full statement of all the school work done in their respective districts for the school year ending the 31st day of July preceding, in such form as may be prescribed by the county school superintendent, with the name, number and grade of each school in the district. Said report shall also state the salary agreed upon to be paid to the teachers of the several schools for the ensuing year, which salary, if confirmed by the superintendent, shall not be increased or diminished during the year without his written consent. The report shall also state the hour prescribed for the opening and closing of the schools and time allowed for intermission. This report shall be forwarded to the superintendent of the county with the forms required by section sixty-eight within the time prescribed by said section.

368. At the October meeting the board shall prepare an estimate showing the amount of money which will be needed in the district during the next school year for providing school-houses, furniture, apparatus, text books for indigent children, and all other means and appliances needful for the successful operation of the schools, with other proper charges. Said estimate shall be filed with the superintendent of schools as the chairman of the county board, to be by him laid before said board at its annual meeting on or before the first Wednesday in November. Page 41, ₴ 66.

369. Boards of school trustees may transact any other business at the annual meeting, and special meetings may be called by the chairman or any two members. Page 41, ₴ 64

District clerks.

370. District clerks are required to make annual reports as provided in section sixty-eight, page forty-two, under heavy penalties for failure

Employment of teachers.

371. Boards of school trustees in all the counties which have not adopted the sub-districting law have the absolute power to employ teachers, whether the one selected is satisfactory to the patrons or not: provided that in all cases teachers must be employed and contracted with at a regular or called meeting of said board. Page 41, ₴ 60.

372. But if the board elects to submit the question of selection of a teacher to the patrons of any school it shall call a meeting of the same by due proclamation and by posting a notice of the time and place of meeting, at least ten days before it is to be held, on the front door of the school-house and at three of the most prominent places in the district, at which meeting the chairman or some other member of the board shall preside, if present; if no member of the board is present the meeting shall elect a chairman. The meeting shall also elect a secretary. The clerk of the board of trustees shall provide the meeting with a list of the

patrons of the school, which shall embrace the names of all those who intend to enroll their children in said school for the current school year. The secretary of the meeting shall ascertain from the list whether or not a majority of the children are represented. If they are, the chairman shall declare the meeting organized and ready to proceed with the election of a teacher.

373. The election shall be by ballot, unless otherwise determined by the meeting.

374. No teacher shall be eligible to be voted for unless he present to the meeting a certificate of qualification of at least as high a grade as the school he desires to teach, granted to him by the superintendent of the county as required by law.

375. Before voting for a teacher the patrons must pledge themselves to support the one selected by the meeting.

376. Immediately upon the adjournment of the meeting the secretary thereof shall report the proceedings to the chairman of the board of school trustees, who, if a teacher has been selected, shall cause a contract to be immediately given him by said board.

377. Should there not have been a majority of the children represented at the meeting the board may either call another meeting or declare its determination to select a teacher independent of the action of the people, but if a majority of the children were represented at the meeting, then the board must be governed by its action.

Page 48, ? 91. 378. Boards of school trustees shall not entertain any proposition from, or enter into correspondence with any party who may desire to teach a public school until said party presents a teacher's certificate, of at least as high a grade as the school he applies for, issued to him by the superintendent of the county in which the school is situated.

Page 48, ? 93. 379. Boards of school trustees *must* enter into written contracts with teachers in a form to be prescribed by the school regulations *before they enter upon their duties.* Any failure on its part to make such contract with the teachers assigned by it to the respective schools will subject its members to such fine as the law directs.

Opening schools.

380. The time for opening and closing schools shall be prescribed by the board of school trustees, subject to the approval of the county superintendent: provided that where an intermission of thirty minutes or more is given no school shall open later than 9 A. M. or close earlier than 4 P. M., and in no event shall a school

open later than 9 A. M. or close earlier than 3 P. M., nor shall any school be taught less than six hours each school day. The time of opening and closing the school, with the intermission to be given, must be stated in the contract made with the teacher.

381. Boards of school trustees shall, immediately upon contracting with a teacher, report the fact in writing to the county superintendent, giving the teacher's name and address, the number of the school he is to teach, and the amount of salary agreed to be paid.

Number of pupils required to form a school.

382. An enrolment of at least twenty pupils, with an average daily attendance of twenty, is required to constitute a public free school, and upon this basis shall teachers' salaries be fixed and paid. But boards of school trustees may enter into contract with teachers to conduct schools with a smaller enrolment and shall pay them a proportional amount for each scholar under twenty in average daily attendance: provided that no public money shall be paid to support any school with a smaller daily average than ten. _{Page 53, § :07.}

383. It shall be the duty of the superintendent to see that no teacher is paid for any excess of twenty or a greater amount than the daily average of his school entitles him to receive, except as hereinafter provided.

384. Boards of school trustees, when satisfied that there is not a sufficient number of children in any school neighborhood to entitle them to a school under the law, and that the geography of the district is such that no judicious rearrangement of the several schools can be made so as to furnish the minorities with proper school facilities, may certify all of these facts, with a diagram of the section to be accommodated, to the county superintendent, who shall forthwith visit the section in question, and if he find that the facts stated are correct and that the contiguous schools are judiciously located and cannot be so arranged as to furnish the minority in question with fair school facilities, may authorize the board of school trustees to reduce the daily average to fifteen for such school; but each case must stand on its own merits, and the legal average of no school can be reduced except as stated.

385. In cases where the average attendance in the 381st regulation is reduced by reason of a factious spirit on the part of one or a few parties, or in consequence of the proper exercise of discipline, the district boards may continue such school if they deem

it advisable to do so: provided that each case be reported to the county superintendent and his written approval obtained.

Discontinued schools.

386. The board of school trustees of any school district in which a public school has been closed, for sufficient cause, before the expiration of the time for which it was required by contract to continue, is hereby authorized, with the written consent of the county superintendent, to pay the teacher of every such school as much of his or her salary as may be due for the time the school was taught.

Improvement of schools.

387. The attention of school officers is called to those portions of the school laws and regulations which refer to the organization, management, appliances and general character of the public free schools; and they are exhorted to tolerate nothing in the schools under their charge that would impair their usefulness or make them in any way a discredit to the state.

388. Officers are specially cautioned against licensing or employing any teacher who is not well qualified for the position he seeks.

389. The teacher's certificate shall state the branches upon which the holder has been examined, and shall be given for only one scholastic year and may be of three grades, and the teacher's professional certificate for two years, provided that any teacher who has previously received it or its equivalent, a first grade certificate, may be re-commissioned for any period not exceeding five years, at the discretion of the county superintendent. The professional certificate shall be bestowed very sparingly, and should always imply tried ability and a general professional spirit and knowledge, in addition to a thorough mastery of the branches taught. It is understood that the difference in these grades is not based upon any difference in the subjects taught, but is intended to represent different grades of ability, experience, attainment and success.

390. County and city superintendents are required to hold in their respective counties and cities at least one teachers' institute during each scholastic year, at which all the teachers employed in the public free schools shall be expected to attend; and should the institute be held whilst any of the schools are in operation, the teachers attending it shall not thereby suffer any diminution of their monthly pay, provided the time thus occupied does not exceed one week. Superintendents may arrange to hold the examination of applicants for teachers' certificates at these institutes

391. School officers and teachers in the counties and cities of the state are instructed to require all children applying for admission into the public free schools to be provided with such books as have been prescribed and duly selected according to the regulations of this board, and none shall be enrolled or taught who are not so provided; and any teacher violating the provisions of this section shall be fined not less than one, nor more than three dollars.

392. Hereafter the school month shall consist of four weeks of five school days each, and deduction shall be made from the pay of teachers for every day they lose, except such days as may have been declared by boards of school trustees to be legal holidays.

School attendance and sub-districts.

393. Pupils may in all cases be admitted into graded schools of more than one teacher by the authorities thereof without reference to the dividing lines of districts, sub-districts or counties, unless forbidden by act of Assembly; in this and all other cases in which pupils attend school outside of their own districts in accordance with these regulations, the rate of tuition to be charged by the district receiving the pupil against the district to which the pupil belongs shall be a matter of previous agreement between the two school boards immediately concerned. Any tuition deemed proper by the school board of the district within which the school is situated may be charged against private parties sending children to such schools.

394. It shall be lawful for any district school board to sub-district its territory or vary its boundary lines with a view to the improvement of its schools or to the better accommodation of particular neighborhoods, and in counties which have failed to adopt the provisions of the act to provide for the division of school districts into sub-districts and for the appointment of school directors, approved March 7th, 1878, the district board or boards above mentioned shall, in carrying out the sub-districting, be governed by such provisions of the aforesaid act of Assembly as pertain to this subject—namely, sections 1, 2, 3, 6 and 10 thereof.

Admission of adults into the public schools.

395. All persons between twenty-one and twenty-five years of age, seeking admission into any public free school, must prepay a tuition fee at the rate of one dollar per month to the school board within whose territorial limits such school is taught, and receive from the school board a permit acknowledging the receipt of

Page 53, § 105.

payment, specifying the school to be attended and the length of time which has been paid for: provided that in cities of the first class the amount of the tuition fee may be fixed by the city school board, but shall not exceed the average cost of tuition per scholar for the school session.

396. No adult shall be enrolled or taught in a public school who has not previously presented to the teacher a permit from the school board of the district. Nor shall any adult be admitted or retained in any school to the detriment of the school or any of its pupils, or to the exclusion from the school of any child between the ages of five and twenty-one years. Nor shall any such adult be allowed to continue in the school after the expiration of the time specified in his permit.

397. Adults received into a public school shall submit to the regulations of the school and to the authority of the teacher in like manner as other pupils, and shall not under any circumstances have the right to claim a return of any part of the tuition fee paid to the school board, unless he has been excluded from the school in order to make room for younger pupils.

398. It shall be the duty of the district clerk to record all permits granted and tuition fees received, and pay over the fees to the county treasurer, who shall give a receipt for same, and shall place the amount to the credit of the district, to be used for the payment of teachers therein.

399. Clerks, treasurers and teachers shall keep their records so that in making their reports the statistics concerning this class of pupils may be given separately, according to such forms as may be prescribed by the Superintendent of Public Instruction.

Nepotism.

400. School officers are cautioned against all appearance of nepotism or favoritism in any form in the employment of teachers.

As to introduction and uniformity of text-books, adopted April, 1882.

401. The text-books for use in the public schools of Virginia on Spelling, Reading, Arithmetic, Grammar, Geography, Penmanship and United States and Virginia History shall be selected from the list prescribed by the State Board of Education.

402. The county school board of each county in the State shall determine which of the books licensed by the State Board of Education shall be used in the public schools of the county, but

shall not adopt more than one book of the same grade on any of the branches required to be taught in the public schools.

403. The county superintendent of each county shall appoint an advisory committee, to consist of not less than three nor more than five of the leading teachers of the county, preference being given to those holding professional certificates, who, in conjunction with the county superintendent, shall meet, examine, and recommend for the consideration of the county school board such text-books as in their judgment would be best adapted to the wants of the public schools of the county; provided, however, that such selection shall be made from the State list only. The county superintendent shall act as chairman of said advisory committee, and shall call the committee together for the performance of its duties at least five days before the assembling of the county board for the adoption of text-books. The report of the advisory committee shall be submitted in writing.

404. The contract between the State Board of Education and the publishers is limited to four years, namely from August 1st, 1882, to August 1st, 1886, but the school board of each county shall, between the dates of August 1st, 1882, and August 1st, 1883, meet, upon the call of the county superintendent, and adopt from the State list a uniform series of text-books to be used in the public schools of the county, and arrange with the publishers for the introduction of the same into the schools: the books to remain in use not less than four years from the date of their adoption and introduction, provided they continue for so long a time on the list licensed by the State Board. The exact date of the meeting of the county board above provided for, shall be fixed by the county superintendent, who shall give timely notice to the members of the board of the day and place selected for the meeting.

405. The new books shall be introduced in the formation of all new classes, and the old books shall be tolerated only when a commencement has previously been made in such books by a majority of the pupils in a class, in such case their use may be continued until the completion of those books by the class; provided, that after August 1st, 1883, only the newly adopted books shall be used. If, however, the publishers of the newly selected books make satisfactory offers in reference to exchange of the new books for the old, the changes may be as sudden and complete as may be deemed advisable by the county board.

406. As soon as the text-books for use in the schools shall have been determined on by the county school board, due public notice

shall be given by the county superintendent of the names, prices and mode of obtaining the books, and of the regulations of the State Board of Education requiring every pupil to be supplied with the proper books before admission into any public school.

407. It shall be the duty of the county superintendent to make early and efficient arrangements whereby supplies of books will be brought within reach of the children and sold on the terms indicated in the contract. He shall furnish each teacher with a copy of the regulations of the Board of Education concerning text-books, and also with a list of the books and prices agreed upon by the county school board, which list the teacher shall keep posted in his school-room.

408. No teacher shall receive or teach any pupil who is not supplied with the proper books, and the faithfulness of the teacher in this particular shall not work to the detriment of the school in the matter of average attendance; that is to say, the schools shall not be closed for lack of the number of pupils required for a lawful school if the deficiency has been occasioned by the rejection of pupils for the reason given above.

409. County superintendents shall require of each teacher explicit statements in reference to text-books in every monthly report, and if any irregularity has been allowed the teacher shall be warned to obey the law, and after warning has been given, if irregularity is continued or repeated, it shall be the duty of the county superintendent to withhold his receipts for the teacher's monthly reports until he is satisfied that the law is observed properly, and should a teacher be contumacious or persistently negligent his license shall be cancelled.

410. It shall be the duty of the county superintendent to see that these regulations are rigidly enforced, and he shall make monthly reports to the Superintendent of Public Instruction in respect to their observance and concerning other matters of duty, according to forms furnished by that officer.

411. Although no teacher or school officer can receive any pay or percentage for supplying books to the children, yet any teacher, trustee, or superintendent may with propriety assist in bringing the books within easy reach of the children, and in receiving the price of the books and transmitting the same to any dealer who may entrust them with a gratuitous agency; and any teacher or officer may with propriety buy with his own money and keep on hand books for the convenience of scholars.

412. The duties and privileges conferred upon county superin-

tendents and county school boards in the foregoing regulations shall apply also to city superintendents and city school boards.

413. All regulations heretofore adopted by the Board of Education in reference to text-books which may be in conflict with the foregoing are hereby repealed.

SUPPLEMENT.

COUNTY SUPERINTENDENTS OF SCHOOLS TO REPORT TO COMMISSIONER OF AGRICULTURE.

414. That the Commissioner of Agriculture be required to receive, in the name of the state, from the county superintendents of schools, and preserve in proper form in his cabinet, any charts, maps, geological sections, mineral specimens, specimens of woods, specimens of the productions of their respective counties, and any written descriptions illustrating or pertaining to the physical structure and mineral or other resources of said counties which the above officers may be able to furnish ; and that the Commissioner of Agriculture shall include in his annual reports so much of the information thus furnished him as may, in his judgment, be conducive to the public interest. 1879–80, c. 184, § 1, p. 174.

415. That the county superintendents of schools be instructed to combine with their regular official visits such examinations of the mineral deposits and geological structure of their respective counties, as far as may be practicable, and which, in their judgment, will not materially interfere with their official duties and which might increase their usefulness, by means of information thus collected and imparted to school teachers, school officers, and the people generally, in regard to the geology, mineralogy and geography of their respective counties and of the state. Id. § 2.

416. That at least once a year the county superintendents of schools shall report to the Commissioner of Agriculture, giving the results of their observations and explorations of their respective counties. Id. § 3.

LAWS PASSED BY LEGISLATURE, SESSION 1883-'84.

SCHOOL COMMISSIONERS.

Appointments of District School Trustees.

[This repeals sections 49, 50, 51, 52, 53, pp. 39—40.]

1883–84, c. 138, p. 177, § 1.
417. The general assembly shall, during the sessions of eighteen hundred and eighty-three-four, and every four years thereafter, proceed to elect three citizens of each county in this commonwealth, to be known as the county board of school commissioners, the members of said board to go into office on the first day of April succeeding their election, having first taken and subscribed the usual oath of office, and to hold their offices for the term of four years, or until their successors are duly elected and qualified.

Id. § 2.
418. The said board shall elect one of their number chairman and another secretary; and any two shall constitute a quorum for the transaction of business; and any vacancy occurring in any of the said county school electoral boards, during the recess of the legislature, shall be filled by appointment of the judge of the circuit court of the county in which such vacancy may occur; said appointee to hold office until thirty days after the next meeting of the general assembly.

Id. § 3.
419. The general assembly may elect said county school electoral boards in a joint resolution for that purpose, embracing all the counties of the commonwealth.

Id. § 4.
420. All vacancies existing or occurring in district boards of school trustees shall be filled by said county school electoral boards: provided that no person who is unable to read and write shall be appointed a school trustee: and provided, further, that nothing in this act shall be construed as giving authority or power to said electoral board to interfere in any way with the appointment, as heretofore, of school trustees by municipal councils, or to disturb in any way the present law bearing on the action of said municipal councils in the premises.

Id. § 5.
421. The said school trustee electoral boards shall have power, and it shall be their duty, to declare vacant and to proceed to fill the office of any trustee in their respective counties who fails to qualify and to deliver to the clerk of the board his official oath, in the usual form, within thirty days after he has been notified of his appointment;

which notification shall be promptly given by the clerk. The board shall also vacate the office of any and every trustee who fails to discharge the duties of his office according to law.

422. Any member of said board may call a meeting by notifying the other two. All proceedings shall be recorded in a bound volume; and such record-book and stationery as may be necessary shall be paid for from the county-school fund: provided the cost of the same shall not exceed five dollars in any one year. It shall also be the duty of the clerk of said board to furnish the board of education with a list of school trustees and such other information as may be called for. Id. ¿6, p. 178.

423. The clerk shall convene the said electoral board promptly when unexpected vacancies occur, and also at least thirty days before the expiration of regular terms of office, so that district boards may be kept full and no members be left to hold over unnecessarily. Id. ¿ 7.

424. All acts and parts of acts inconsistent herewith are hereby repealed. Id. § 8.

SCHOOL TRUSTEES IN CITIES AND INCORPORATED TOWNS OF FIVE THOUSAND INHABITANTS AND OVER.

425. That section seven of chapter seventy-nine of the Code of eighteen hundred and seventy-three be and the same is hereby repealed. 1883–84, c. 258, ¿ 1, p. 344.

426. That the places of all trustees now in office, in towns and cities of five thousand inhabitants and over, be and become vacant on the expiration of thirty days from the passage of this act. Id. § 2.

427. That the councils of such cities and towns shall, as soon as may be after the passage of this act, elect trustees, not exceeding three for each school district of their respective corporations, and shall designate which of such trustees shall go out of office in one year, which in two, and which in three years: provided, however, that the foregoing provisions of this and the whole of the fourth and fifth sections of this act shall not apply to the city of Winchester, but in lieu thereof, the corporation court of Winchester shall, as soon as may be after the passage of this act, choose the trustees for said city. In all other respects this act shall apply to the city of Winchester. Id. § 3.

428. The term of all trustees so elected shall begin on the thirty-first day after the passage of this act: provided, however, that the provisions of section two, three, and four shall not apply to the cities of Norfolk and Alexandria, and shall not apply to the city of Petersburg until on and after July second, eighteen hundred and eighty-four. Id. ¿ 4, p. 345.

429. All vacancies in the school board, arising from whatever cause, shall be filled by the councils of such cities or towns. Id. ¿ 5.

STATE FEMALE NORMAL SCHOOL.

430. There shall be established, as hereinafter provided, a normal school expressly for the training and education of white female teachers for public schools. 1883–84, Id. ¿ 1, p. 417.

PUBLIC FREE SCHOOL LAW.

Id. § 2. 431. The school shall be under the supervision, management, and government of W. H. Ruffner, J. L. M. Curry, John B. Minor, R. M. Manly, L. R. Holland, John L. Buchanan, L. A. Michie, F. N. Watkins, S. C. Armstrong, W. B. Taliaferro, George O. Conrad, W. E. Gaines, and W. W. Herbert, as a board of trustees. In case of any vacancy, caused by death, resignation, or otherwise, the successor shall be appointed by the governor. The superintendent of public instruction shall be *ex-officio* a member of the board of trustees.

Id. § 3. 432. Said trustees shall, from time to time, make all needful rules and regulations for the good government and management of the school, to fix the number and compensation of teachers and others to be employed in the school, and to prescribe the preliminary examination and conditions on which students shall be received and instructed therein. They may appoint an executive committee, of whom the superintendent shall be one, for the care, management, and government of said school, under the rules and regulations prescribed as aforesaid. The trustees shall annually transmit to the governor a full account of their proceedings under this act, together with a report of the progress, condition, and prospects of the school.

Id. § 4. 433. The trustees shall establish said school at Farmville, in the county of Prince Edward: provided said town shall cause to be conveyed to the state of Virginia, by proper deed, the property in said town known as the Farmville female college; and if the said property be not so conveyed, then the said trustees shall establish said school in such other place as shall convey to the state suitable grounds and buildings for the purposes of said school.

Id. § 5, p. 418. 434. Each city of five thousand inhabitants, and each county in the state, shall be entitled to one pupil, and one for each additional representative in the house of delegates above one, who shall receive gratuitous instruction. The trustees shall prescribe rules for the selection of such pupils and for their examination, and shall require each pupil selected to give satisfactory evidence of an intention to teach in the public schools of the state for at least two years after leaving the said normal school.

Id. § 6. 435. The sum of five thousand dollars is hereby appropriated to defray the expense of establishing and continuing said school. The money shall be expended for that purpose under the direction of the trustees, upon whose requisition the governor is hereby authorized to draw his warrant on the treasury.

Id. § 7. 436. There shall be appropriated annually, out of the treasury of the state, the sum of ten thousand dollars to pay incidental expenses, the salaries of officers and teachers, and to maintain the efficiency of the school, said sum to be paid out of the public free school fund: provided, however, that the commonwealth will not in any instance be responsible for any debt contracted or expenditure made by the institution in excess of the appropriation herein made.

437. The superintendent of public instruction shall render to the second auditor an annual account of the expenditures under this act. Id. ? 8.

PROVIDING FOR AN EIGHT WEEKS' COURSE OF INSTRUCTION, FOR THE COLORED TEACHERS IN THIS STATE, AT THE VIRGINIA NORMAL AND COLLEGIATE INSTITUTE.

438. The president and faculty of the Virginia Normal and Collegiate Institute shall be required, during each and every year, to conduct a normal course of instruction for the benefit of the colored teachers in the public schools of this state, or those who expect to make teaching a profession—said normal course to commence on some day between the eighteenth and twenty-fifth days of July, to be fixed by the state superintendent of public instruction, and continue for eight weeks. 1883-84, ? 1, p. 442.

439. The president of the said Normal and Collegiate Institute, who shall be appointed for a term of three years by the state board of education, with the superintendent of public instruction of this state, may so divide the said faculty as that a part of it may relieve the other from the class-room during the aforementioned eight weeks' normal course of instruction. Id. ? 2.

440. The annual salary paid the instructors in the said normal school shall be regarded as covering the time in which they are engaged in giving instruction in the said normal course: provided this shall not prohibit the superintendent of public instruction from employing competent and skilled normal school lecturers to assist the regular faculty in conducting the normal course, or from supplementing the salary of the said faculty from any funds that may be at his disposal for the purpose of conducting normal institutes: provided the money so to do comes from some other than state school funds. Id. ? 3, p. 443.

441. When any county or city superintendent of schools shall be notified of the time of the commencement of said normal course, he shall notify all the colored school teachers in his city or county, and said teachers shall be required to attend said normal course at least one month in each year, except prevented by sickness; and should any teacher fail to attend any session, or any part of said normal course, for five consecutive school years, then the superintendent shall revoke said teacher's license, and he shall not be allowed to again enter the profession as a teacher until after he or she shall have attended at least one session of said normal course of instruction, unless excused by the board of education: provided this section shall not include married women. Id. ? 4.

442. The teachers, in attending such normal course, may occupy the rooms of the school, and in all respects have the same accommodations as the regular students have during the regular sessions of instruction, and subject to the rules and regulations made for their government by Id. ? 5.

the board of education. They shall receive certificates for proficiency and attendance, and such other marks for distinction as the board of education may think proper and by rules establish.

Id. § 6. 443 The charge for board shall not exceed eight dollars per month while attending said sessions, and should it exceed that sum, the deficiency shall be paid from the annuity to this school.

Id. § 7. 444. All the normal school buildings, the regular employees, and so forth, shall be placed at the disposal of the board of education for this purpose during the above mentioned eight weeks, without additional cost, except that nothing herein shall be construed to prevent the superintendent of public instruction from using any money at his disposal to further and promote the objects of this normal course of instruction among the colored teachers in any other part of the state.

NORFOLK CITY SCHOOL BOARD.*

1883-84, § 70, p. 49. 445. The board of school trustees for the city of Norfolk shall consist of two members from each ward of said city, together with the president of the common council, and the president of the select council, who shall be *ex-officio* members of said board.

Id. § 71. 446. There shall be elected by the qualified voters in each ward of said city, on the fourth Thursday of May, eighteen hundred and eighty-four, and *biennially* thereafter, one elector as a member of the board of school trustees, who shall be a resident of the ward during his term of office, to serve for *two years* and until his successor is appointed and qualified. The persons so elected in eighteen hundred and eighty-four, shall succeed the members of the present board, whose term will expire on the first day of July, eighteen hundred and eighty-four.

Id. § 72. 447. And the persons elected on the fourth Thursday of May, eighteen hundred and eighty-six, shall succeed the members of the present board, whose terms will expire on the first day of July, eighteen hundred and eighty-six. In case of a vacancy in the board, the members thereof shall elect a qualified person to fill the same, from the ward in which such vacancy exists, for the unexpired term.

Id. § 73. 448. The said board of school trustees shall have and exercise all the powers and duties which have been heretofore, or may hereafter, be vested in the school board of said city, by law or ordinance.

SCHOOL TAX—HOW PAID.

1883-84, § 113, p. 603. 449. All taxes assessed on property, real or personal, by this act, and by it dedicated to the maintenance of the public free schools of the state, shall be paid and collected only in lawful money of the United

---

*This act is clearly unconstitutional. Second clause of section 3 of art. 7 of the Constitution says: "In each school district there shall be elected or appointed *annually* one school trustee, who shall hold his office *three* years: provided that at the first election held under this provision there shall be three trustees elected, whose terms shall be one, two, and three years respectively."

States, and shall be paid into the treasury to the credit of the free school fund, and shall be used for no other purpose whatsoever. And to this end the auditor of public accounts shall have the books of the commissioners of the revenue prepared with reference to the separate assessment and collection of said school tax, and the several treasurers of the commonwealth shall have the tax bills in their counties or corporations so made out as to specify the amount of tax due from each tax-payer to the said public free school fund, including the capitation tax and school taxes of whatever kind or nature, and to keep said capitation tax and school taxes separate and distinct from all other taxes or revenues so collected by him, and forward the same, thus separate and distinct, to auditor of public accounts, which shall be kept separate and distinct by him from all other taxes or revenues until paid to the public free schools.

A NON-RESIDENT OF A CITY—HOW TO SEND HIS CHILDREN TO CITY SCHOOL.

450. It shall be lawful for any person who is a tax-payer and citizen of Virginia, owning real estate to the assessed value of fifteen hundred dollars in any city, town or county school district of the commonwealth, to send his children to any public free school in any city, town, county, or school district, subject to the laws regulating public free schools therein, as though said tax-payer resided in such city, town, or school district; and any guardian who is owner of such real estate and tax-payer for his ward or wards as aforesaid, shall be entitled to the privileges above named for his ward or wards, if such ward or wards be residents of the state. *Id. § 1, p. 669.*

HOLDING OF CERTAIN OFFICES INCOMPATIBLE.

451. No person holding the office of attorney for the commonwealth, judge of the county court, clerk of the county or circuit court, or sheriff, county or city treasurer, or superintendent of public schools for any county or corporation, shall hold any other office elective by the people; and if any person shall be elected to two or more of such offices, his qualification in one shall be a bar to his qualification in any other, and they shall be filled as other vacancies. *Id. § 5, p. 671.*

TEACHERS' INSTITUTES.

452. The board of education shall have power, at its discretion, to invite and encourage meetings of teachers at convenient places, and to provide addresses to be made before such meetings touching the processes of school organization, discipline, and instruction: provided that no public money shall be expended for the purposes of this section; that no such meeting of teachers shall be held during the period of the year when the schools are or should be open; that no teachers shall be compelled to attend such meetings, nor be paid for attendance. *Id. § 47, p. 672.*

DECLARING VACANT THE OFFICES OF SUPERINTENDENTS IN CERTAIN CASES, &c.

Id. § 1, p. 684.

453. The office of superintendent of public free schools and the office of city superintendent of schools, in any of the counties or districts or cities of the commonwealth, shall be deemed vacant in the following cases, and upon the happening of any one of the following events: The refusal of the senate to confirm his nomination, his death, resignation, or removal from the county or city for which he was appointed such superintendent, the expiration of his term of office, or his removal from office by competent authority.

Id. § 2.

454. It shall not be lawful for the board of education, or the governor, during the periods when the senate is not in session, to appoint as school superintendent, for any county or city of this commonwealth, any person who, having been previously nominated by said board for the position of superintendent of schools, has been rejected by the senate.

PROHIBITING THE ACTIVE PARTICIPATION IN POLITICS OF CERTAIN OFFICERS OF THE STATE GOVERNMENT.

Id. § 1, p. 698.

455. It shall not be lawful for the judge of any court, the superintendent of public instruction, any superintendent of schools, the superintendent, manager, or any employee of any asylum or state institution of learning, actively to induce or procure, either directly or indirectly, or to attempt either directly or indirectly to induce or procure any qualified elector to vote in any election for any particular candidate, or in favor of any particular political party, or to vote against any particular candidate, or against any particular political party.

Id. § 2.

456. It shall not be lawful for any of the officers or employees mentioned in the foregoing section to participate actively in politics, and making political speeches, or the active or official participation in political meetings, shall be deemed to be an active participation in politics within the meaning of this section.

Id. § 3.

457. Any person offending under either of the foregoing sections shall be deemed guilty of a misdemeanor, and upon conviction thereof shall be fined no less than fifty dollars nor more than five hundred dollars for each offence. Any person prosecuted under section one of this act may be examined as a witness in his own behalf.

Id. § 4.

458. Any person convicted under this act shall forfeit the office or appointment held by him, and it shall be the duty of the court, wherein such party is convicted, to declare the office or appointment so held by such person vacated, and such vacancy shall be filled in the mode prescribed by law for filling vacancies occurring in such office.

PROVIDING FOR CERTIFICATES OF ELECTION FOR CERTAIN OFFICERS ELECTED BY THE GENERAL ASSEMBLY.

459. It shall be the duty of the keeper of the rolls, immediately after any election by the general assembly of any officers mentioned in this act, to cause a list of all school commissioners, who may be elected under the act entitled an act to amend and re-enact an act approved January eleventh, eighteen hundred and seventy-seven, entitled an act to provide for the appointment and removal of district school trustees, and to repeal the fourth clause of the seventh section of the seventy-eighth chapter of the Code of eighteen hundred and seventy-three, which became a law on the twentieth of February, eighteen hundred and eighty-four, and all members of the county or city electoral boards, who may be chosen under the act in force February fourteenth, eighteen hundred and eighty-four, entitled an act to provide for the manner of choosing registrars and judges and clerks of election, and to repeal sections eight and twenty-four of chapter eight, and sections two and three of chapter seven of the Code of eighteen hundred and seventy-three, and the keeper of the rolls will certify such lists to the secretary of the commonwealth. It shall be the duty of the secretary of the commonwealth, upon the receipt of any such list, to make out, sign, and mail to each person so elected, a certificate, setting forth the fact of such election, the name of the person elected, and the office and term for which he was elected; which certificate shall be evidence of the facts therein stated, and to which shall be appended the oath to be taken by such person.

Id. § 1, p. 433.

INDEX.

ALEXANDRIA COUNTY.

Section.		Page.
122.	May impose an additional tax for school purposes.............	56-57

APPEALS.

100.	From action of District Board in locating school-house or discontinuing school; how taken.................................	50
27.	From decisions of Superintendent Public Instruction............	35
44.	From decision by County Superintendents......................	38
152.	From action of District Boards in forming sub-districts; how taken..	67-68
152.	How taken from action of County Boards in forming sub-districts from districts belonging to different counties............	68
159.	From action of School Directors and District Board; how taken..	70
160.	From action of District Boards in extending lines of separate school districts..	71
334.	From action of City Superintendent...........................	121

ATTORNEY FOR COMMONWEALTH.

149.	To act as Attorney for County School Board...................	66
90.	To prosecute for fines.......................................	47-48
49.	Member of Trustee Electoral Board............................	39

AUDITOR OF PUBLIC ACCOUNTS.

129.	Duty of with reference to Commissioners of Revenue books and school levies..	59
131.	To make estimate of funds upon receipt of Commissioners' books and report to Superintendent of Public Instruction ninety per centum as basis for distribution. Superintendent to furnish the Auditor with statement of amounts due counties and corporations on this basis........................	60
131.	Warrant to issue to Superintendents..........................	60
135.	To furnish Superintendents with blank warrants...............	61
137.	To pay arrearages of State fund quarterly....................	61-62

Section.		Page.
138.	Chapters 248 of Acts 1877-8 and 127 of Acts 1878-9 repealed,	62
139.	To return to schools a portion of moneys diverted therefrom	62-63
142.	Requisition for State money from Superintendents	63-64
288.	To pay annual appropriation to Virginia Normal and Collegiate Institute	108

BOARD OF EDUCATION.

3.	Of whom composed	32
4.	Place and time of meeting	32
5.	Record of proceedings	32
6.	Literary funds, how recoverable	32-33
7.	To make by-laws and regulations for its government	32
8.	To suggest improvements in system to General Assembly	32
9.	To invest unappropriated capital and income of Literary Fund,	32
10.	To appoint and remove county Superintendents of schools	33
11.	To decide appeals from decisions of Superintendent Public Instruction	33
12.	To determine contingent expenses of Superintendent's office and examine accounts of same	33
13.	To audit claims and issue warrants on Second Auditor	33
14.	To approve appointments of first and second clerks and fix their salaries	33
15.	To regulate all matters pertaining to the system not otherwise provided for	33
16.	To make annual report to Legislature	34
17.	To punish county Superintendents for neglect of duty	34
64.	To fix time of meetings of Board of School Trustees	41
87.	Members of shall not be interested in supplying text books, &c.	47
96.	Teachers meetings to be encouraged	48
105.	Power to remove Superintendents for violation of this section or discrimination in pay of teachers	53
114.	To provide uniformity of text-books	54-55
116.	To establish number of schools according to amount of funds available	55
117.	To guard against multiplication of schools without sufficient funds	55
118.	Literary Fund invested in	55
140.	To apportion moneys received from Norfolk and Western Railroad Company	63
161.	To provide regulations for carrying out the provisions of act of Legislature 1877-'8, chapter 161	71
162.	May relieve counties of Fairfax and Loudoun from the operation of the sub-districting act	71
234.	Authorized to sell land scrip donated by United States, proceeds, how invested	92

Section.		Page.
254.	To turn over funds to Board of Visitors of Virginia Agricultural and Mechanical College........	97
265.	Members of corporation "The Miller Manual Labor School of Albemarle"........	101
268.	Duty as to fund, etc., of "Miller Manual Labor School"........	102
269.	To keep and preserve funds, stocks, securities, etc., of Miller Fund; liability therefor........	102–103
271.	To execute deed of release in reference to estate of Samuel Miller........	103
275.	Commission to select site for Virginia Normal and Collegiate Institute to report to........	105
278.	To fill vacancies in Board of Visitors of Virginia Normal and Collegiate Institute........	106
279.	Board of Visitors of Virginia Normal and Collegiate Institute to make annual report to........	106
285.	To approve salaries of professors and teachers of Virginia Normal and Collegiate Institute........	107
286.	To approve bond of treasurer of Virginia Normal and Collegiate Institute........	108–109
288.	State Treasurer to place to credit of Board appropriation for Virginia Normal and Collegiate Institute; how paid........	108
327.	To fill vacancies in city School Trustees when........	119
331.	To appoint separate City Superintendent when........	121
337.	To appoint and remove City Superintendent........	121
339.	Authority in reference to text-books in Richmond, Petersburg and Norfolk........	122
349.	Refusal of Superintendent to examine teachers to be reported to........	125
400.	To prescribe list of text-books........	134
403.	Contract as to text-books limited........	135
412.	Regulations in reference to text-books heretofore adopted in conflict with new repealed........	136–7

BOARD OF SUPERVISORS.

123.	County School Board, on or before first Wednesday in November, to file an estimate of money needed for support of schools in county........	57
124.	County School Board, on or before first Wednesday in November, to file separate estimates of money needed in each school district........	57
125.	To meet on request of Superintendent of Schools, when........	58
126.	To levy tax for county and district free schools........	58
127.	Authority given to levy tax on roadway and track, depots, &c., of any railroad company and its telegraph lines—assessment, how based........	58

BOARD OF REFERENCE.

Section.		Page.
100.	How formed, duties, &c..	50
152.	To decide appeals from action of District Boards in forming sub-districts from two or more districts...........................	67
152.	How formed in case of appeals from action of County Boards in forming sub-districts from parts of two or more counties...	68
159.	Appeals to, from action of District Boards.........................	71

CENSUS.

75.	To be taken every five years..	43
154.	To be taken of sub-districts, when.....................................	69–70

CITY SUPERINTENDENTS.

132.	To endorse Auditor's warrant and deposit with Treasurer of corporation..	60
331.	By whom appointed...	120–121
332.	Compensation...	121
333.	May teach in public schools...	121
334.	May suspend or dismiss pupils, subject to appeal................	121
335.	Privileges in meetings of School Boards............................	121
336.	Under same regulations as county Superintendents............	121
337.	How appointed or removed...	121
133.	To take up warrants of School Board and issue new ones, limit of aggregate amount..	60
135.	Auditor to furnish blank warrants to...................................	61
342.	Must file oath of office with Superintendent of Public Instruction...	123
342.	United States officers prohibited from holding office of Superintendent..	123
346.	Must enforce regulations...	124
347.	To make monthly reports to Superintendent of Public Instruction—when due—fine for failure................................	124
348.	To fix times for examining teachers—prohibited from examining at other times—may admit public................................	124
349.	Duties in examining teachers—may refuse to examine—in case of refusal must report to Board of Education........................	125
350.	To prepare list of questions for examination of teachers and forward copy of same to Superintendent Public Instruction,	125
351.	Examination papers to be endorsed and filed: to furnish copy..	125–6
354.	To issue warrants on Treasurer for school fund apportioned under Grandstaff Act...	126
355.	To apportion school money...	126

Section.   *Page.*

359. To see that books of District Clerk are correctly kept and school funds properly applied 127
360. To require Treasurer to make stated reports in reference to school funds 127
361. To require annual report from Treasurer 127
363. To enter reports of Treasurer and apportionments of school funds in record book 128
364. To keep a record of applicants for teachers' certificates 128
367. Boards to furnish at August meeting an annual detailed report of work done 128-9
389. To hold Institute at least annually—may examine teachers at same 132
411. Duties and privileges conferred in reference to regulations of Board of Education 136

CITY SCHOOL BOARDS.

323. Powers to prescribe number and boundaries of school districts, number of trustees, etc. 118
324. Incorporated, style of corporation 118-119
325. Authority; quorum; clerk and his pay 119
326. Who ineligible as Superintendent; eligibility of members of Council on City School Boards 119
327. How constituted; vacancies, how filled; Council failing to act on vacancies; appointment by State Board 119
328. Cannot raise or use funds for any school that is not a part of the free-school system 120
329. To make estimate for Council of school funds needed 120
330. State funds for cities; how apportioned and disbursed 120
334. Appeals from action of Superintendent in suspending or dismissing pupils to 121
335. Superintendent's privileges in meetings of 121
336. Subject to same rules as District Boards 121
338. Powers and duties of 121
339. Shall prescribe text-books 122
411. Duties and privileges conferred in reference to regulations of Board of Education 136

CITY COUNCILS.

323. To approve number and boundaries of school districts, number of trustees, etc. 118
326. Member of ineligible to act as Superintendent; may serve as a member of School Board; number limited 118-119
327. To fill vacancies in School Trustees; failure to do so, how appointed 119
328. To levy tax for public schools 120

INDEX.

Section.		Page.
329.	School Board to furnish estimate of school funds needed to...	120
340.	To make appropriations for school purposes; tax limited; Council of Richmond given same discretion as to school funds as County Supervisors......................................	121

CLERK OF DISTRICT SCHOOL BOARD.

68.	Penalty for failure to make report to Board........................	42
74.	Duties of..	43
76.	To keep record of proceedings of Board, official acts, &c.....	43
77.	Compensation...	44
75.	To take school census and submit same to District Board, compensation therefor...	43
87.	Cannot be interested in supplying text-books, &c................	47
88.	Penalty for failure to turn over papers, books, &c., to successor..	47
104.	To file with Superintendent certificate as to length of time schools have been in operation..................................	52
145.	Compensation, how drawn...	64
147.	To report to County School Board annually all official transactions...	65
148.	Penalty for failing to make annual report to County Board.....	65-66
154.	To furnish copy of act to meeting for election of school directors...	68-69
156.	To take census of sub-districts, when............................	69-70
362.	Superintendent to notify of apportionment of district funds...	127
371.	To furnish list of patrons of school when needed for a meeting...	129
397.	To record permits and receive tuition fees......................	134
398.	Records concerning admission of adults in schools, how kept,	134

CLERK COUNTY SCHOOL BOARD.

81.	How appointed, compensation.....................................	45
88.	Penalty for failure to turn over books, &c., to successor........	47
148.	To enter fine against delinquent county treasurer or clerk District Board...	65-66

COUNTY SUPERINTENDENTS.

34.	How appointed, term of service...................................	36-37
35.	Compensation, how determined....................................	37
36 and 144.	Salaries, how paid.. 37	and 64
37.	Duties...	37
38.	To explain system...	37
39.	To prepare scheme for apportioning State and county school funds and furnish copies thereof................................	37

INDEX.

Section.		Page.
40.	To examine teachers and grant certificates	37-38
41.	To promote improvement and efficiency of teachers	38
42.	To assist in organizing boards of district school trustees	38
43.	To visit and examine schools and school districts, examine records and official papers of school districts, advise and counsel teachers, &c	38
44.	To decide appeals or complaints	38
45.	To administer oaths and take testimony	38
46.	To keep record of official acts	38
47.	To require reports from clerks of boards annually or oftener	38-39
48.	To observe regulations prescribed by Superintendent Public Instruction and make reports	39
49.	A member of Trustee Electoral Board	39
51.	Clerk of Electoral Board	40
53.	To report failure of clerk District Board to make annual report	40
57.	To call first meeting of Board of School Trustees	41
70.	To name and number school districts	42
75.	To require clerk District Board to take census	43
78.	A member of County School Board	44
79.	Is President of Board	44
87.	Cannot be interested in supplying text-books, &c	47
100.	To appoint Board of Reference to decide appeals from action of District Boards in locating school houses or discontinuing schools	50
102.	To condemn school-houses. Trustees must consult Superintendent in reference to building school houses	51
125.	Salary of Superintendent of Nelson county may be increased and paid out of county and district fund, when	57
132.	To endorse Auditor's warrant and deposit with Treasurer of county	60
133.	To take up warrants of District School Board and issue new ones, aggregate amount not to exceed amount of Auditor's warrant; penalty for exceeding	60
135.	Auditor to furnish Superintendents with blank warrants	61
146.	County Treasurer to render annual account of school money received and disbursed; account to be forwarded to Superintendent Public Instruction	65
148.	To visit and examine books, &c., of delinquent clerks before forwarding annual report	65-66
156.	Report of census of sub-districts to be reported to	70
160.	Authority in respect to teachers and schools not interfered with,	71
342.	Must file oath of office with Superintendent Public Instruction,	123
343.	United States officers prohibited from holding office of Superintendent	124
344.	Prohibited from teaching in public schools	124

Section.		Page.
346.	Must enforce laws and regulations..................................	124
347.	To make monthly report to Superintendent Public Instruction—when due—fine for failure................................	124
348.	To fix time for examining teachers—prohibited from examining on other dates—may admit the public.....................	124-5
349.	Duties in examining teachers; may refuse to examine; in case of refusal must report to Board Education................	125
350.	To prepare list of questions for examinations and forward copy of same to Superintendent Public Instruction............	125
351.	How examination papers to be endorsed and filed; to furnish copy..	125
354.	To issue warrants on Treasurer for apportionment of school funds under Grandstaff act	126
355.	To apportion State money to districts................................	126
359.	To see that the books of district clerks are correctly kept and school fund properly applied....................................	127
360.	To require County Treasurer to make stated reports in reference to school funds...	127
361.	To require annual report from Treasurer..........................	127
362.	To apportion district funds and notify clerks of District Boards..	127
363.	To enter reports of Treasurers and apportionments of school fund in record-book...	128
364.	To keep a record of applicants for teacher's certificate...........	128
367.	Boards at any meeting to furnish detailed report of year's school work, etc.; salary of teachers to be reported and confirmed...	128
368.	Boards at October meeting to make and forward estimate of funds needed in district, to be submitted to County Board....	129
379.	To approve time fixed for opening and closing school...........	130
380.	Boards to report when contracting with teacher..................	130
382.	To see that no teacher is paid for more than the average attendance...	131
383.	Duties of in certain cases where average cannot be obtained...	131
384.	Report to be made when average is reduced from certain causes...	131
388.	May renew professional certificate...................................	132
389.	To hold institute at least annually; may examine teachers at same...	132
402.	To appoint advisory committee to select text-books, and act as chairman of same; time of meeting..........................	134
403.	To fix time of meeting of County Board to select text-books ..	135
405.	To give public notice of adoption of text-books..................	135
406.	To make arrangements for sale of text-books, each teacher to be furnished with copy of regulations of Board of Education and price-list of books................................	135

INDEX. 147

Section.		Page.
408.	To require report from teacher as to use of text-books, and to withhold receipt for monthly report for violations	136
409.	To see that the regulations of Board of Education are enforced and make monthly reports to Superintendent Public Instruction	136

COUNTY SCHOOL BOARDS.

78.	How formed	44
79.	To elect Vice-President	44
80.	President to call meetings	44
81.	Record of proceedings, by-laws, appointment and compensation of clerk, etc.	45
82.	Annual meeting	45
83.	Property vested in Board	45-46
84.	Annual report to Superintendent Public Instruction	46
85.	County Treasurer to collect, disburse or invest funds under direction of Board	46
98.	Donations of property to county vested in	49
111.	May sanction introduction of higher branches in school	54
123.	Estimate of school fund needed for county to be furnished Board of Supervisors	57
124.	Separate estimate of district funds to be laid before Board of Supervisors	57
125.	President to request Board of Supervisors to meet to examine estimates	57
134.	At annual meeting in August to compare warrants of District Board with those issued by Superintendent and report to State Superintendent	61
147.	County Treasurer and clerks of District Boards to make annual report	65
148.	Penalty for failure of County Treasurer and Clerk of District Board to make annual report	65-66
149.	To institute legal proceedings against delinquent County Treasurer, clerks of District Boards, or other officials, when necessary	66
152.	May form sub-districts from districts of different counties	68
162.	May adopt at their discretion act of 1878, chapter 161, providing for the division of school districts into sub-districts and appointment of School Directors (except Fairfax and Loudoun)	161
162.	County Boards of Fairfax and Loudoun may apply for relief from provisions of this act when	161
328.	Cannot use school funds for school not a part of the free-school system	120
365.	To hold two meetings each year; date of said meetings	128

Section. Page.

368. Superintendents to submit estimates for funds needed in each district.. 129
401. To make selection of text books................................ 134
403. Time of meeting to adopt text-books.......................... 135

COUNTY TREASURERS.

85. To collect, disburse or invest funds under control of County School Boards, compensation therefor, liable on official bond for proper application 46
130. To receive, collect and disburse all funds for school purposes, keep district, State and county funds separate, compensation, &c.. 59
131. To accept Auditor's warrant from Superintendents............ 60
132. To credit Superintendent Schools with amount of warrant from Auditor... 60
133. Not to pay warrants on State fund unless issued by Superintendent, nor exceed amount to credit of Superintendent; penalty for violation.. 60–61
142. To notify County Superintendent of receipt of State funds..... 63–64
144. To transmit warrant for pay of Superintendents to Superintendent Public Instruction when correctness doubted......... 64
146. To render to County Superintendents account of receipts and disbursement of school moneys annually or oftener............ 65
147. To furnish County School Board report of transactions in receipt and disbursement of school funds....................... 65
148. Penalty for failure to make annual report..................... 65–66
354. To pay warrants of Superintendents on fund apportioned under Grandstaff act 126
360. To make stated reports to Superintendent..................... 127
361. To make annual report to Superintendent..................... 127
398. Records regarding tuition fees received; how kept............ 134

COUNTY COURT OF ALBEMARLE.

268. Duty of as to Miller Fund, expensés, etc., of Miller Manual Labor School... 102

COMMISSIONERS OF REVENUE.

129. To keep separate the tax for each school district............ 58–59

CONSTITUTION OF VIRGINIA.

Preamble to Constitution... 1–3
Art. 1—Bill of rights.. 3–5
Art. 2—Division of power between departments........................ 5–6

INDEX. 149

Section. *Page.*
Art. 3—Elective franchise and qualification for office.............. 6–7
Art. 4—Executive department. 7–10
Art. 5—Legislative department 10–14
Art. 6—Judiciary department.. 15
       Court of Appeals.. 15
       Circuit Courts... 16–17
       County Courts.. 17
       Government of cities and towns. 17–20
Art. 7—County organization... 20
       Magisterial districts.. 20
       School districts... 20–21
Art. 8—Education... 21–23
Art. 9—Militia... 23
Art. 10—Taxation and Finance.. 23–26
Art. 11—Miscellaneous provisions... 26
       Homestead and other exemptions........................ 26–27
       Church property 27
       Heirship of property... 27
Art. 12—Future changes in Constitution................................. 27–28
       Schedule.. 28–29
       Common law and present statutes in force....... 28
Writs, remedies, rights, prosecutions and charters continued.. 28
Indictments proceeded with... 28–29
Courts to have their jurisdiction.. 29
Fines, penalties, forfeitures, and escheats to accrue to State..... 29
Recognizances, bonds, obligations, &c., entered into to State or
    county, &c., binding; rights and liabilities continue.......... 29
Crimes to be prosecuted and punished otherwise provided........ 29

DISTRICT BOARDS.

57. Quorum and officers... 41
58. Duties prescribed... 41
59. To enforce school laws and regulations........................ 41
60. To employ and dismiss teachers.................................... 41
61. To suspend or dismiss pupils.. 41
62. To provide indigent scholars with text-books............... 41
63. To require the taking of census of school children...... 41
64. Times of meetings fixed by Board of Education; special
    meetings, how called... 41
65. To call meetings of the people for consultation in regard to
    school interests... 41
66. To prepare estimate of funds needed in the district for pro-
    viding school houses, etc... 41–42
67. To care for and control school property in district 42
68. To report annually to Superintendent Schools; penalty for
    failure of clerk to make report................................... 42

Section.		Page.
69.	To visit schools of district	42
74.	Must notify County Treasurer when money is borrowed	43
75.	To examine clerk's list of school children	43
98.	Donations of property to district vested in	49
100.	Shall provide suitable school houses, furniture and appliances; may hire, purchase or build; appeal from action of Board in locating school house, how taken, etc	50
101.	May condemn land for school houses; mode of procedure	50-51
102.	Trustees to consult county Superintendent before building school house	51
104.	Clerk of, to file with county Superintendent certificate as to length of time schools have been in operation	52
110.	May introduce higher branches and require fee	54
122.	Excess of levy may be applied to teachers' salaries	57
145.	To audit teachers' and clerks' pay—cost of providing school houses, furniture, text-books, &c.	64
147.	Clerk of, to make annual report to County Board	65
151.	To form Sub-Districts—how numbered	67
152.	Sub-Districts from parts of two or more Districts—how formed—by failing to agree, how determined	67-68
153.	May grant permit for pupils to enter from outside limits of a Sub-District upon certain conditions	68
154.	To appoint meetings for election of School Directors—who to preside, how conducted, &c	68-69
155.	May make contribution for contingent expenses of school	69
156.	Clerk to take census of Sub-Districts, when	69-70
157.	Opening and closing of schools, pay of teachers, &c., under control of	70
159.	To decide appeals from action of Directors—Directors to report violations of law to	70-71
160.	May extend lines of separate school districts, when	71
355.	To issue warrants on School Fund for pay of teachers	126
357.	District school tax under control of, and how used	126
358.	Excess of District levy, how to be applied	126-7
366.	To hold two regular meetings; time of said meetings	128
367.	To prepare detailed report of work done during the year at August meeting and furnish same to Superintendent	128
368.	At October meeting to prepare estimate of district funds needed and forward to Superintendent	129
369.	May transact any other business at annual meeting; special meetings, how called	129
370.	Have absolute power to employ teachers	129
371 to 376.	May refer selection of teachers to patrons; mode of procedure, etc., must be governed by its action if teacher is selected, when	129-30
378.	Cannot employ teacher unless he holds certificate of Superintendent for current year	130

Section. *Page.*

379. Must enter into written contracts with teachers; failure to do so subjects members to fine... 130
380. Must prescribe time of opening and closing school, subject to approval of Superintendent, and state in contract............... 130
381. Report to be made to Superintendent when contracting with teacher... 131
382. May contract with teachers with less than average................ 131
384. May reduce the average; when... 131
385. May continue school not making average; when................. 131-2
386. Authorized to pay amount due teacher whose school has been closed... 132
392. May designate holidays... 133
393. May authorize admission of pupils in graded schools from different districts.. 133
394. May sub-district its territory... 133
395. Audults must pay tuition fee; permit authorized................. 133

DISTRICT SCHOOL TRUSTEES.

49. How appointed, qualifications, &c..................................... 39
54. Who eligible.. 40
55. Must be a resident of School District................................ 40
56. Exempt from service on juries and militia duty................... 41
73. May borrow money... 43
78. To constitute County Board... 44
83. Holding property, to make report to County Board when called upon... 46
87. Cannot be interested in supplying text-books, &c................ 47'
98. Authority over property donated to District....................... 49
99. Permission to use unoccupied school-houses by any teacher for school purposes may be granted.............................. 49
101. To condemn land for school-houses, mode of procedure........ 50-51
102. To consult Superintendent Schools before building school-house.. 51
149. County Board may petition court for removal of, for cause.... 66
240. Selection of students to Virginia, Agricultural and Mechanical College... 93
343. United States officer cannot be a School Trustee................ 124
344. Cannot teach in public schools.. 124

EXAMINATION OF TEACHERS.

349. What to consist of. How conducted................................. 125
350. Superintendent to prepare list of questions, &c................. 125
351. Examination papers, how endorsed................................... 125

GENERAL RULES FOR OFFICERS.

Section. Page.
86. Higher officers may, temporarily, discharge the duties of the lower in certain cases.. 46-47

GRADED SCHOOLS.

115. Preference given to... 55
392. Pupils how admitted.. 133

HAMPTON NORMAL AND AGRICULTURAL INSTITUTE.

255. Appropriation, conditions of; curators, how appointed, term of service, etc... 97-98
256. Students, how selected, privileges................................. 98
257. Treasurer, how appointed, compensation............................ 98
258. Funds of Institute; interest on State debt held, to be paid..... 98-99
259. Annual report; when made; contents................................ 99
260. Reservation of control by Legislature............................. 99
262. Prohibition of sale of liquor to students; penalty for viola-
     tion... 99-100
263. Conviction for sale of liquor to students: County Court to
     revoke license... 99-100
291. Protection to State institutions, public trusts and funds....... 109

INSTITUTION FOR DEAF AND DUMB AND THE BLIND.

224. Act of incorporation; its powers................................... 89
225. Visitors, how appointed, term of service; vacancies, how
     filled.. 89
226. Appointment of President and Secretary............................. 89
227. Duties of Board; removal of a professor............................ 89
228. Annual meeting; special meetings, how called...................... 90
229. Fiscal year, end of; annual report, when and to whom to be
     made.. 90
230. Schools for deaf and for blind; how pupils selected............... 90
231. Arbitrators authorized; how appointed.............................. 90
239. Annual appropriation; how paid..................................... 91
291. Protection of State institutions, public trusts and funds........ 109

MILLER MANUAL LABOR SCHOOL OF ALBEMARLE.

264. Incorporated... 101
265. Who members of corporation, corporate powers...................... 101
266. Meetings, who authorized to call................................... 101

INDEX. 153

Section.   *Page.*

267. General Assembly to designate corporators in case of officers being changed or abolished, power given Legislature to change organization.. 101
268. Corporation to hold property; duties of Board of Education, Second Auditor, and County Court of Albemarle as to funds and expenses for support of school; expenses, how allowed and paid; duty of clerk of court; duties of district school trustees... 102
269. Funds, stock, securities, &c., of school, how kept and preserved 102–103
270. Rate of interest on bonds.. 103
271. Board of Education to execute deed of release, &c............. 103
272. Rights of the heirs of Samuel Miller not affected................ 104
273. Status of case if compromise fails..................................... 104
291. Protection to institutions of State, public trusts and funds...... 109

OATHS OF OFFICE.

341. Form of oath of school officers.. 123

SCHOOL FUNDS.

13. Claims against, how audited... 33
83. What moneys vested in County Board.............................. 45–46
103. District first to provide school houses before receiving any... 52
104. When State funds to be paid for school purposes................. 52
116. Number of schools regulated by amount of funds................ 55
118. Literary fund, how received, collected and disbursed........... 55–56
119. What to consist of... 56
120. State funds, how derived... 56
121. County funds how raised... 56
122. District funds, how levied... 56
123. Estimate of amount needed, to be submitted to Board of Supervisors... 57
125. County and District cannot be used to pay Superintendents salaries (Nelson county excepted)..................................... 57
126. Board of Supervisors to levy tax for County and District free school purposes.. 58
127. Board of Supervisors authorized to levy tax on roadway and track, depots, &c., of any railroad company and its telegraph lines, in county... 58
128. School taxes, how assessed... 58
129. Duty of Commissioner of Revenue as to school tax levied.... 58–59
130. County Treasurer receives and disburses, District, State and County funds to be kept separate..................................... 59
131. and 142. How State funds placed in County Treasury......... 60 and 65

21

Section.		Page.
136.	Excess of approximate amount of Auditor to be distributed as law provides............	61
133.	State fund, how drawn from county treasury............	60
137.	Arrearages of State funds, how paid............	61
139	and 140. Auditor to return portions of moneys diverted.......	62-63
141.	Fund for normal school for colored teachers............	63
144	and 145. Pay of Superintendent, teachers, &c., how drawn...	64
146.	Treasurer to render account annually to County Superintendent............	65
150.	Unexpended, how disposed of............	67
156.	When census of sub-districts affects population of county, how apportioned............	69
160.	When lines of separate school districts are extended, how apportioned............	71
328.	Cannot be used for any school not a part of the public free school system............	120
330.	For city, how apportioned, by whom received and disbursed...	120
340.	Duty of City Council to make appropriation............	122
352.	How classified............	126
353.	How used............	126
354.	How paid out............	126
355.	How apportioned to districts and how paid............	126
356.	When county fund apportioned and for what used............	126
357.	District tax, for what purpose used, under control of District Board............	126
358.	Excess of district levy, how used............	126
382.	Cannot be used to support school with less average than ten...	131

SCHOOL DIRECTORS.

154.	Mode of election, term of service, vacancies how filled, who eligible, &c............	68-69
157.	To choose teachers, who eligible; report made to the District Board, &c............	70
158.	Duties of............	70
159.	To report violations of law to District Board, appeal may be taken to Board of Reference............	70-71
162.	Act providing for may be adopted at the discretion of County Boards, except in Fairfax and Loudoun............	71

SCHOOL OFFICERS.

88.	To turn over to successors all papers, books, &c.; penalty for failure............	47
386.	To enforce laws and regulations............	132
387.	Caution as to employment of inefficient teachers............	132

Section.		Page.
390.	To require pupils to be provided with books prescribed by school law..	132
399	Caution as to Nepotism...	134
410.	May assist in furnishing text-books...................................	136

SCHOOL PROPERTY.

97.	Vested in and held by each School District........................	49
98.	Donations to county vested in County Board, and to district in District Board...	49
101.	Condemnation of land for school-house............................	50-51

SCHOOL HOUSES.

99.	Trustees may permit use of by teachers of other than of the public free school, under certain circumstances...................	49
100.	Board of school trústees to provide; appeal from action in locating, how taken...	50
101.	Condemnation of land for..	50-51
102.	Style and expense..	51
145.	Cost of providing, repairs, furniture, &c.; how paid............	64
152.	Doubts arising as to location in sub-districts, how decided......	68

SCHOOLS.

1.	Uniform system to be adopted...	31
2.	Authority for administering system...................................	31
105.	Who admitted into, pupils from an adjoining district, white and colored separate, etc...	52
106.	Privileges of sending children to, who entitled....................	53
107.	Number of pupils required to form a school fixed by Board of Education...	53
108.	Persons suffering from contagious diseases excluded from, vaccination required..	53-54
109.	Branches to be taught in..	54
110.	Higher branches may be taught in...................................	54
111.	Introduction of higher branches to receive approval of County Board..	54
112.	Introduction of higher branches not to interfere with elementary branches...	54
113.	Two teachers may be employed, when...............................	54
114.	Uniformity of text-books to be provided............................	54-55
115.	Preference given to graded schools...................................	55
116.	Number of schools regulated by amount of funds.................	55
117.	Board of Education to guard against multiplication of schools without sufficient funds..	55
153.	Pupils may be received from beyond limits of sub-district, how	68

Section.		Page.
154.	Contingent Expenses, how provided for..................................	69
155.	District Boards may provide for contingent expenses..............	69
157.	Opening and closing, terms and pay of teachers under control of District Board..	70
381.	Average required to constitute...	131
383.	Average may be reduced, when...	131
384.	With less than the average, how continued...........................	131
394 and 395.	Adults may be admitted, how................................	133

SCHOOL DISTRICTS

70.	How named and numbered, record of...............................	42
71.	Corporate powers..	42
72.	Boundaries of, towns of 500 may form separate Districts, and Council appoint trustees...	42
103.	Not entitled to funds unless provision be made for school-houses, etc..	52
151.	Sub-Districts, how formed...	67
152.	Sub-Districts from Districts of same or different counties, how formed...	67-68
160.	Separate School Districts may extend their lines beyond corporate limits, when...	71
163.	Act of 1875, providing for division into Sub-Districts, repealed	71

SCHOOLS IN CITIES AND TOWNS.

321.	How established..	118
322.	How classified..	118
328.	Tax levied by City Council for support...............................	120
329.	Estimate for their maintenance..	120
330.	State funds, how apportioned..	120

SECOND AUDITOR.

174.	Board of Visitors, University of Virginia, to make annual report to, contents...	74
187.	Visitors, trustees, &c., of any college or academy, established by the State to make annual report to before October 1......	77
188.	Visitors, trustees, &c., failing to make annual report, penalty therefor...	78
189.	Interest on State stock to be paid.....................................	78
229.	Report of Board of Visitors, Deaf Dumb and Blind Institute....	90
254.	To pay Virginia Agricultural and Mechanical College interest on State debt, held by College.....................................	97
265.	A member of corporation of "The Miller Manual Labor School of Albemarle"...	101
268.	Duty as to fund, &c., of Miller Manual Labor School"...........	102

INDEX. 157

SUPERINTENDENT OF PUBLIC INSTRUCTION.

Section.		Page.
18.	Election and term of service, vacancy how filled................................	34
19.	Salary, how paid, expenses, &c..	34
20.	Office to be provided for..	34
21.	Chief Executive of the system...	35
22.	Enforcement of school laws..	35
23.	To decide questions of law and regulations.....................................	35
24.	Preparation of blanks, &c...	
25.	Reports from County Superintendents..	35
26.	Visit to schools...	35
27.	Decide appeals from decisions of Superintendents...........................	35
28.	Preserve copies of decisions...	35
29.	Preserve documents, books, &c., from other States received...	35-36
30.	Apportionment of State funds..	36
31.	Official seal...	36
32.	Annual report of...	36
33.	Discharge of other duties...	36
131.	To furnish statement to Auditor Public Accounts, of amount due each county and corporation upon basis furnished by Auditor...	
134.	County School Boards to report result of comparison of District and County Superintendents' warrants annually to......	63
144.	County Treasurers to transmit warrant for pay of Superintendents, where doubt exists as to correctness...........................	64
146.	Treasurer's annual accounts of receipts to be forwarded by Superintendent..	64
148.	County Superintendent to report on accounts of delinquent clerks of District Boards...	65-66
156.	Report of census of sub-district to be made, when........................	69-70
244.	A member of the Board of Visitors of Virginia Agricultural and Mechanical College, and of Board of Curators of Hampton Normal and Agricultural Institute................................	94-95
259.	Annual report from Virginia Agricultural and Mechanical College and Hampton Normal and Agricultural Institute...	99
265.	A member of corporation, "The Miller Manual Labor School of Albemarle"...	101
282.	A member of Board of Visitors of Virginia Normal and Collegiate Institute, and chairman...	106
283.	Board of Visitors of Virginia Normal and Collegiate Institute, a corporate body..	107
316.	To appoint to scholarships in Nashville University.........................	117
320.	To give information pertaining to University at Nashville..............	117
323.	Report of school districts in cities..	118
342.	Superintendents to file oaths of office..	123
347.	Superintendents to make monthly reports.....................................	124

Section.		Page.
350.	Superintendents to furnish copy of list of questions in examining teachers...	125
398.	To prescribe form for report of statistics regarding admission of adults in public schools..	134
409.	County Superintendents to make monthly reports in respect to observance of regulations of Board of Education............	136

SUB-DISTRICTS.

151.	How formed, record of boundaries..	67
152.	From two or more districts, how formed..................................	67
152.	From districts belonging to different counties, how formed.....	68
157.	Teachers in, how chosen...	70
162.	Act providing for division into may be adopted at discretion of County Board, except in Fairfax and Loudoun.................	71
163.	Act approved February 5, 1875, in reference to division of districts into, repealed...	71
393.	District Boards may form sub-districts.......................................	133

TEACHERS.

91.	Must hold certificate of County Superintendent.........................	48
92.	To keep daily record of facts pertaining to school and deliver to clerk School Board...	48
93.	Written contract made before entering upon duties................	48
94.	May suspend scholars, subject to decision of Board of School Trustees..	48
95.	Same exemptions as School Trustees..	48
95.	Institutes for teachers...	48
112.	To give not less than five hours to instruction in elementary branches where but one is employed..................................	54
113.	Two teachers may be employed, when....................................	54
145.	How paid..	64
157.	How chosen; compensation, how fixed, etc..............................	70
159.	May appeal from action of School Directors, or District Board	70-71
345.	Must be at least eighteen years of age.....................................	124
349.	Examination, of what to consist of..	125
351.	May obtain copy of examination papers...................................	125
370.	By whom employed...	129
371.	May be selected by patrons, when and how............................	129
377.	Must hold certificate of Superintendent....................................	130
378.	Boards of Trustees to give written contracts............................	130
381.	Basis of salary of...	131
382.	Cannot be paid for excess of average.......................................	131
386.	Duties in reference to improvement of schools........................	132
389.	Pay continues while attending institute....................................	132

Section.		Page.
390.	Must require pupils to use books prescribed, penalty for violation of this law..	132
391.	Deduction from pay for time lost..	133
396.	Adults must submit to authority of..	134
398.	Records regarding admission of adults, how kept........................	134
406.	Copy of regulations of Board of Education concerning text-books to be furnished..	135
407.	Prohibited from receiving pupils not supplied with proper books...	136
408.	To report irregularity to Superintendent, receipt for monthly report withheld, when..	136
410.	May assist in furnishing text-books...	136

TEACHERS' INSTITUTES.

389.	Pay of Teachers continues while attending..................................	132
398.	Superintendents required to hold at least one annually...............	134

TRUSTEE ELECTORAL BOARD.

49.	Who compose...	39
50.	Powers and duties, Clerk to notify trustees of their appointment...	39-40
51.	Chairman and Clerk, record of proceedings, expenses, how paid, list of trustees to be furnished Board of Education.....	40
52.	Duties of Clerk and penalty for neglect.......................................	40
53.	Failure of Clerk and District Board to make annual report to be reported to Electoral Board and penalty therefor...............	40

TREASURER OF COMMONWEALTH.

204.	To pay appropriation to Virginia Military Institute...................	84
288.	To retain portion of funds due Commonwealth from Atlantic, Mississippi and Ohio Railroad for benefit of Virginia Normal and Collegiate Institute..	108

UNIVERSITY OF VIRGINIA.

164.	Continued, style of corporation, &c...	72
165.	Board of Visitors, number and term of service...........................	72
166.	Vacancies in Board of Visitors declared.....................................	72
167.	Vacancies in Board of Visitors, how, and when filled...............	72
168.	Time and place of meeting of Board of Visitors, special meetings, how called...	73
169.	How office of Visitor vacated, and vacancy filled.......................	73
170.	Appointment of Rector and other officers..................................	73
171	and 172. Duties of Board of Visitors...	73-74

Section.		Page.
173.	Expenses, how paid..	74
174.	Annual report to Second Auditor......................................	74
175.	Salaries of Professors, &c..	74
176.	What branches of learning to be taught...........................	74
177.	Board of Visitors authorized to issue bonds.....................	74–75
178.	Amount limited, proceeds, how applied...........................	75
179.	Payment of bonds, how secured.......................................	75
180.	Annual appropriation, amount, conditions, &c................	75
181.	Necessary repairs and interest, how paid, sinking fund established, how applied...	76–77
182.	Bequests legalized, how invested and applied.................	76
183.	Bequests specifying particular objects, funds, how invested....	76
184.	Donations irrevocable, disposition in case of non-acceptance	77
185.	Donor reserving right to nominate to any professorship, scholarship, &c., failing to do so in six months, Board of Visitors to act..	77
186.	State of Virginia constituted trustee for safe keeping, and application of funds. Treasurer liable on bond for funds deposited, &c..	77
187.	Visitors or trustees of any academy established by the State to make report annually to Second Auditor before October 1st. Nature of report..	77
188.	Penalty for failing to make report.....................................	78
189.	Second Auditor to pay interest on State stock.................	78
190.	Provisions apply to Dawson fund and dividends of James River Company..	79
191.	Scholarships, how established...	79
192.	Scholarship funds to be invested; donations irrevocable; donor's right to nominate pupils.......................................	80
193.	If donor fail to nominate, Board of Visitors or trustees may appropriate income...	80

UNITED STATES MILITARY ACADEMY.

292.	Appointment of cadets, how made...................................	110
293.	Manner of making application..	110
294.	Date of appointment..	110
295.	Alternates..	110–111
296.	Preliminary examinations..	111
297 and 298.	Qualifications..	111
299.	Required to take oath..	111
300.	Form of oath required...	112

UNITED STATES NAVAL ACADEMY.

301.	Number of cadets, limit...	113
302.	Mode of nomination...	113

Section.		Page.
303.	Vacancies, how filled	113
304.	Nominations, when made	113
305.	Qualifications	114
306.	Students from Japan received	114
307.	Examination requirements	114
308.	Medical examination	114
309.	Cause for rejection of candidate	114–115
310.	Examination in reading, writing, &c	115
311.	Examinations must be written	115
312.	Rejected candidates, privileges of	115

UNIVERSITY AT NASHVILLE.

313.	Objects of the Institution, connection with public-school system of Virginia	116
314.	Scholarships, how apportioned	116
315.	Examination of applicants for scholarships	116–117
316.	Appointments, by whom made	117
317.	Pledge to teach in public schools	117
318.	Under whose control	117
319.	Number Virginia entitled to, vacancies, conditions of granting scholarships	117
320.	Information in reference to	117

VIRGINIA MILITARY INSTITUTE.

195.	Name; its annuity for support	81
196.	Board of Visitors vacated; vacancies, how filled; number; how selected; term of office, quorum, etc	82
197.	Meeting of Board to fix salaries, power to remove officers, etc.	82–83
198.	Board to meet annually; special meetings, how called	83
199.	Vacancy on Board, how filled	83
200.	Expenses of Board, how paid	83
201.	Power of Board to make laws	83
202.	The arsenal and grounds vested in institute	83
203.	Power of Board to borrow money and secure its payment	83–84
204.	For relief of the Institute	84
205.	Title of property, how vested	84
206.	Bonds, how secured	84–85
207.	Annual expense of Institute	85
208.	Treasurer, how appointed, bond, etc	85
209.	Annual report of Treasurer	85
210.	Professors, how appointed	85
211.	The Governor to Commission officers	85
212.	Board of visitors to prescribe terms of admission for cadets	86
213.	Board may admit cadets free of charge, number, how selected, etc.; vacancies, how filled	86

Section.		Page.
214.	Power given to Board to arrange with Washington and Lee University as to admission of students..................................	86
215.	How commissioned officer of militia may become a student...	86
216.	Cadets to be guards to Institute..	87
217.	Duty of Superintendent as to arms...	87
218.	Superintendent's annual report, to whom made, contents, etc.	87
219.	How degree of graduate is conferred.......................................	87
220.	Cadet to act as a teacher...	87
221.	Annual inspection by Board of Visitors, report to Governor...	87
222.	Enlistment and pay of musicians..	88
223.	Authority to condemn lands and springs..................................	88
291.	Protection to State Institutions, public trusts and funds..........	109

VIRGINIA AGRICULTURAL AND MECHANICAL COLLEGE.

233.	Donation of public lands by the United States accepted.........	92
234.	Board of Education to sell land scrip.......................................	92
235.	Interest on proceeds of land scrip, how appropriated..............	93
236.	Conditions upon grant of the annuity......................................	93
237.	Name of Preston and Olin Institute changed to Virginia Agricultural and Mechanical College..	93
238.	Trustees to convey property to College....................................	93
239.	Appropriation from the county of Montgomery, how expended...	93
240.	Apportionment of students, and how selected.........................	93
241.	Property to revert to trustees and county of Montgomery, when...	93–94
242.	What to be taught at College..	94
243.	Students, when selected; their term at College.......................	94
244.	Board of Visitors, how and when appointed, term of office; vacancies, how filled, &c...	94–95
245.	Office of Visitors, how vacated and refilled.............................	95
246.	Appointment of rector and clerk..	95
247.	Meetings of Board, time and place; special meetings, how called...	95
248.	Duties of Board, President and Professors, agents and servants; pay of Visitors...	95–96
249.	Salaries of professors, fees of students...................................	96
250.	Property to be valued and transferred to Visitors....................	96
251.	Lands for experimental farms..	96–97
252.	College incorporated; general powers......................................	97
253.	Pay of rector; bond of Treasurer...	97
254.	Funds to be turned over to Board, interest on State debt held to be paid...	97
256.	Trustees to select students to Hampton Normal and Agricultural Institute...	98

Section. *Page.*

259. Annual report to Superintendent of Public Instruction............ 99
260. Reservation of control by Legislature 99
261. Board may accept subscriptions to College; how held, and when to revert to subscribers.. 99
291. Protection to State institutions, public trusts and funds........... 109

VIRGINIA NORMAL AND COLLEGIATE INSTITUTE.

141. Fund provided for erection and maintenance.......................... 63
274. Governor to appoint Commission to select site....................... 105
275. Duties of Commission, report to Board of Education................ 105
276. Board of Visitors to proceed to build, limit of cost................ 105
277. Name of Institute, how governed, Visitors how appointed, meetings, &c.. 105-106
278. Quorum of Board, vacancies, how filled................................ 106
279. Duties of Board Visitors, annual report to Board of Education 106
280. Normal department, branches taught, &c.............................. 106
281. College to be established, Board of Visitors to prescribe branches... 106
282. Board of Visitors to appoint and remove Professors, other duties... 106-107
283. Board of Visitors made a corporate body, authority &c............. 107
284. Institute under control of Legislature, Visitors, when appointed.. 107
285. Board to fix number of professors and teachers' salaries.......... 107
286. Treasurer, how appointed, bond, compensation..................... 107-108
287. Students, how admitted.. 108
288. Funds, how received and paid out..................................... 108
289. Board of Visitors to note progress of students. Expenses of Visitors, how paid.. 108-109
290. Bequests, how invested... 109
291. Protection of Institutions of State, public trusts and funds...... 109

INDEX TO SUPPLEMENT.

AUDITOR OF PUBLIC ACCOUNTS.

Section.		Page.
449.	To prepare Commissioners' Books, with reference to separate assessment and collection of school tax................................	145
449.	To keep school taxes separate..	145

BOARD OF EDUCATION.

439.	To appoint President of Virginia Normal and Collegiate Institute..	143
444.	Employees of Institute placed at disposal of Board for normal course..	144
422.	Clerk of Board of School Commissioners to furnish list of trustees.	141
454.	Prohibited from appointing persons rejected by Senate..............	146

BOARD OF SCHOOL COMMISSIONERS.

417.	How elected, term of office, &c...	140
418.	Board, how organized; quorum; vacancies, how filled..............	140
420.	To fill vacancies in Board of District Trustees............................	140
421.	Clerk to notify trustees of their appointment...........................	140
422.	Meetings, how called; clerk to furnish list of trustees to Board of Education...	141
423.	Clerk to convene Board; when...	141
459.	Secretary Commonwealth to furnish certificates of election.........	147

CITY COUNCILS.

| 427. | To elect trustees... | 141 |

CITY SCHOOL BOARD.

425.	Section 7, of chapter 79, Code 1873, repealed.........................	141
426.	Offices of trustees declared vacant..	141
427.	Councils to elect; Winchester excepted....................................	141
428.	Terms of trustees; when to commence; Norfolk and Alexandria excepted..	141
429.	Vacancies, how filled...	141

c

INDEX TO SUPPLEMENT.

CITY SUPERINTENDENT OF SCHOOLS.

Section. Page.
441. To notify colored teachers to attend normal course of instruction;
to revoke license of teachers for failure to attend................... 143
451. Cannot hold any other office elective by the people................. 145
456. Prohibited from actively engaging in politics......................... 146
457. Penalty for violating this law....................................... 146

CLERK OF BOARD SCHOOL COMMISSIONERS.

418. How elected.. 140
421. Trustees to file oath of office with; notification to be given
promptly of appointment... 140
422. To record proceedings and furnish Board of Education with
list of trustees and other information............................. 141
423. To convene Board of Commissioners................................... 141

CLERK HOUSE OF DELEGATES.

459. To certify election of School Commissioners to Secretary
Commonwealth.. 147

COUNTY SUPERINTENDENT.

415. To collect information in regard to the geology, mineralogy,
and geography of their counties..................................... 139
441. To notify colored teachers to attend normal course of instruction;
to revoke license of teacher for failure to attend.................. 143
416. To report annually to the Commissioner of Agriculture.............. 139
451. Cannot hold any other office elective by the people................ 145
453. Office to be declared vacant in certain cases....................... 146
454. Board of Education prohibited from appointing persons who have
been rejected by Senate... 146
456. Prohibited from actively engaging in politics....................... 146
457. Penalty for violating this law...................................... 146

COUNTY TREASURER.

449. To collect and keep separate the school tax......................... 144

DISTRICT SCHOOL TRUSTEES.

420. How appointed; qualifications....................................... 140
421. To file oath with Board of Commissioners........................... 140
427. In cities, how appointed; terms of office.......................... 141

INDEX TO SUPPLEMENT.

NORFOLK CITY SCHOOL BOARD.

Section.	Page.
445. Of whom composed..	144
446. How and when elected..	144
447. Vacancies, how filled...	144
448. Powers and duties..	144

SCHOOLS.

450. Non-resident of city or town may send children to public school therein; when... 145

SCHOOL FUNDS.

449. To be paid in lawful money of United States; treasurer to collect and keep separate from other taxes........................... 144

SECRETARY OF THE COMMONWEALTH.

459. To furnish certificate of election to School Commissioners......... 147

STATE FEMALE NORMAL SCHOOL.

430. Established...	141
431. Board of Trustees; vacancies, how filled; Superintendent Public Instruction a member of...................................	142
432. Duties of Board; annual report to Governor.......................	142
433. Where located...	142
434. Pupils; trustees to prescribe rules and regulations for selection and examination...................................	142
435. Appropriation for expense of establishing........................	142
436. Annual appropriation for support of.............................	142

SUPERINTENDENT PUBLIC INSTRUCTION.

431. A member of Board of Trustees State Female Normal School......	142
432. One of the Executive Committee...................................	142
437. Annual report to Second Auditor.................................	143
438. To fix time for commencement of normal course of instruction for colored teachers...	143
440. To employ skilled normal school lecturers to assist faculty of Virginia Normal and Collegiate Institute in conducting normal course...	143
455. Prohibited from actively engaging in politics.....................	146
457. Penalty for violating this law...................................	146

INDEX TO SUPPLEMENT.

TEACHERS.

Section.		Page.
438.	Normal course of instruction provided for colored teachers.........	143
441.	Required to attend; penalty for failure...............................	143
442.	Subject to regulations provided by Board of Education...............	143

TEACHERS' INSTITUTES.

452.	Act relating thereto amended..	145

VIRGINIA NORMAL AND COLLEGIATE INSTITUTE.

438.	President and Faculty to conduct a normal course of instruction for colored teachers; when to commence, and length of same...	143
439.	President appointed by Board of Education............................	143
440.	Annual salary of instructors to cover time engaged in instructing in normal course...	143
444.	Employees placed at disposal of Board Education for normal course	144

WE ARE INDEBTED TO GENERAL JOHN EATON, UNITED STATES COMMISSIONER OF EDUCATION, FOR THE FOLLOWING CIRCULAR OF INFORMATION, WHICH IS OF IMPORTANCE TO SCHOOL OFFICERS.

CIRCULARS OF INFORMATION

OF THE

BUREAU OF EDUCATION.

No. 4–1883.

RECENT SCHOOL LAW DECISIONS: COMPILED BY
LYNDON A. SMITH, A. B., LL. M.

WASHINGTON:
GOVERNMENT PRINTING OFFICE.
1883.

CONTENTS.

	Page.
Letter of the Commissioner of Education to the Secretary of the Interior	5
Table of cases cited	7–20

CHAPTER I.— POWERS OF LEGISLATURES.

Section.
1-2. To establish schools and school systems 21–22
3. To establish reform schools and authorize commitments 22–23
4. Over public school districts and corporations 23–24
5. Respecting taxation and appropriations 24–25
6. Over school funds 25

CHAPTER II.— SCHOOL DISTRICTS.

7. Organization of districts 26–27
8. Alteration of districts 27–28
9-10. Powers of districts 28–30
11. District meetings 30–31
12. Liabilities of districts on contracts 31–33
13. Liabilities of districts for injuries 33–34

CHAPTER III.—TAXATION.

14. Subjects of taxation 34
15. Purposes of taxation 34–35
16. Powers of taxation 35
17. Collection of taxes 35–36
18-20. Exemption of school property from taxation 36–39
21. Local assessment of school property 39–40

CHAPTER IV.— SCHOOL PROPERTY.

22-23. School funds 41–43
24-25. Sites and buildings 43–44
26. Use of buildings 44–46
27. Insurance, repair, and furnishing of school-houses 46–47

CHAPTER V.— OFFICERS.

28. Quasi-judicial powers of officers 47–48
29. Same. Limitation of appeals 48–49
30. County superintendents 49
31. Directors, trustees, &c. Organization 49–50
32-33. Same. Requisites to valid action of a school board 50–52
34. Same. Power to employ and dismiss teachers 52–53
35. Same. Power to repair, expend money, &c 53–55
36. Same. General liability 55–56

Section.	Page.
37. Same. Liabilities for negligence	56–57
38. Same. Removal from office	57–58
39. Treasurer	58–59
40. Assessors	59–60
41. Collector	60

CHAPTER VI.—SCHOOLS AND STUDIES.

42. Public schools in general	60–61
43. High schools	61
44–46. Colored schools	61–64
47. Studies	64–65
48. Text books	65

CHAPTER VII.—TEACHERS.

49. License prerequisite to a valid contract	66
50–51. Contracts	66–68
52–53. Recovery of wages. When impossible	68–70
54–55. Same. When possible	70–71
56–57. Dismissal	71–73
58. Complaints against candidates for teachers' positions	73

CHAPTER VIII.—ADMINISTRATION.

59. Rules and regulations	73
60. Regulations respecting studies	73–74
61–62. Regulations respecting attendance	74–76
63–64. Suspension of pupils in the absence of rules	76–77
65. Corporal punishment	77–78
Index	79–82

LETTER.

DEPARTMENT OF THE INTERIOR,
BUREAU OF EDUCATION,
Washington, D. C., October 5, 1883.

SIR: The leading courts of the various States render many opinions in which general principles of law intimately affecting school officers and educational interests are discussed and determined.

A knowledge of the points decided in these opinions must tend to expedite school business and diminish future controversies. For this reason and in response to a popular demand for such information, I assigned to Lyndon A. Smith, esq., an employé of this office and a member of the city bar, the collection and compilation of recent decisions and discussions most pertinent to school affairs.

The cases cited have been decided since the beginning of my present term of office. The principal questions of school law have been before the courts during this time, and their determination is usually stated as briefly as possible in the compilation. Quotations from earlier cases, from text books, and from State statutes are given in foot notes where a peculiarly important point has seemed to need further explanation. Decisions concerning school lands, rules of evidence, and court practice have not been included.

This document is of value chiefly as supplementing State school laws, which are generally distributed by the States to school officers and contain the ordinary rules for official action; but statutory provisions are excellently illustrated, explained, and interpreted by judicial decisions and opinions. The table of cases is arranged so that a list of those which have been decided in any State can be easily distinguished.

I hereby recommend the publication of this compilation as a circular of information.

I have the honor to be, very respectfully, your obedient servant,

JOHN EATON,
Commissioner.

The Hon. SECRETARY OF THE INTERIOR.
Publication approved.

H. M. TELLER,
Secretary.

TABLE OF CASES CITED.

NOTE.—When a place or institution is mentioned in the title of a case, its name is considered the leading word and generally determines the entry of the case in the table; for example, City of Fort Worth v. Davis is entered Fort Worth, City of, v. Davis.

Title of case.	Report.	Cited on page—
Abbott, Thompson v.	61 Mo., 176	32
Abercrombie v. Ely	60 Mo., 23	46
Adams v. State	82 Ill., 132	58
Adams, School Commissioners of Alleghany County v.	43 Md., 349	69
Adams County (School District 4 of), State ex rel. Kimball v.	13 Nebr., 82	30
Adams County (School District 24 of), State ex rel. Gregory v.	13 Nebr., 78	26, 30
Adkins v. Mitchell	67 Ill., 511	67
Ætna Insurance Company, School District 6 of Dresden v.	62 Me., 330	46
Aikman v. School District 16 of Butler County.	27 Kans., 129	50
Akron (Town Board of), Hazen v.	48 Mich., 188	58
Akron (Town Board of), McLaren v.	48 Mich., 189	47, 58
Albin v. Directors Independent District of West Branch.	58 Iowa, 77	42
Albright v. Riker	22 Hun (N. Y.), 367	44, 53
Alleghany County, School Commissioners of, v. Adams.	43 Md., 349	69
Alleghany County (School Commissioners of), Wiley v.	51 Md., 401	41, 47, 48, 61
Allegheny (Sixth Ward School District of), Ferree v.	76 Pa. St., 376	44
Allen v. Frink	32 Mich., 96	59
Allen, People ex rel. Schenectady Astronomical Observatory v.	42 N. Y. App., 404	25
American Insurance Company v. District Townships Willow and Grand Meadow.	55 Iowa, 606	46
Andover, Jenkins v.	103 Mass., 94	41
Andress, Sheffield School Township v.	56 Ind., 157	29
Armstrong v. Union School District	28 Kans., 345	72
Arrington v. Cotton	1 Baxter (Tenn.), 316	21
Assessors, St. Joseph's Church v.	12 R. I., 19	38, 60
Auditor v. Holland	14 Bush (Ky.), 143	25, 41
Babcock, Burdick v.	31 Iowa, 562	74, 77
Bailey v. Ewart	52 Iowa, 111	49
Barnes, Bedell v.	17 Hun (N. Y.), 353	60
Barry, Burditt v.	6 Hun (N. Y.), 657	68
Bartlett v. Board of Education of Freeport School District.	59 Ill., 364	58
Bassett v. Fish	75 N. Y. App., 303	57
Batchellor, McKay v.	2 Colo., 591	36
Bays v. State	6 Nebr., 167	52, 71
Beach v. Leahy	11 Kans., 23	28
Bealey v. Dickinson	48 Vt., 599	31

Title of case.	Report.	Cited on page
Beaver, Thompson v.	63 Ill., 353.	27, 76
Beck, Pierce v.	61 Ga., 413.	69
Beckwith, Mount Pleasant v.	100 U. S. Sup. Ct., 528.	32
Bedell v. Barnes.	17 Hun (N. Y.), 353.	60
Bellmeyer v. Ind. District of Marshalltown.	44 Iowa, 564.	44
Berlin (School District 12 of), Cashen v.	50 Vt., 30.	70
Betts v. Betts	4 Abbott's N. C. (N. Y.), 412	42, 54, 60
Blain, State ex rel. Riley v.	36 Ohio St., 429.	71
Bluff Creek, District Township of, v. Hardinbrook.	40 Iowa, 130.	58
Board of Education, Peers v.	72 Ill., 508.	47, 52
Board of Education, People v.	101 Ill., 308; 40 Am. Rep., 196.	62, 64
Board of Education, Powell v.	97 Ill., 375; 37 Am. Rep., 123.	34, 64
Board of Trustees, Potter v.	10 Ill. App., 343.	50
Boget, Davis v.	50 Iowa, 11.	45
Bohenblost, Woodhull v.	4 Hun (N. Y.), 399.	60
Boston (City of), Davis v.	133 Mass, 103.	77
Boston, (City of) Hill v.	122 Mass., 344.	33
Boston (School Committee of), Peabody v.	115 Mass., 383.	50
Bourbon County, School District 29 of, v. Perkins.	21 Kans., 536; 30 Am. Rep., 447.	46
Bouton v. Rice.	10 Phil. Rep., 559.	50
Boutwell, Greenbanks v.	43 Vt., 207.	26, 28, 34
Boynton v. Newton.	34 Iowa, 510.	54
Braner, Trustees, &c., of Morgan County v.	71 Ill., 546.	42
Bremond, State v.	38 Tex., 116.	24
Briggs v. Johnson County.	4 Dillon (U. S. C. Ct.), 148.	22
Brody v. Penn.	32 Mich., 272.	48
Brownfield, Taylor v.	41 Iowa, 264.	30
Bryce, Dent v.	16 S. C., 1.	35
Bulmer, Estate of.	59 Cal., 131.	42
Buntin, United States v.	10 Fed. Rep., 730.	61, 62
Burdick v. Babcock.	31 Iowa, 562.	74, 77
Burditt v. Barry.	6 Hun (N. Y.), 657.	68
Burr Oak (Independent District of), District Township of Hesper v.	34 Iowa, 306.	31
Burt, McCormick v.	95 Ill., 263; 35 Am. Rep., 163.	56, 77
Burton, Directors of Subdistrict 7 of Moulton v.	26 Ohio St., 421.	55
Burton, State ex rel. Burpee v.	45 Wis., 150; 30 Am. Rep., 706.	47, 76
Butler v. Haines.	79 Ind., 575.	55, 66
Butterfield v. District 6 of Prospect.	61 Me., 583.	27
Cabaniss, Danielly v.	52 Ga., 211.	45
Cairo and Fulton R. R. Co. v. Parks.	32 Ark., 131.	35
Campbell v. Board of Commissioners of Monroe County.	71 Ind., 185.	49
Cannon (School District 2 of), Everett v.	30 Mich., 249.	67
Carsner, Oliver v.	39 Texas, 396.	35
Carter, Cory v.	48 Ind., 327; 17 Am. Rep.,738.	62, 63
Cashen v. School District 12 of Berlin.	50 Vt., 30.	70
Champaign County, Illinois Industrial University v.	76 Ill., 184.	24, 41
Chelmsford, Spalding v.	117 Mass., 393.	43
Chicago, City of, v. People ex rel. Miller.	80 Ill., 384.	36, 41
Churchman, Stuckey v.	2 Ill. App., 584.	68
Cincinnati, Board of Education of, v. Minor.	23 Ohio St., 211; 13 Am. Rep., 233.	22
Cist v. State ex rel. Wilder.	21 Ohio St., 339.	27
Citizens' Bank, Johnson School Township v.	81 Ind., 515.	29
Clark v. Board of Directors of Muscatine.	24 Iowa, 266.	62, 64
Clark v. Nichols.	52 N. H., 298.	32
Clement v. Everest.	29 Mich., 19.	26, 54

RECENT SCHOOL LAW DECISIONS. 9

Title of case.	Report.	Cited on page
Cleveland Public School Board, Waterhouse v.	9 Baxter (Tenn.), 398	24
Cobb, State ex rel. Dunton v	8 N. S. Rich. (S. C.), 123	25
Coe, Pennington v	57 Ill., 118	35
Coffin's Grove (District Township of), Monticello Bank v.	51 Iowa, 350	46
Coleman, Loomis v	51 Mo., 21	52, 53
Coleman, Pickering v	53 N. H., 424	34
Colfax (District Township of), Place v	56 Iowa, 573	69
Colfax County (School District 15 of), Ward v.	10 Nebr., 293	58
Collins v. Henderson	11 Bush (Ky.), 74	25
Colvin, School District v	10 Kans., 283	73
Commissioners v. Raleigh	88 N. C., 120	43
Commonwealth of Pennsylvania v. Davis	10 W. N. C., 156	62
Commonwealth (Pa.), Kaine v	27 Al. L. Journal, 283	62
Commonwealth v. Secl	5 Pa. L. J. Rep., 78	77
Commonwealth ex rel. Acker v. Thomas	10 Phil. Rep., 600	50
Commonwealth ex rel. Swartz v. Wickersham.	66 Pa. St., 134	51
Conklin v. School District 37 of Lyon County.	22 Kans., 521	53
Cook v. Ind. School District of North McGregor.	40 Iowa, 444	68
Cook, State ex rel. Brawford v	72 Mo., 496	55
Cooper (ex parte)	3 Tex. App., 489	25
Cornes, Gordon v	47 N. Y. App., 608	25
Corwin, District Township of, v. Moorehead	43 Iowa, 466	44
Cory v. Carter	48 Ind., 327; 17 Am. Rep., 738.	62, 63
Cotton, Arrington v	1 Baxter (Tenn.), 316	21
Cottrell, Appeal of	10 R. I., 615	47, 48
Cowee, School District 25 of Hall County v.	9 Nebr., 53	68
Crawfordsville, City of, v. Hays	42 Ind., 200	{ 52,67, 69, 71
Crocker, Perkins v	109 Mass., 128	27
Crowl, St. Mary's College v	10 Kans., 442	36
Curryer v. Merrill	25 Minn., 1; 33 Am. Rep., 450.	{ 21,22, 65
Dakota County (District 13 of), Ryan v	27 Minn., 433	66
Dakota County (District 45 of), McKinney v..	20 Minn., 72	66
Dallas v. Fosdick	40 How. Pr. (N. Y.), 249	62
Dauenhofter v. State	69 Ind., 295; 35 Am. Rep., 216.	77
Danielly v. Cabaniss	52 Ga., 211	45
Dannat v. Mayor N. Y. City	6 Hun (N. Y.), 88	{ 31,54, 57
Davies, Holland v	36 Ark., 446	30
Davis v. Boget	50 Iowa, 11	46
Davis v. Boston	133 Mass., 103	77
Davis, City of Fort Worth v	57 Texas, 225	24
Davis, Commonwealth v	10 W. N. C., 156	62
Davis, Littleworth v	50 Miss., 403	42
Davis v. School Directors	92 Ill., 293	52
Day, Weir v	35 Ohio St., 143	45
Dean, Lipscomb v	1 Lea (Tenn.), 546	24
Defiance (Board of Education of), Sewell v	29 Ohio St., 89	74
Dennison, School District of, v. Padden	89 Pa. St., 395	50, 53
Dent v. Bryce	16 S. C., 1	35
Dewey v. Union District, Alpena	43 Mich., 480	71
Dickinson, Bealey v	48 Vt., 599	31
Dilman, School District 2 of Oxford v	22 Ohio St., 194	66
Directors, &c., v. Trustees, &c	66 Ill., 247	27
Dixon County, School District 2 of, v. Stough.	4 Nebr., 357	44, 54
Donelly v. Duras	11 Nebr., 283	58
Donovan v. Board of Education of New York City	44 N. Y. Sup. Ct., 53	57
Donovan v. McAlpin	85 N. Y. App., 185; 39 Am. Rep., 649.	57
Donovan, Marshal v	10 Bush (Ky.), 681	25
Dorr Township Board, Wenzel v	49 Mich., 25	58

167

Title of case.	Report.	Cited on page
Dorton v. Hearne	67 Mo., 301	45
Dove v. Ind. School District, Keokuk	41 Iowa, 689	62
Dresden, School District 6 of, v. Ætna Ins. Co.	62 Me., 330	46
Dritt v. Snodgrass	66 Mo., 286; 27 Am. Rep., 343.	55
Duffy, State ex rel. Stoutmeyer v	7 Nev., 342; 8 Am. Rep., 713.	61
Dupuyt, People ex rel. C. & St. L. R'y Co. v...	71 Ill., 651	34
Duras, Donelly v	11 Nebr., 283	58
Duryea (collector), State v	40 N. J. L., 266	34
East Bridgeport School District, Wilson v	36 Conn., 280	52, 53
Easton, State ex rel. Dietz v	13 Abb. Pr. N. S. (N. Y.), 159.	61
East St. Louis v. Trustees of Schools	102 Ill., 489	25
Eddy v. Wilson	43 Vt., 363	28, 31
Ely, Abercrombie v	60 Mo., 23	46
Erie, School District of City of, v. Fuess	98 Pa. St., 600	33
Erwin v. St. Joseph Board of Public Schools..	2 McCrary (U. S. Cir. Ct.), 608.	54
Essex School District, Heck v	49 Mich., 551	43
Estes, School District 8 of Dodge County v...	13 Nebr., 52	70
Everest, Clement v	29 Mich., 19	26, 54
Everett v. School District 2 of Cannon	30 Mich., 249	67
Every, Lord v	38 Mich., 405	26
Ewart, Bailey v	52 Iowa, 111	49
Ewing v. School Directors	2 Ill. App., 458	69
Exeter, Trustees of Phillips Exeter Academy v.	58 N. H., 306; 42 Am. Rep., 589.	37
Fairfax (School District 2 of), Scott v	46 Vt., 452	66, 70, 71
Fairfield, Board of Education of, v. Ladd	26 Ohio St., 210	42
Faris, Ratcliff v	6 Nebr., 539	49
Farnum's petition	51 N. H., 376	23, 27
Faulkner, Holbrook v	55 N. H., 311	31
Ferree v. School District, Allegheny	76 Pa. St., 376	44
Ferriter v. Tyler	43 Vt., 444; 21 Am. Rep., 133.	74, 75
Fifield v. Swett	56 N. H., 435	27, 34
Finch v. Board of Education of Toledo	30 Ohio St., 37	56
Fish, Bassett v	75 N. Y. App., 303	57
Fleishell & Kimsey v. Hightower	62 Ga., 324	23, 45, 46
Flint River Ind. District v. Kelley	35 Iowa, 568	54
Flood, Ward v	48 Cal., 36; 17 Am. Rep., 405.	61, 62, 63
Fogleman, School Directors v	76 Ill., 189	35
Fort Worth, City of, v. Davis	57 Tex., 225	24
Fosdick, Dallas v	40 How. Pr. (N. Y.), 249	62
Freeport School District (Board of Education of), Bartlett v.	59 Ill., 364	58
Fremont (District Township of), Templin & Son v.	36 Iowa, 411	47
Frink, Allen v	32 Mich., 96	59
Fry, Hodgkin v	33 Ark., 716	30
Fuess, School District of City of Erie v	98 Pa. St., 600	33
Fuller, Long v	68 Pa. St., 170	43
Furniture Company v. Harvey	45 Iowa, 466	25
Gage, School District 4 of Marathon v	39 Mich., 480	28, 71
Gallagher, People ex rel. King v	11 Abb. N. C., 187	62
Garrett, Overton v	5 Lans. (N. Y.), 156	60
Garvey, Trustees of Common Schools v	— Ky	31
Geddes v. Thomastown	46 Mich., 316	58
Gehling v. School District 56 of Richardson County.	10 Nebr., 239	54
Genesee Township v. McDonald	98 Pa. St., 444	68

168

RECENT SCHOOL LAW DECISIONS.

Title of case.	Report.	Cited on page
Gerke v. Purcell	25 Ohio St., 229	38, 43
German Township School District v. Sangston.	74 Pa. St., 454	42
Gibbs, State v	25 Ohio St., 256	26
Gibson v. School District 5 of Vevay	36 Mich., 404	46
Gillis v. Space	63 Barbour (N. Y.), 177	52, 53
Goodell, Hughes v	3 Pittsburgh (Pa.), 264	56
Gordon v. Cornes	47 N. Y. App., 608	25
Graham, State ex rel. Straight University v	25 La. Ann., 440	60
Grant, State v	74 Mo., 33	70
Greenbanks v. Boutwell	43 Vt., 207	26, 28, 34
Greenleaf (Collector), State v	34 N. J. L., 441	35
Greenwood (School District 1 of), Todd v	40 Mich., 294	43
Griswold College, Trustees of, v. State	46 Iowa, 275	37
Grubb, State ex rel. Oliver v	85 Ind., 213	64
Hackman, Township Board of Education v	48 Mo., 243	43
Hagan, Townsend v	35 Iowa, 194	45
Haile v. Young	6 Lea (Tenn.), 501	49
Haines, Butler v	79 Ind., 575	55, 66
Halbert v. School Districts of Watertown	36 Mich., 421	32
Halbert v. Sparks	9 Bush (Ky.), 259	25
Hall & Julius v. District Township of Pleasant Valley.	41 Iowa, 494	68
Hamilton County (District 5 of), District 9 v.	9 Nebr., 331	34
Hamtramck Board v. Holihan	46 Mich., 127	47, 58
Harbison, Murphy v	29 Ark., 340	35
Hardinbrook, District Township' of Bluff Creek v.	40 Iowa, 130	58
Hartford, City of, v. West Middle District	45 Conn., 462; 29 Am. Rep., 687.	39
Harvey, Furniture Co. v	45 Iowa, 466	35
Harvey, People ex rel. Danielwitz v	58 Cal., 337	50
Hathaway v. New Baltimore and Lake School District.	48 Mich., 257	43
Hays, City of Crawfordsville v	42 Ind., 200	52, 67, 69, 71
Hazen v. Lerche	47 Mich, 626	51
Hazen v. Town Board of Akron	48 Mich., 188	58
Head v. The University of Missouri	19 Wall. (U. S. Sup. Ct.), 526.	24
Hearne, Dorton v	67 Mo., 301	45
Heck v. Essex School District	49 Mich., 551	43
Henderson, Collins v.	11 Bush (Ky.), 74	25
Herrington v. District Township of Liston	47 Iowa, 11	51
Hesper, District Township of, v. Independent District of Burr Oak.	34 Iowa, 306	31
Hightower, Fleishell & Kimsey v	62 Ga., 324	28, 45, 46
Hightower v. Slayton	54 Ga., 108; 21 Am. Rep., 273.	23
Hill v. City of Boston	122 Mass., 344	33
Hodge, People ex rel. McMillan v	4 Nebr., 265	27
Hodgkin v. Fry	33 Ark., 716	30
Hodgkins v. Rockport	105 Mass., 475	77
Holbrook v. Faulkner	55 N. H., 311	31
Holihan, Hamtramck Board v	46 Mich., 127	47, 58
Holland, Auditor v	14 Bush (Ky.), 143	25, 41
Holland v. Davies	36 Ark., 446	30
Holmes, Simmons v	49 Miss., 134	31, 49
Howard, Robinson v	87 N. C., 151	55
Hudson, School Directors v	88 Ill., 563	67
Hughes v. Goodell	3 Pittsburgh (Pa.), 264	56
Hurff, State v	38 N. J. L., 312	30
Hyde, People ex rel. Gilmour v	89 N. Y. App., 11	72

Title of case.	Report.	Cited on page—
Illinois Industrial University v. Champaign County.	76 Ill., 184	24, 41
Independent Districts, District Township of Knoxville v.	26 Iowa, 420	32
Independent Districts, State v.	46 Iowa, 425	27
Indianapolis, School Commissioners of, v. Magner.	84 Ind., 67	35
Inspectors, Parman v.	49 Mich., 63	26
Irvington (Town of), Putnam v.	69 Ind., 80	66
Jackson (District Township of), Williams v.	36 Iowa, 216	44
Jamison v. Senter	56 Miss., 194	69
Jefferson City School Board, King v.	71 Mo., 628; 36 Am. Rep., 499.	73, 74
Jenkins v. Andover	103 Mass., 94	41
Jennings, School Directors v.	10 Ill. App., 645	51, 66
Johnson v. School Directors	67 Mo., 319	47
Johnson v. Smith	64 Ind., 275	42
Johnson, State v.	55 Mo., 80	42
Johnson County, Briggs v.	4 Dillon (U. S. C. Ct.), 148.	22
Johnson School Township v. Citizens' Bank	81 Ind., 515	29
Joint School District (Caledonia and Mt. Pleasant), Scott v.	51 Wis., 554	70
Joint School District, Spencer v.	15 Kans., 259	44
Jones v. Nebraska City	1 Nebr., 176	71
Jones v. School District 47 of Neosho County	8 Kans., 362	67
Jones v. Wright	34 Mich., 371	58, 59
Judd v. Thompson	125 Mass., 553	60
Kaine v. Commonwealth (Pa.)	27 Al. L. J., 283	62
Kalamazoo School District No. 1, Stuart v.	30 Mich., 69	22, 26, 34, 52, 61
Kane v. School District	52 Wis., 502	47
Kelley, Flint River Independent District v.	55 Iowa, 568	54
Keokuk (Independent School District of), Dove v.	41 Iowa, 689	62
Kesler, School Committee of Providence v.	67 N. C., 443	32, 44
King v. Jefferson City School Board	71 Mo., 628; 36 Am. Rep., 499.	73, 74
Kirkpatrick v. Independent School District of Liberty.	53 Iowa, 585	69
Knox, Woodbury v.	74 Me., 462	68, 72
Knoxville, District Township of, v. Independent Districts.	36 Iowa, 420	32
Knoxville National Bank v. Independent District of Washington.	40 Iowa, 612	32
Kuhn v. Board of Education of Wellsburg	4 W. Va., 499	21
Ladd, Board of Education of Fairfield v.	26 Ohio St., 210	42
Lake View, Trustees of Schools of, v. People	87 Ill., 303; 29 Am. Rep., 55.	64, 74
Lamar (Board of Education of), School District v.	73 Mo., 627	28
Lamkin, Otken v.	56 Miss., 758	25, 41, 61
Lander v. Seaver	32 Vt., 114	77
Lane v. District Township of Woodbury	58 Iowa, 462	33
Laverty, Van Arsdale v.	69 Pa. St., 103	73
Leahy, Beach v.	11 Kans., 23	28
Learock v. Putnam	111 Mass., 499	55
Lee's Summit (Board of Education of), Wilson v.	63 Mo., 161	67
Le Grand (Independent School District of), Mann v.	52 Iowa, 130	67
Leonard, State v.	3 Tenn. Chan., 177	51, 67
Lerche, Hazen v.	47 Mich., 626	51
Lewis (Collector), State v.	35 N. J. L., 377	31

170

RECENT SCHOOL LAW DECISIONS. 13

Title of case.	Report.	Cited on page—
Liberty (Independent School District of), Kirkpatrick v.	53 Iowa, 585	69
Liberty Township (Treasurer of), State ex rel. Steinbeck v.	22 Ohio St., 144	29, 50
Lipscomb v. Dean	1 Lea (Tenn.), 546	24
Liston (District Township of), Herrington v.	47 Iowa, 11	51
Littleworth v. Davis	50 Miss., 403	42
Long v. Fuller	68 Pa. St., 170	43
Loomis v. Coleman	51 Mo., 21	52, 53
Lord v. Every	38 Mich., 405	26
Lovingston v. School Trustees	99 Ill., 564	58
Lower Allen School District v. Shiremanstown School District.	91 Pa. St., 182	27
Lynnfield, Russell v	116 Mass., 365	73
Lyon County (School District 37 of), Conklin v.	22 Kans., 521	53
Mabee, Wieman v	45 Mich., 484	73
McAlpin, Donovan v	85 N. Y. App., 185; 39 Am. Rep., 649.	57
McCann, State ex rel. Garnes v	21 Ohio St., 198	62, 63
McClelland, Rice v	58 Mo., 116	{ 26,51, 52
McCormick v. Burt	95 Ill., 263; 35 Am. Rep., 163.	56, 77
McCutcheon v. Windsor	55 Mo., 149	{ 52,56, 69
McDonald, Genesee Township v.	98 Pa. St., 444	68
McFarland, Morrison v	51 Ind., 206	55
McKay v. Batchellor	2 Colo., 591	36
McKeesport, School District of, v. Miller	1 Pa. Sup. Ct., 510	44
McKenney, Marble v	60 Me., 332	34
McKinney v. School District 45 of Dakota Co.	20 Minn., 72	66
McLaren v. Township Board of Akron	48 Mich., 189	47, 58
Magner, School Commissioners of Indianapolis v.	84 Ind., 67	25
Manchester, Warde v.	56 N. H.,508; 22 Am.Rep.,504.	38
Mann v. Ind. School District, Le Grand	52 Iowa, 130	67
Marathon, School District 4 of, v. Gage	39 Mich., 480	28, 71
Marble v. McKenney	60 Me., 332	34
Marengo (Directors Ind. District of), Murphy v.	30 Iowa, 429	77
Marshall v. Donovan	10 Bush (Ky.), 681	25
Marshall (Ind. District of), National Bank of Mount Pleasant v.	39 Iowa, 490	29
Marshalltown (Ind. District of), Bellmeyer v	44 Iowa, 564	46
Mason v. Fractional District, Scio and Webster	34 Mich., 230	59, 60
Mason City, Ind. District of, v. Reichard	50 Iowa, 98	55
Maynard v. Woodward	36 Mich., 423	29
Merrill, Curryer v	25 Minn., 1; 33 Am. Rep., 450.	{ 21,22, 65
Merrill v. Town of Monticello	14 Fed. Rep., 628	29
Midland (School District 5 of), School District 9 v.	40 Mich., 551	31
Miller, School Directors v	54 Ill., 338	54
Miller, School District of McKeesport v	1 Pa. Sup. Ct., 510	44
Miller, Sharp v	65 Mo., 50	22
Milton (School District 2 of), Smith v	40 Mich., 143	43
Milwaukee Industrial School v. Supervisors	40 Wis., 328	22
Minor, Board of Education of Cincinnati v.	23 Ohio St., 211; 13 Am. Rep., 233.	22
Mitchell, Adkins v	67 Ill., 511	67
Mizner, State v	45 Iowa, 248; 24 Am. Rep., 769; 50 Iowa, 145; 32 Am. Rep., 128.	77, 78
Mobile School Commissioners v. Putnam	44 Ala., 506	{ 23,41, 47

171

Title of case.	Report.	Cited on page—
Monaghan v. School District 1 of Randall	38 Wis., 101	31,67, 68
Monroe County (Board of Commissioners of), Campbell v.	71 Ind., 185	49
Monticello Bank v. District Township of Coffin's Grove.	51 Iowa, 350	46
Monticello Seminary v. People	106 Ill., 398	37
Monticello (Town of), Merrill v.	14 Fed. Rep., 628	29
Moore v. Ind. District of Toledo City	55 Iowa, 654	55
Moorehead, District Township of Corwin v.	43 Iowa, 466	44
Morgan County, Trustees, &c., of, v. Braner	71 Ind., 546	42
Morley v. Power	5 Lea (Tenn.), 691	72
Morrison v. McFarland	51 Ind., 206	55
Morrow v. Wood	35 Wis., 64; 17 Am. Rep., 741.	65, 78
Morton, District Township of Taylor v.	37 Iowa, 553	59
Moulton, Directors of Subdistrict 7 of, v. Burton.	26 Ohio St., 421	55
Moundville, Probasco v	11 W. Va., 501	36
Mt. Pleasant v. Beckwith	100 U. S. Sup. Ct., 528	32
Mt. Pleasant, National Bank of, v. Ind. District Marshall.	39 Iowa, 490	29
Murphy v. Directors I) d. District of Marengo.	30 Iowa, 429	77
Murphy v. Harbison	29 Ark., 340	35
Muscatine (Board of Directors of) Clark v	24 Iowa, 266	62, 64
Nebraska City, Jones v	1 Nebr., 176	71
Neosho County (District 47 of), Jones v.	8 Kans., 362	67
New Baltimore and Lake School District, Hathaway v.	48 Mich., 257	43
Newton, Boynton v	34 Iowa, 510	54
New York City (Board of Education of), Donovan v.	44 N. Y. Sup. Ct., 53	57
New York City (Board of Education of), State ex rel. Murphy v.	3 Hun (N. Y.), 177	47
New York City (Commissioners of Taxes of), People ex rel. Academy of the Sacred Heart v:	6 Hun (N. Y.), 109	38
New York City (Mayor of), Dannat v	6 Hun (N. Y.), 88	31,54, 57
Nichols, Clark v	52 N. H., 298	32
Nichols v. School Directors	93 Ill., 61; 34 Am. Rep., 160.	46
North McGregor (Independent School District of), Cook v.	40 Iowa, 444	68
Northumberland, First National Bank of, v. Rush School District.	81* Pa. St., 307	29
Norton v. Perry	65 Me., 103	43, 44
Nuckolls County (District 9 of), State ex rel. Phillips v.	10 Nebr., 544	31
Oakland (Board of Education of), People ex rel. Beckwith v.	55 Cal., 331	65
Oliver v. Carsner	39 Tex., 396	35
Opinion of justices	68 Me., 582	21, 24
Otken v. Lamkin	56 Miss., 758	25,41, 61
Ottawa, Board of Education of, v. Tinnon	26 Kans., 1	62, 64
Overton v. Garrett	5 Lans. (N. Y.), 156	60
Oxford, School District 2 of, v. Dilman	22 Ohio St., 194	66
Padden, School District of Dennison v	89 Pa. St., 395	50, 53
Palmer, State v	39 N. J. L., 250	31
Parker v. School District	5 Lea (Tenn.), 525	71, 76
Parks, Cairo and Fulton Railroad Company v.	32 Ark., 131	35
Parman v. School Inspectors	49 Mich., 63	26
Patten, St. Joseph Board of Public Schools v.	62 Mo., 444	25
Peabody v. School Committee of Boston	115 Mass., 383	50

172

Title of case.	Report.	Cited on page
Peachy v. Redmond	59 Cal., 326	49
Peck v. Smith	41 Conn., 442	78
Peers v. Board of Education, District 3, Madison County.	72 Ill., 508	47, 52
Penn, Brody v	32 Mich., 272	48
Pennington v. Coe	57 Ill., 118	35
People v. Board of Education	101 Ill., 308; 40 Am. Rep., 196.	62, 64
People, Monticello Seminary v	106 Ill., 398	37
People r. Sisson	98 Ill., 335	35
People, Trumbo v	75 Ill., 561	35
People, Trustees of Schools of Lake View r.	87 Ill., 303; 29 Am. Rep., 55.	64, 74
People, Wells v	71 Ill., 532	66
People ex rel. Academy of the Sacred Heart r. Commissioners of Taxes of New York City.	6 Hun (N. Y.), 109	38
People ex rel. Beckwith r. Board of Education of Oakland.	55 Cal., 331	65
People ex rel. Bellmer r. State Board of Education.	49 Cal., 684	65
People ex rel. Brewer, Rogers r	68 Ill., 154	32
People ex rel. C. & St. L. Railway Company r. Dupuyt.	71 Ill., 651	34
People ex rel. C. & St. L. Railroad Company v. Trustees of Schools.	78 Ill., 136	28
People ex rel. Danielwitz v. Harvey	58 Cal., 337	50
People ex rel. Dietz v. Easton	13 Abb. Pr. N. s. (N. Y.), 159	61
People ex rel. Gilmour v. Hyde	89 N. Y. App., 11	72
People ex rel. Hunter v. Peters	4 Nebr., 254	51
People ex rel. Johnson, Thacher v	98 Ill., 632	35
People ex rel. King r. Gallagher	11 Abb. N. C., 187	62
People ex rel. McMillan v. Hodge	4 Nebr., 265	27
People ex rel. Miller, City of Chicago v	80 Ill., 384	36, 41
People ex rel. Murphy v. Board of Education of New York City.	3 Hun (N. Y.), 177	47
People ex rel. Schenectady Astronomical Observatory v. Allen.	42 N. Y. App., 404	25
People ex rel. T., W. & W. Railway Company, Trustees of Schools r.	63 Ill., 299	24, 34
People of Illinois, Northwestern University v	99 U. S. Sup. Ct., 309	36
Perkins v. Crocker	109 Mass., 128	27
Perkins r. Directors Independent District, West Des Moines.	56 Iowa, 476	49, 75
Perkins, School District 29 of Bourbon County r.	21 Kans.,536; 30 Am.Rep.,447	46
Perrott r. Philadelphia	83 Pa. St., 479	69
Perry, Norton v	65 Me., 103	43, 44
Peters, People ex rel. Hunter v	4 Nebr., 254	51
Philadelphia, Perrott v	83 Pa. St., 479	69
Phillips, Shankland v	3 Tenn. Chan., 556	31
Phillips Exeter Academy, Trustees of, v. Exeter.	58 N. H.,306; 42 Am. Rep.,589	37
Pickering v. Coleman	53 N. H., 424	34
Pickett r. School District 1 of Wiota	25 Wis., 551	54
Pierce v. Beck	61 Ga., 413	69
Place v. District Township of Colfax	56 Iowa, 573	69
Pleasant Valley (District Township of), Hall & Julius r.	41 Iowa, 494	68
Pleasant Valley (Ind. District of), Wolf & Son v.	51 Iowa, 432; 30 Am. Rep., 450, n.	46
Post, Rulison v	79 Ill., 567	74
Potter v. Board of Trustees	10 Ill. App., 343	50
Powell r. Board of Education	97 Ill., 375; 37 Am. Rep., 123.	34, 64
Powell v. Board of Supervisors, Saint Croix County.	46 Wis., 210	36
Powell, State v	67 Mo., 395	58
Power, Morley r	5 Lea (Tenn.), 691	72
Powers, State v	38 Ohio St., 54	21, 28

Title of case.	Report.	Cited on page—
Power's petition	52 Mo., 218	34
Probasco v. Moundville	11 W. Va., 501	36
Prospect (District 6 of), Butterfield v	61 Me., 583	27
Providence, School Committee of, v. Kesler	67 N. C., 443	32, 44
Purcell, Gerke v	25 Ohio St., 229	38, 43
Puterbaugh v. Township Board of Education	53 Mo., 472	55
Putnam, Learock v	111 Mass., 499	55
Putnam, Mobile School Commissioners v	44 Ala., 506	23,41, 47
Putnam v. Town of Irvington	69 Ind., 80	66
Randall (School District 1 of), Monaghan v	38 Wis., 101	31,67, 68
Raleigh, Commissioners v	88 N. C., 120	43
Ratcliff v. Faris	6 Nebr., 539	49
Rawson v. Spencer	113 Mass., 40	23
Rawson v. Van Riper	1 N. Y. Sup. Ct., 370	27
Ray, Wait v	5 Hun (N. Y.), 649	52
Raymond, Richards v	92 Ill., 612	22,34, 61
Redmond, Peachy v	59 Cal., 326	49
Reichard, Ind. District of Mason City v	50 Iowa, 98	55
Rice, Bouton v	10 Phil. Reports, 559	50
Rice v. McClelland	58 Mo., 116	26,51, 52
Richards v. Raymond	92 Ill., 612	22,34, 61
Richardson County (District 56 of), Gehling v.	10 Nebr., 239	54
Riker, Albright v	22 Hun (N. Y.), 367	44, 53
Roach v. St. Louis School Board	7 Mo. App., 567	60, 61
Robinson v. Howard	87 N. C., 151	55
Rockport, Hodgkins v	105 Mass., 475	77
Rogers v. People ex rel. Brewer	68 Ill., 154	32
Rulison v. Post	79 Ill., 567	74
Rush, School District 4 of, v. Wing	30 Mich., 351	47
Rush School District, First Nat. Bank of Northumberland v.	81* Pa. St., 307	29
Russell v. Lynnfield	116 Mass., 365	73
Ryan v. School District 13 of Dakota County	27 Minn., 433	66
St. Croix County (Board of Supervisors of), Powell v.	46 Wis., 210	36
St. Joseph Board of Public Schools, Erwin v	2 McCrary (U. S. C. Ct.), 608	54
St. Joseph Board of Public Schools v. Patten	62 Mo., 444	25
St. Joseph's Church v. Assessors	12 R. I., 19	38, 60
St. Louis, Kansas City & Northern Railway Company, State ex rel. Board of Education of Moberly v.	74 Mo., 163	25
St. Louis School Board, Roach v	7 Mo. App., 567	60, 61
St. Mary's College v. Crowl	10 Kans., 442	36
Saugston, German Township School District v.	74 Pa. St., 454	42
School Directors, Davis v	92 Ill., 293	52
School Directors, Ewing v	2 Ill. App., 458	69
School Directors v. Fogleman	76 Ill., 189	35
School Directors v. Hudson	88 Ill., 563	67
School Directors v. Jennings	10 Ill. App., 645	51, 66
School Directors, Johnson v	67 Mo., 319	47
School Directors v. Miller	54 Ill., 338	54
School Directors, Nichols v	93 Ill., 61; 34 Am. Rep., 160	46
School District, Aikman v	27 Kans., 129	50
School District v. Board of Education of Lamar	73 Mo., 627	28
School District v. Colvin	10 Kans., 283	73
School District, Kane v	52 Wis., 502	47
School District, Parker v	5 Lea (Tenn.), 525	71, 76

RECENT SCHOOL LAW DECISIONS. 17

Title of case.	Report.	Cited on page—
School District, Stevenson v............	87 Ill., 255............	52,53, 66
School District 1 of Reno County v. Shadduck.	25 Kans., 467............	65
School District 5, Stackpole v............	9 Oreg., 508............	33
School District 8 of Dodge County v. Estes....	13 Nebr., 52............	70
School District 9 v. School District 5 of Hamilton County.	9 Nebr., 331............	34
School District 9 v. School District 5 of Midland.	40 Mich., 551............	31
School District 25 of Hall County v. Cowee...	9 Nebr., 53............	68
School Trustees, Lovingston v............	99 Ill., 564............	58
School Trustees, State v............	43 N. J. L., 312............	30
School Trustees, Townsend v............	41 N. J. L., 312............	50, 51
Scio and Webster (Fractional District of), Mason v.	34 Mich., 230............	59, 60
Scott v. Joint School District............	51 Wis., 554............	70
Scott v. School District 2 of Fairfax............	46 Vt., 452............	66, 70, 71
Seaver, Lander v............	32 Vt., 114............	77
Seed, Commonwealth v............	5 Pa. L. J. Rep., 78.........	77
Senter, Jamison v............	56 Miss., 194............	69
Sewell v. Board of Education of Defiance......	29 Ohio St., 89............	74
Shadduck, School District 1 of Reno County v.	25 Kans., 467............	65
Shankland v. Phillips............	3 Tenn. Chan., 556............	31
Shawnee County (Commissioners of), Washburn College v.	8 Kans., 344............	36
Sharp v. Miller............	65 Mo., 50............	22
Sheffield School Township v. Andress.........	56 Ind., 157............	29
Sherlock v. Winnetka............	68 Ill., 530............	45
Shiremanstown School District, Lower Allen School District v.	91 Pa. St., 182............	27
Silsbee, Stockle v............	41 Mich., 615............	26
Simmons v. Holmes............	49 Miss., 134............	31, 41
Sisson, People v............	98 Ill., 335............	35
Slayton, Hightower v............	54 Ga., 108; 21 Am. Rep., 273	28
Smith v. District No. 2 of Milton............	40 Mich., 143............	43
Smith, District Township of Union v.........	39 Iowa, 9............	50
Smith, Johnson v............	64 Ind., 275............	42
Smith, Peck v............	41 Conn., 442............	78
Smith, Sproul v............	40 N. J. L., 314............	32
Smith v. Township Board of Education........	58 Mo., 297............	27
Snodgrass, Dritt v............	66 Mo., 286; 27 Am. Rep., 343.	55
South Bend v. University of Notre Dame du Lac.	69 Ind., 344............	35, 36
Space, Gillis v............	63 Barbour (N. Y.), 177......	52, 53
Spalding v. Chelmsford............	117 Mass., 393............	43
Sparks, Halbert v............	9 Bush (Ky.), 259......'.....	25
Spencer v. Joint School District............	15 Kans., 259............	44
Spencer, Rawson v............	113 Mass., 40............	23
Spring v. Wright............	63 Ill., 90............	52
Springfield School Directors, State ex rel. Roberts v.	74 Mo., 21............	65
Sproul v. Smith............	40 N. J. L., 314............	32
Stackpole v. School District 5............	9 Oreg., 508............	33
State, Adams v............	82 Ill., 132............	58
State, Baughart, pros., v. Sullivan............	36 N. J. L., 89............	35
State, Bays v............	6 Nebr., 167............	52, 71
State v. Bremond............	38 Tex., 116............	24
State, Corrigan, pros., v. Duryea............	40 N. J. L., 266............	35
State, Danenhoffer v............	69 Ind., 295; 35 Am. Rep., 216.	77
State, Duryee, pros., v. Greenleaf............	34 N. J. L., 441............	35
State v. Gibbs............	25 Ohio St., 256............	26
State v. Grant............	74 Mo., 33............	70

175

2——5032

Title of case.	Report.	Cited on page—
State v. Independent School Districts	46 Iowa, 425	27
State, Lamb, pros., v. Hurff	38 N. J. L., 312	30
State v. Leonard	3 Tenn. Chan., 177	51, 67
State v. Mizner	45 Iowa, 248; 24 Am. Rep., 769; 50 Iowa, 145; 32 Am. Rep., 128.	77, 78
State v. Powell	67 Mo., 395	58
State v. Powers (New London District)	38 Ohio St., [4	21, 28
State v. School Trustees	43 N. J. L., 312	30
State, Slack, pros., v. Palmer	39 N. J. L., 250	31
State v. Tiedemann	69 Mo., 306	55
State, Trustees of District 4, pros., v. Lewis	35 N. J. L., 377	31
State, Trustees of Griswold College v	46 Iowa, 275	37
State, Yazoo City v	48 Miss., 440	25
State v. Young	23 Minn., 551	42
State Board of Education, People ex rel. Bellmer v.	49 Cal., 684	65
State ex rel. Board of Education of Moberly v. St. Louis, Kansas City & Northern R. R. Co.	74 Mo., 163	25
State ex rel. Brawford v. Cook	72 Mo., 496	58
State ex rel. Burpee v. Burton	45 Wis., 150; 30 Am. Rep., 706.	47, 76
State ex rel. Dunton v. Cobb	8 Rich., N. S. (S. C.), 123	25
State ex rel. Garnes v. McCann	21 Ohio St., 198	62, 63
State ex rel. Gregory v. School District 24 of Adams County.	13 Nebr., 78	26, 30
State ex rel. Kimball v. School District 4 of Adams County.	13 Nebr., 82	30
State ex rel. Moreland v. Whitford	54 Wis., 154	22, 47, 48
State ex rel. Oliver v. Grubb	85 Ind., 213	64
State ex rel. Phillips v. Dist. 9 of Nuckolls Co.	10 Nebr., 544	31
State ex rel. Riley v. Blain	36 Ohio St., 429	71
State ex rel. Roberts v. School Directors of Springfield.	74 Mo., 21	65
State ex rel. School District 2 of West Bend v. Wolfrom.	25 Wis., 468	26
State ex rel. Stallard v. White et al	82 Ind., 283; 42 Am. Rep., 496.	60, 73, 74
State ex rel. Steinbeck v. Treasurer of Liberty Township.	22 Ohio St., 144	29, 50
State ex rel. Stoutmeyer v. Duffy	7 Nev., 342; 8 Am. Rep., 713.	61
State ex rel. Straight University v. Graham	25 La. Ann., 440	60
State ex rel. Werden v. Williams	29 Ohio St., 161	52
State ex rel. Wilder, Cist v	21 Ohio St., 339	27
State of Missouri v. Tiedemann	3 McCrary(U. S. C. Ct.),309.	46
State to use of Maries County v. Johnson	55 Mo., 80	42
Storricker, Union School District v	86 Ill., 595	70
Stevenson v. School District	87 Ill., 255	52,53, 66
Stevenson & Rice v. Township of Summit	35 Iowa, 462	32, 54
Stevens' Point, Stroud v	37 Wis., 367	28, 32
Stockdale v. Wayland School District	47 Mich., 226	29
Stoure v. Silsbee	41 Mich., 615	26
Story County, Whitney & Keemer v	54 Iowa, 81	46
Stough, School District 2 of Dixon County v.	4 Nebr., 357	44, 54
Stow, Whitney v	111 Mass., 368	24, 29
Stroud v. Stevens' Point	37 Wis., 367	28, 32
Stuart v. School District No. 1 of Kalamazoo	30 Mich., 69	22,26, 34,52, 61
Stuckey v. Churchman	2 Ill. App., 584	68
Sullivan (Collector), State v	36 N. J. L., 89	35
Summit (District Township of), Stevenson & Rice v	35 Iowa, 462	32, 54

176

RECENT SCHOOL LAW DECISIONS. 19

Title of case.	Report.	Cited on page
Supervisors, Milwaukee Industrial School v...	40 Wis., 328	22
Sutton Manufacturing Company v. Sutton	108 Mass., 106	27
Swett, Fifield v	56 N. H., 435	27, 34
Taylor v. Brownfield	41 Iowa, 264	30
Taylor, District Township of, v. Morton	37 Iowa, 553	59
Templin & Son v. District Township of Fremont.	36 Iowa, 411	47
Thacher v. People ex rel. Johnson	98 Ill., 632	35
Thomas, Commonwealth v	10 Phil. Reports, 600	50
Thomastown, Geddes v	46 Mich., 316	58
Thompson v. Abbott	61 Mo., 176	32
Thompson v. Beaver	63 Ill., 353	27, 76
Thompson, Judd v	125 Mass., 553	60
Tiedemann, State v	69 Mo., 306	55
Tiedemann, State of Missouri v	3 McCrary (U. S. C. Ct.), 399	46
Tinnon, Board of Education of Ottawa v	26 Kans., 1	62, 64
Todd v. School District 1 of Greenwood	40 Mich., 294	43
Toledo (Board of Education of), Finch v	30 Ohio St., 37	56
Toledo City (Independent District of), Moore v.	55 Iowa, 654	55
Townsend v. Hagan	35 Iowa, 194	45
Townsend v. Trustees District 12, Essex County.	41 N. J. L., 312	50, 51
Township Board of Education v. Hackman	48 Mo., 243	43
Township Board of Education, Puterbaugh v.	53 Mo., 472	55
Township Board of Education, Smith v	58 Mo., 297	27
Tripp v. School District 3 of Utica	50 Wis., 651	72
Trumbo v. People	75 Ill., 561	35
Trustees of Common Schools v. Garvey	— Ky., —	31
Trustees, &c., Directors v	66 Ill., 247	27
Trustees of Schools, East St. Louis v	102 Ill., 489	25
Trustees of Schools v. People	87 Ill., 303; 29 Am. Rep., 55.	64, 74
Trustees of Schools, People ex rel. C. & St. L. R. R. Co. v.	78 Ill., 136	28
Trustees of Schools v. People ex rel. T., W. & W. R. R. Co.	63 Ill., 299	24, 34
Tyler, Ferriter v.	48 Vt., 444; 21 Am. Rep., 133.	74, 75
Union, District Township of, v. Smith	39 Iowa, 9	59
Union District (Alpena), Dewey v	43 Mich., 480	71
Union School District, Armstrong v	28 Kans., 345	72
Union School District v. Sterricker	86 Ill., 595	70
United States v. Buntin	10 Fed. Rep., 730	61, 62
University (Northwestern) v. People of Illinois.	99 U. S. Sup. Ct., 309	36
University of Iowa, Weary v	42 Iowa, 339	24
University of Missouri, Head v	19 Wall. (U. S. Sup. Ct.), 526.	24
University of Notre Dame du Lac, South Bend v.	69 Ind., 344	35, 36
Utica (School District 3 of), Tripp v	50 Wis., 651	72
Van Arsdale v. Laverty	69 Pa. St., 103	73
Van Riper, Rawson v	1 N. Y. Sup. Ct., 370	27
Vevay (School District 5 of), Gibson v	36 Mich., 404 ......,.........	46
Wait v. Ray	5 Hun (N. Y.), 649	52
Waltersville School District, Wilson v	46 Conn., 400	51
Ward v. Flood	48 Cal., 36; 17 Am. Rep., 405.	61,62, 63
Ward v. School District 15 of Colfax County..	10 Nebr., 293	58
Warde v. Manchester	56 N. H.,508; 22 Am.Rep.,504.	38
Washburn College v. Commissioners of Shawnee County.	8 Kans., 344	36
Washington (Independent District of), Knoxville National Bank v	40 Iowa, 612	32
Waterhouse v. Cleveland Public School Board.	9 Baxter (Tenn.), 398	24
Watertown (School District of), Halbert v	36 Mich., 421 ..,..........	32

Title of case.	Report.	Cited on page —
Wayland School District, Stockdale v.........	47 Mich., 226	29
Weary v. University of Iowa.................	42 Iowa, 338.................	24
Weir v. Day	35 Ohio St., 143..............	45
Wells v. People	71 Ill.,532...................	66
Wellsburg (Board of Education of), Kuhn v...	4 W. Va., 499	21
Wenzel v. Dorr Township Board.............	49 Mich.,25	5d
West Branch (Directors Independent District of), Albin v.	58 Iowa, 77	42
West Des Moines (Directors Independent District of), Perkins v.	56 Iowa, 476	49, 75
White et al., State ex rel. Stallard v..........	82 Ind., 283; 42 Am. Rep., 496.	60,73, 74
Whitford, State ex rel. Moreland v............	54 Wis., 154	22,47, 48
Whitney v. Stow.............................	111 Mass.,368................	24, 29
Whitney & Keemer v. Story County	54 Iowa, 81.................	46
Wickersham, Commonwealth ex rel. Swartz v..	66 Pa. St., 134	51
Wieman v. Mabee............................	45 Mich., 484	73
Wiley v. School Commissioners of Alleghany Co.	51 Md., 401	41,47, 48, 61
Wiley v. Wilson.............................	44 Vt., 404.................	30
Williams, District Township of, v. Jackson...	36 Iowa, 216	44
Williams, State ex rel. Werden v.............	29 Ohio St., 161.............	52
Willow and Grand Meadow District Townships, American Insurance Company v.	55 Iowa, 606................	46
Wilson v. Board of Education of Lee's Summit.	63 Mo., 167	67
Wilson v. East Bridgeport School District	36 Conn.,280	52,53
Wilson, Eddy v	43 Vt., 363..................	28, 31
Wilson v. Waltersville School District	46 Conn., 400	51
Wilson, Wiley v.............................	44 Vt., 404.................	30
Windsor, McCutcheon v	55 Mo., 149	52,56, 69
Wing, School District 4 of Rush v.............	30 Mich., 351	47
Winnetka, Sherlock v	68 Ill., 530..................	45
Wiota (School District 1 of), Pickett v........	25 Wis., 551	54
Wolf & Son v. Independent District of Pleasant Valley.	51 Iowa, 432; 30 Am. Rep., 450, n.	46
Wolfrom, State ex rel. School District 2 of West Bend v.	25 Wis., 468	26
Wood, Morrow v	35 Wis., 64 ; 17 Am. Rep.,741.	65, 78
Woodbury v. Knox...........................	74 Me., 462	68, 72
Woodbury (District Township of), Lane v	58 Iowa, 462................	33
Woodhull v. Bohenblost......................	4 Hun (N. Y.), 399	60
Woodward, Maynard v	36 Mich., 423	29
Wright, Jones v.............................	34 Mich., 371...............	58, 59
Wright, Spring v............................	63 Ill.,90...................	52
Yazoo City v. State	48 Miss.,440	25
Young, Haile v.............................	6 Lea (Tenn.), 501	49
Young, State v	23 Minn., 551	42

RECENT SCHOOL LAW DECISIONS.

CHAPTER I.—POWERS OF LEGISLATURES.

§ 1. **Powers of legislatures to establish schools and school systems.**—The constitutionality of legislative statutes is often inquired into by the courts. A statute will not be construed as unconstitutional if, by any fair and rational construction, it may be brought within the constitutional power of the legislature.[1] In the absence of any constitutional prohibition the whole matter of the establishment of public schools, the course of instruction to be pursued therein, how they shall be supported, upon what terms and conditions people shall be permitted to participate in the benefits they afford—in fine, all matters pertaining to their government and administration come within the range of proper legislative authority.[2] Directions in a constitution that the legislature shall provide "for the establishment of a thorough and efficient system of free schools" and "for the organization of such institutions of learning as the best interests of general education in the State may demand," give that body power to create independent school districts without the assent of the citizens residing therein, to authorize the election of a board of education by the qualified voters of the district, and to give the board power to make annual levies for buildings and the support of schools.[3] Where school laws are passed to "secure a thorough and efficient system of common schools throughout the State," they are of a general nature; and a special act relative to a school district is prohibited by a further provision of the constitution that "All laws of a general nature shall have a uniform operation throughout the State." The court said:[4] "It was a wise provision in the constitution that the system of common schools should be controlled and governed by general laws, so that the whole State may enjoy the benefits of the best system which the experience and wisdom of the legislature can devise. It does not require a prophetic eye to see that local legislation to suit the views of this locality and of that would soon impair the efficiency of our public schools; that, while in some places they might be elevated, in others they would be degraded. True, in some localities, from density of population and other causes, different necessities may exist requiring modi-

[1] Arrington v. Cotton, 1 Baxter (Tenn.), 316; Opinion of Justices, 68 Me., 582.
[2] Curryer v. Merrill, 25 Minn., 1; s. c., 33 Am. Rep., 450.
[3] Kuhn v. Board of Education, 4 W. Va., 499.
[4] State v. Powers, 38 Ohio St., 54, 64.

fications in the management of schools in order to attain the greatest efficiency; but for all such cases ample provision can be made by judicious classification and discrimination in general laws."

§ 2. Same.—High schools may be established when there is a provision of the constitution directing the legislature to provide a thorough and efficient system of free schools for the conferring of a good common school education[1] and when their existence is in accordance with the educational policy of a State.[2] Normal schools may be provided, though a State constitution mentions only free schools and a university. In an opinion maintaining this ground, Judge Krekel said:[3] "The constitution having vested all legislative power not prohibited by the Constitution of the United States in the general assembly, the establishing of normal or other schools than those named, it is fair to presume, was intended to be left with the legislature. That normal schools are public institutions, useful and necessary for the full development of free schools, is not disputed." When the legislature has placed the management of the public schools under the exclusive control of directors, trustees, or boards of education, the courts have no authority to interfere in matters of instruction,[4] nor will they consider a statute unconstitutional which imposes upon a State superintendent quasi-judicial powers, such as authority to hear appeals from the decisions of township boards respecting the division of school districts.[5] The legislature may maintain schools for a longer period than the time required by the constitution. The specifying of time does not negative the right of the legislature to provide for maintaining schools longer.[6] Though there is a clause in the constitution prescribing a uniform system of public schools, a legislature may organize various kinds of school districts, such as independent, special, and common school, and may prescribe text books for their schools, uniform only for a single class of districts.[7]

§ 3. Power of legislature to establish reform schools and authorize commitments.—The establishment of reform and industrial schools is proper, and the commitment to them of specified classes of pauper, disorderly, and vagrant children does not involve any improper interference with the relation of parent and child, nor imprisonment such as ought not to be inflicted except for crime.[8] In an elaborate opinion, Ryan, C. J., said:[9] "We cannot understand that the detention of the child at one of these schools should be considered as imprisonment any more than its detention in the poorhouse, any more than the detention of any child

---
[1] Richards v. Raymond, 92 Ill., 612.
[2] Stuart v. School District No. 1 of Kalamazoo, 30 Mich., 69.
[3] Briggs v. Johnson County, 4 Dillon (U. S. C. Ct.), 148.
[4] Board of Education of Cincinnati v. Minor, 23 Ohio St., 211 ; s. c., 13 Am. Rep., 233.
[5] State v. Whitford, 54 Wis., 150.
[6] Sharp v. Miller, 65 Mo., 50.
[7] Curryer v. Merrill, 25 Minn., 1.
[8] Milwaukee Industrial School v. Supervisors, 40 Wis., 328.
[9] Ibid., 337, 339.

at any boarding school standing for the time *in loco parentis* to the child. Parental authority implies restraint, not imprisonment; and every school must necessarily exercise some measure of the parental power of restraint over children committed to it. And when the State, as *parens patriæ*, is compelled by the misfortune of a child to assume for it parental duty and to charge itself with its nurture, it is compelled also to assume parental authority over it. This authority must necessarily be delegated to those to whom the State delegates the nurture and education of the child. The State does not, indeed we might say could not, intrude this assumption of authority between parent and child standing in no need of it. It assumes it only upon the destitution and necessity of the child, arising from want or default of parents. And, in exercising a wholesome parental restraint over the child, it can be properly said to imprison the child no more than the tenderest parent exercising like power of restraint over children.

"When a parent or other proper guardian should be able to show that the disability or default on which the child's commitment proceeded was accidental or temporary and no longer exists, and that he is * * * not otherwise unsuitable for the custody of the child, his right to the custody should prevail over the commitment to which he was not a party."

§ 4. **Powers of legislatures to control public school districts and corporations.**—As the legislature can establish school districts, so it can change or abolish them. The inhabitants of a school district have no rights in the existence or in any of the corporate functions of the district which can be regarded as vested rights or which can be set up as beyond legislative control.[1] This question arose in Massachusetts in consequence of the enactment of statutes abolishing school districts and creating town systems. The court decided that the statutes were not unconstitutional as taking the property of districts without compensation or as impairing the obligation of contracts.[2]

"Before their enactment," said Colt, J.,[3] "school districts were indeed *quasi*-corporations, with the power to hold property, to raise money by taxation for the support of schools, and with certain defined public duties. But they were public and political as distinguished from private corporations, and their rights and powers were held at the will of the legislature, to be modified or abolished, as public welfare might require. The property held by them for public use was subject to such disposition in the promotion of the objects for which it was held as the supreme legislative power might see fit to make. The laws in question

---

[1] Farnum's petition, 51 N. H., 376. In this case the legislature, within a month after the location of a school-house "for five years," provided for an appeal from the action of the committee that had located it. See, also, Mobile School Commissioners *v.* Putnam, 44 Ala., 506.
[2] Rawson *v.* Spencer, 113 Mass., 40.
[3] Ibid., 45.

do nothing more; they provide for the transfer of public property and of a public duty connected with its use from one public corporation to another." The debts of such abolished districts may be imposed upon the town.[1] The legislature has powers over a State university similar to those over school districts. Though it has appointed trustees for the institution it may, through agents other than the trustees, sell and dispose of the property of the university, or at pleasure amend or even repeal the charter, as public policy or the interests of the university may require.[2] It can discharge at any time a professor who has been employed for a specified time "subject to law." In delivering the opinion of the Supreme Court of the United States in this case Mr. Justice Hunt said:[3] "That he and his office and contract were subject to the laws in existence at the time of making it was sufficiently evident without any declaration on the point. All persons and all contracts are in that condition. But that he would be subject to future legislative action, to the extent of an immediate removal and without cause, was not so evident. It was to make that point clear, and for no other purpose, that his employment for six years * * * was declared to be 'subject to law.'"

§ 5. **Powers of legislatures respecting taxation and appropriations.**—The power to tax falls naturally, and usually by constitutional allotment, to the legislature, and it cannot delegate this power to another body, as, for example, to city school authorities, except by permission given or implied in the constitution.[4] The question arose in Maine whether the legislature had authority to assess a general tax on the property of the State for the support of common schools. The opinion of the justices of the supreme court was asked. They said that, education being of benefit to the people and taxation being incidental and essential to its successful promotion, the tax for educational purposes must be regarded as constitutional, inasmuch as it was not repugnant to the constitution and was authorized by the grant to the legislature of "full power to make and establish all reasonable laws and regulations for the defence and benefit of the people of this State."[5] A legislature cannot authorize a school district to levy taxes for other than educational purposes. On this ground the several provisions of an act which authorized the trustees of schools in townships in Illinois to hold an election, subscribe for stock, and issue and deliver bonds to aid in the construction of railroads, and the voters in such township to vote in favor of such subscription, have been declared unconstitutional.[6] Though the constitution

---

[1] Whitney v. Stow, 111 Mass., 368.
[2] Illinois Industrial University v. Champaign County, 76 Ill., 184. See, also, Weary v. State University, 42 Iowa, 338.
[3] Head v. The University of Missouri, 19 Wall., U. S., 526.
[4] Lipscomb v. Dean, 1 Lea (Tenn.), 546; Waterhouse v. Cleveland Public School Board, 9 Baxter (Tenn.), 398; City of Fort Worth v. Davis, 57 Texas, 225. See State v. Bremond, 33 Texas, 116.
[5] Opinion of Justices, 68 Me., 582.
[6] Trustees of Schools v. People ex rel. T., W. and W. Railway Company, 63 Ill., 299.

prohibits the application of more than a specified portion of the general revenue to school purposes, the legislature may set apart for the same object special taxes, such as a dog tax or license fees.[1] A license fee is not a tax.[2] A constitutional limitation of a school tax is self-executing,[3] but a proviso permitting the tax to be increased under certain circumstances requires legislation to put it into operation.[4] A legislature can and ought to provide for the support of normal schools which it has lawfully established, and whose support has failed through the unconstitutional appropriation of a part of the revenue of the common school fund for their maintenance.[5] Rapallo, J., said:[6] "By establishing them and inducing contributions from others for that purpose, it assumed the duty of supporting them, and if the particular provision which it has attempted to make for such support is objectionable it must be assumed that the legislature will regard it as their duty to provide a substitute."

§ 6. **Power of legislatures over school funds.**—The diverting, by a statute or by a city ordinance, of any part of the school fund provided by the constitution of a State to other than the purposes specified therein is unconstitutional and void.[7]

For this reason the respective acts or parts of acts have been declared unconstitutional which provided for the purchase with school moneys of a State history for each district not voting against receiving it,[8] which allowed a pro rata share of the money received from the common school fund to be paid for pupils in a private school,[9] which gave to counties money which had become a part of the general school fund through their failure to draw it in the way prescribed by the constitution,[10] which authorized the president of an academy to receive half the public moneys due a common school which was given into his charge,[11] and which appropriated common school revenues to normal schools.[12] A legislature may direct that school funds may be used in the payment of overdue claims.[13] A complaint that the legislative power as exercised in the expenditure of the school fund provided by the constitution is unwarranted will not be heard from one receiving a full share of the benefits of that fund.[14]

---

[1] *Ex parte* Cooper, 3 Texas App., 489.
[2] East St. Louis *v.* Trustees of Schools, 102 Ill., 489.
[3] St. Joseph Board of Public Schools *v.* Patten, 62 Mo., 444.
[4] State *v.* St. Louis, Kansas City and Northern Railway Company, 74 Mo., 163.
[5] Gordon *v.* Cornes, 47 N. Y., 608.
[6] Ibid, p. 617.
[7] People *v.* Allen, 42 N. Y., 404 ; Yazoo City *v.* State, 48 Miss., 440.
[8] Collins *v.* Henderson, 11 Bush (Ky.), 74.
[9] Otken *v.* Lamkin, 56 Miss., 758.
[10] Auditor *v.* Holland, 14 Bush (Ky.), 143.
[11] Halbert *v.* Sparks, 9 Bush (Ky.), 259.
[12] Gordon *v.* Cornes, 47 N. Y., 608.
[13] State *v.* Cobb, 8 Richardson (S. C.), 123.
[14] Marshall *v.* Donovan, 10 Bush (Ky.), 681.

CHAPTER II.—SCHOOL DISTRICTS.

§ 7. **Organization of districts.**—The legal organization of a school district will be presumed after it has enjoyed the franchises and privileges of a regularly organized corporation for a considerable time.[1] In Michigan the legislature has recognized this principle, and has not only deemed it important that the power of school districts should not be questioned after any considerable lapse of time, but has even established what is in effect a very short act of limitation for the purpose.[2] It is too late to revive proceedings against the formation of a district after its organization has been completed, a tax voted, and a contract made for building a schoolhouse, and interests have been established which cannot be overturned without public inconvenience and injury and private damage.[3] In a Missouri case Vories, J., said:[4] "The evidence shows that this sub-district had been organized, conducting business of every kind pertaining to such an organization for thirteen years. This, we think, was sufficient to show that such a district existed in fact, without showing their organization by record evidence." Where a complainant employed a dilatory remedy against the organization of a district, neglecting a speedy one, and the district had consequently enjoyed its franchises five years, the court refused to review its organization.[5] The legality of organization cannot be collaterally attacked if a district exists in fact and is in full exercise of corporate powers.[6] Judge Campbell, of Michigan, said:[7] "It would be dangerous and wrong to permit the existence of municipalities to depend on the result of private litigation. Irregularities are common and unavoidable in the organization of such bodies, and both law and policy require that they shall not be disturbed, except by some direct process authorized by law, and then only for very grave reasons." A new organization is not necessary when one district is enlarged by the addition of the whole or part of another.[8] The incorporation of a village constituting a part only of a school district creates, by operation of law, a joint village and township district.[9] The creation of new school districts from territory lying in different towns must be by the coöperation of the towns in their corporate capacities after due notice to the inhabit-

---

[1] Stuart v. School District No. 1 of Kalamazoo, 30 Mich., 69.
[2] Ibid., 73, Comp. L. 1871, § 3591: "Every school district shall, in all cases, be presumed to have been legally organized when it shall have exercised the franchises and privileges of a district for the term of two years." The limit is placed at one year in Nebraska. See State v. School District 24 of Adams County, 13 Nebr., 78.
[3] Parman v. School Inspectors, 49 Mich., 63.
[4] Rice v. McClelland, 58 Mo., 121.
[5] Lord v. Every, 38 Mich., 405.
[6] Stockle v. Silsbee, 41 Mich., 615.
[7] Clement v. Everest, 29 Mich., 19, 22.
[8] Greenbanks v. Boutwell, 43 Vt., 207; State v. Gibbs, 25 Ohio St., 256.
[9] State v. Wolfrom, 25 Wis., 468.

ants.¹ In Missouri it is the duty of township boards of education, in organizing a subdistrict lying in different townships, to meet together and so effect its organization; and action by one board alone will not suffice, although other boards may have relinquished their right to the territory under consideration.² The courts will not supervise the action of authorized school officers in dividing a township into school districts, unless it appears that they are acting corruptly or from improper motives or that the division is grossly unequal and unjust.³ Where a township system of schools has superseded a district system, a vote to reëstablish the school district system reëstablishes the several districts as they were when the township system was adopted. A district which had constituted with another district in an adjacent town a union district is revived as it was before its union.⁴

§ 8. **Alteration of districts.**—School districts exist only by authority derived from the legislature. After they have been created and invested with the rights, privileges, and powers incident to that class of corporations to which such districts belong, the legislature may put an end to their corporate existence and take away or modify all the school rights and privileges the inhabitants before possessed.⁵ An order altering a school district, though irregular, is binding upon subordinate officers and persons on whom it operates until reversed by regular proceedings.⁶ The incorporation of a village does not remove it from the school jurisdiction of the township,⁷ nor does the extension of the territorial limits of a municipality enlarge the school district previously existing within it.⁸ When a district is divided a different part cannot be set off than that specified in the warrant for the meeting at which the division is made.⁹ Where a new school district is created out of a portion of an old one, it is entitled to a pro rata share of the State appropriation for school purposes for the current year.¹⁰ It cannot make an agreement with the old district for a disposition of property contrary to that provided for by law.¹¹ It is to be presumed by a court that the tribunal to which is intrusted the power of changing the lines of school districts will examine carefully into all the equities of each case; that the private rights and interests to be affected by their action, as well as the public convenience and welfare, will receive due consideration and regard.¹²

---

¹ Butterfield v. Dist. 6 of Prospect, 61 Me., 583.
² Smith v. Township Board of Education, 58 Mo., 297.
³ Thompson v. Beaver, 63 Ill., 353; Directors, &c., v. Trustees, &c., 66 Ill., 247.
⁴ Sutton Manufacturing Co. v. Sutton, 108 Mass., 106; Perkins v. Crocker, 109 Mass., 128.
⁵ Farnum's petition, 51 N. H., 376.
⁶ Rawson r. Van Riper, 1 N. Y. Sup. Ct., 370.
⁷ Cist v. State of Ohio, 21 Ohio St., 339.
⁸ State v. Ind. School District, 46 Iowa, 425.
⁹ Butterfield v. School District No. 6 of Prospect, 61 Me., 583.
¹⁰ Lower Allen School District v. Shiremanstown School District, 91 Pa. St., 182.
¹¹ People v. Hodge, 4 Nebr., 265.
¹² Fifield v. Swett, 56 N. H., 435. See § 15, *post*.

The portion of a divided district which obtains the school-house ought to contribute to the erection of one in the other portion.[1]

§ 9. Powers of districts.—The powers of school districts are those belonging to the most restricted quasi-corporations. They have corporate existence by force only of their public functions.[2] They are primarily political subdivisions and agencies in the administration of civil government,[3] and not corporations within the reason or meaning of a constitutional inhibition against special acts "conferring corporate power."[4] Neither are they municipal in their nature or purpose;[5] but they are so far municipal that they cannot be garnished,[6] even by their own consent, unless the debtor also consents.[7] The principal acts they may perform are the establishment of schools, the erection of necessary buildings, the raising of money for school purposes and its expenditure for the same.[8] A district may unite with other parties in the erection of a building, one part to be owned by the district as a school-house and the other part to be owned by the other party and used for purposes disconnected with the schools of the district.[9] The nature of the building a school district may erect and whether or not it may include a hall were discussed in a Vermont case by Barrett, J., as follows:[10] "While, therefore, for the legitimate and proper purposes of a district school, the district might make as part of its school-house more or fewer rooms, and for more or less use, and different rooms for different uses, nevertheless it would not be competent for the district, in connection with the construction of a school-house, and, as a part of the structure, to make lofts or rooms that were not designed nor needed for use in connection with and for the accommodation of the schools of the district. In the present case, if the hall was designed to accommodate the schools and the inhabitants of the district for the purpose of examinations and exhibitions and other such things as are proper and customary in connection with district schools, and it was adopted in that view, the purpose was legitimate and within the province of the district to carry out by making the hall. On the other hand, if the view and purpose were not such, but the design was to use the occasion of building a school-house as a pretext for making a public hall for town meetings, religious meetings, lectures, concerts, dances, picnics, and the other uses to which such halls are ordinarily

---

[1] School District v. Board of Education of Lamar, 73 Mo., 627.
[2] Stroud v. Stevens' Point, 37 Wis., 367.
[3] Beach v. Leahy, 11 Kans., 23, 29.
[4] State v. Powers, 38 Ohio St., 54.
[5] People v. Trustees of Schools, 78 Ill., 136.
[6] Fleishell & Kimsey v. Hightower, 62 Ga., 324; Hightower v. Slayton, 54 Ga., 108; s. c., 21 Am. Rep., 273.
[7] School Dist. No. 4 of Marathon v. Gage, 39 Mich., 484.
[8] People v. Trustees of Schools, 78 Ill., 136. See § 34, 35, *post*.
[9] Eddy v. Wilson, 43 Vt., 363.
[10] Greenbanks v. Boutwell, 43 Vt., 217.

put, then the district was doing what it had no lawful authority to do. If, again, the hall was designed and adapted to serve the interests of the district in respect to its schools, the making of the hall would not be rendered illegal if, when not wanted for school purposes, the district should permit it to be used for other purposes, having no relation to the schools.

"We think it best to say further that, in the building of a school-house to serve present needs, it is entirely proper for the district to have a wise and prudent forecast as to its prospective needs; and in serving present needs it would be proper to go beyond the immediate necessity, and make reasonable provision for what the district seems likely soon to need for the service and accommodation of the increasing population and scholars. Common providence and the obvious dictates of economy may often require this."

§ 10. **Same.**—A school district may accept a bequest which does not materially increase its burdens.[1] It may lawfully recognize and pay equitable claims, though they are not legal demands.[2] Being vested with powers coextensive with the duties imposed upon it by statute or usage, it may do so reasonable an act as to execute a promissory note for a debt legally contracted for the benefit of its property or for money borrowed[3] (if it has power to borrow), but the note is not governed by the law merchant; an assignee takes it subject to all defences.[4] The payment of such a note cannot be resisted on the ground that it was given for unnecessary furniture purchased at an exorbitant price, unless fraud is shown and an offer is duly made to return the goods.[5] A school order does not possess the characteristics of negotiable paper.[6] The supreme court of Pennsylvania gave the following opinion on this point:[7] "Orders drawn by a president of a board of school directors on the treasurer of a school district, under the school law, are not negotiable bills or orders, but mere warrants for the payment of money to the persons to whom they are issued, to be disbursed by the treasurer under authority of law. They therefore do not authorize a subsequent holder to maintain suit in his own name, as upon a promissory note, bill, or order. They do not possess the ordinary properties of a mere contract, but are a statutory means of drawing the public money out of the hands of the legal custodian of the funds of the district." The power to bor-

---

[1] Maynard v. Woodward, 36 Mich., 423.
[2] Stockdale v. Wayland School District, 47 Mich., 226. See, also, Greenbanks v. Boutwell, 43 Vt., 215.
[3] Whitney v. Stow, 111 Mass., 368.
[4] Sheffield School Township v. Andress, 56 Ind., 157. See Merrill v. Town of Monticello, 14 Fed. Rep., 628.
[5] Johnson School Township v. Citizens' Bank, 81 Ind., 515.
[6] National Bank of Mt. Pleasant v. Ind. District, Marshall, 39 Iowa, 490; Ohio ex rel. Steinbeck v. Treasurer of Liberty Township, 22 Ohio St., 144.
[7] First National Bank of Northumberland v. Rush School District, 81* Pa. St., 307, 310.

row money, given expressly and without direction or restraint as to the mode of doing it, implies everything necessary to make that power effectual or requisite to attain the end in view, and authorizes the issuing and sale of school district bonds.[1] In another similar case in Nebraska the court said:[2] "The power to borrow necessarily implies authority to determine the time of payment and the character of the evidence of indebtedness that will be issued, whether in the form of notes or bonds payable in the future. The fact that the bonds were sold on the market, instead of being given to the person furnishing the money, does not make them illegal. The object of the law was to enable school districts to raise means to build school-houses therein. This being the object it was to be attained in the best practicable method. These districts, many of them on the frontier, with but little taxable property therein and no capital to be invested in loans, would have been unable for years to have effected a loan unless they had pursued the course adopted in this case, namely, issued their bonds." Bonds issued to facilitate the erection of a school-house are not invalidated by the facts that the site for it is undesirable and that their issuance was refused at a meeting held shortly before the one at which they were voted.[3]

§ 11. **District meetings.**—District meetings should be held after due notice and conducted according to legal forms.[4] The notice of a school meeting should be exact and explicit, and broad enough in its terms to include the business actually done.[5] Special meetings must be called by the proper officers regularly convened;[6] the notice of an annual meeting may be given by two of three directors.[7] When the date of the meeting is prescribed by statute, all are bound to take notice of it, and it need not be specified in the warning.[8] If the hour of meeting is fixed by statute, a meeting called later in the day is illegal. Trustees have no power to order an election at another time than that authorized by

[1] State v. School District 24 of Adams Co., 13 Nebr., 78.
[2] State v. School District 4, 13 Nebr., 82, 88.
[3] Taylor v. Brownfield, 41 Iowa, 264.
[4] In some States much of the business of school districts is directly voted upon by the electors; in others it is conducted by trustees, directors, or other officers. The meetings of the electors are considered here; those of officers are treated of in § 32, *post*. The formalities of school meetings are determined by statute and vary greatly in different States. Consequently, few decisions have extra-State application.
[5] See Wiley v. Wilson, 44 Vt., 404; State v. Hurff, 38 N. J. L., 312.
[6] State v. School Trustees, 43 N. J. L., 358.
[7] Holland v. Davies, 36 Ark., 446. Apparently a more formal notice is required for a special than for an annual meeting. The customary regulations respecting the calling of a special meeting are given by Judge Cooley, in his work on Taxation, page 246: "That the meeting shall be called by the officers of the municipality either on their own motion or on the application of a certain number of the voters or freeholders; that it shall be notified either by a warning delivered or its contents stated to the several voters, or by notice published or posted in a manner particularly indicated by the statute; and that the subjects to be considered at the meeting shall be specified in the warning or notice."
[8] Hodgkin v. Fry, 33 Ark., 716.

law.¹ A question as to whether a notice was given in due time may be settled by parol evidence, there being no date upon the notice.² In New Hampshire a meeting cannot act excepting on articles distinctly stated in the warrant.³ In New Jersey a greater sum of money cannot be raised than is designated in the warrant.⁴ A mere irregularity in conducting a meeting will not authorize judicial interference with its proceedings.⁵ Strict proof of the regularity of proceedings authorizing money to be collected cannot be required of a district by a defendant who has wrongfully received a portion of it.⁶ It is no objection to an appropriation for a specified object that it was made at a special meeting duly called, after the same appropriation had been refused at the annual meeting.⁷ Bonds issued in accordance with proceedings at a meeting held surreptitiously and without notice are void in the hands of even an innocent purchaser.⁸ The best evidence of business transacted at a school meeting is its records, and a court may reject oral evidence when the records of proceedings are furnished.⁹

§ 12. **Liabilities of districts ex contractu.**—A debt of a common school district, legally created by an existing directory or board of education, will, in the absence of any legislative intent to the contrary, continue binding on the district and enforceable against a subsequent set of officers, although the legislature may have repeatedly changed the organization of the directory or board by repealing old laws and enacting new ones, the district itself continuing to occupy the same territorial limits.¹⁰ Where one corporation goes entirely out of existence by being annexed to or merged in another, as when a consolidation of districts occurs, the new corporation will be entitled to the property and will be subject

¹ District Township of Hesper v. Independent District of Burr Oak, 34 Iowa, 306.
² Bealey v. Dickinson, 48 Vt., 599.
³ Holbrook v. Faulkner, 55 N. H., 311.
⁴ See State v. Palmer, 39 N. J. L., 250.
⁵ Trustees Common Schools of Dist. 88 v. Garvey; reported by State superintendent to Bureau of Education. Judge McCrary, in his work on Elections, says: "The principle is that irregularities which do not tend to affect results are not to defeat the will of the majority; the will of the majority is to be respected even when irregularly expressed." (Sec. 127.) Cooley on Taxation, p. 249, says: "Informalities are to be overlooked and disregarded if the substantial requisites of a vote appear." See § 36, *post*.
⁶ School Dist. 9 v. School Dist. 5 of Midland, 40 Mich., 551.
⁷ State v. Lewis, 35 N. J. L., 377.
⁸ State v. School District 9 of Nuckolls Co., 10 Nebr., 544.
⁹ Monaghan v. School Dist. 1 of Randall, 38 Wis., 101; Eddy v. Wilson, 43 Vt., 363.
"A distinction has sometimes been drawn between evidence to contradict facts stated on the record and evidence to show facts *omitted* to be stated upon the record. Parol evidence of the latter kind is receivable, unless the law expressly and imperatively requires all matters to appear of record and makes the record the only evidence." 1 Dillon's Municipal Corporations, sec. 300.
¹⁰ Shankland v. Phillips, 3 Tenn. Chancery, 556. See Dannat v. Mayor N. Y. City, 6 Hun (N. Y.), 88, and Simmons v. Holmes, 49 Miss., 134.

to the liabilities of the former corporation.[1] "Equity and justice," said Dalrimple, J., "require that the consolidated district shall discharge the liabilities of the several districts which it absorbed and of which it is now composed." Similarly, where a city or village school system supersedes a district, it acquires its property and is burdened with its liabilities.[2] In a case involving this question, the court said:[3] "Where one corporation goes entirely out of existence by being annexed to or merged in another corporation, if no arrangements are made respecting the property and liabilities of the corporation that ceases to exist, the subsisting corporation will be entitled to all the property and answerable for all the liabilities." The law on this subject has been stated in Illinois substantially as follows, in a case arising out of the redistricting of a township: It was not within the power of the township trustees, by any action in the reorganization of the township, to impair the obligation of the directors of an old district to pay a teacher the compensation to which she was entitled under a contract they had made with her for services in behalf of the district. If the indebtedness from the old district had been apportioned among and laid upon the new organizations, thus securing its payment, the law would accept the substituted mode and the old district would be discharged; but, that not having been done, it remains bound, and for all purposes of a remedy will still be deemed to exist.[4] If a school district is parcelled out among existing districts, the latter are liable for a debt of the former district, and the obligation is not joint but several.[5] In an Iowa case a township was organized into independent districts after it had incurred a liability, and it was held that recovery could be had of all the independent districts united, and they could determine between themselves the amount for which each should be responsible.[6]

An action will not lie against a school district on account of a claim

[1] Sproul v. Smith, 40 N. J. L., 314. It is otherwise in New Hampshire. See Gen. Laws, 1878, Chap. 86, sec. 28, and Clark v. Nichols, 52 N. H., 298.

[2] Thompson v. Abbott, 61 Mo., 176; Strond v. Stevens' Point, 37 Wis., 367; School Committee of Providence v. Kesler, 67 N. C., 443.

[3] Thompson v. Abbott, 61 Mo., 177.

[4] Rogers v. People, 68 Ill., 154, 156.

[5] Halbert v. School Districts, Watertown, 36 Mich., 421. This case came under a State statute, but the principle contained in the first proposition stated has been affirmed recently (1879) by the United States Supreme Court, as follows: "In such a case [the annexing of portions of a defunct municipal corporation to existing ones], if no legislative arrangements are made, the effect of the annulment and annexation will be that the two enlarged corporations will be entitled to all the public property and immunities of the one that ceases to exist, and that they will become liable for all the legal debts contracted by her prior to the time when the annexation is carried into operation." Three justices dissented on the ground that it requires legislation to make a legal obligation against the enlarged municipalities and to apportion the debts. Mount Pleasant v. Beckwith, 100 U. S., 528, 535.

[6] Knoxville National Bank v. Independent District of Washington, 40 Iowa, 612. See, also, District Township of Knoxville v. Independent Districts, 36 Iowa, 420, and Stevenson v. Township of Summit, 35 Iowa, 462.

which has not been presented for allowance to the proper officer of the district.[1]

§ 13. **Liabilities of districts ex delicto.**—A school district or a city is not liable for personal injuries sustained on account of the negligent construction of its school-houses or negligence in keeping them in repair.[2]

A noteworthy case has recently been decided in Pennsylvania:

A school district employed a contractor to make certain repairs to the school-house. It was expressly agreed that he should not enter upon the work until the school was dismissed for the season. By permission of the supervising architect, the work was commenced earlier. The supports of the first floor were weakened by excavating around them, so that an iron column in the school room above became loosened and falling over injured a child. Suit was brought against the district to recover damages for the injury. The court decided that although the board of directors took no measures to prevent the excavation which caused the damage, and of which some of them were aware, the persons who caused the injury were liable and not the school district. Trunkey, J., in giving the opinion, said:[3]

"School districts are corporations of a lower grade and less power than a city, have less the characteristics of private corporations and more of a mere agent of the State. They are territorial divisions for the purposes of the common school laws, and their officers have no power except by express statutory grant and necessary implication, and these are for the establishment and maintenance of the public schools. The common school system partakes much of the nature of a public charity, extends over the whole State, is sustained by the public moneys, and the directors, who devote much time and labor for the public benefit, receive no compensation for their services. Unless exempted by the act of incorporation or by law, a private corporation is liable for the wrongful acts and neglects of its officers, done in the course and within the scope of

---

[1] Stackpole v. School District No. 5, 9 Oreg., 508.

[2] Lane v. District Township of Woodbury, 58 Iowa, 462; Hill v. City of Boston, 122 Mass., 344. In the latter case Gray, C. J., ably reviews the law of the liability of municipal and quasi-corporations for neglect of corporate duty. "The school district or the road district is usually invested, by general enactments operating throughout the State, with a corporate character, the better to perform within and for the locality its special function, which is indicated by its name. It is but an instrumentality of the State, and the State incorporates it that it may the more effectually discharge its appointed duty. * * * The bodies above named rank low down in the scale or grade of corporate existence, and hence have been frequently called quasi-corporations. * * * Many of the courts have drawn a marked line of distinction between municipal corporations and quasi-corporations in respect to their liability to persons injured by their neglect of duty, holding the former liable, without an express statute giving the action, in cases in which the latter are not considered liable unless made so by express legislative enactment." 1 Dillon's Municipal Corporations, secs. 25, 26. In the recent case of Wixom v. City of Newport (13 R. I., 454; 43 Am. Rep., 35) it was was held that the city was not liable for an injury caused by a defect in the heating apparatus in a public school.

[3] School District of City of Erie v. Fuess, 98 Pa. St., 600. See § 37, *post.*

their employment, the same as a natural person is for the acts and neglects of his servant or agent. A less stringent rule applies to public corporations, and least stringent of all should be applied to school districts, whose officers have limited and defined powers in a system exclusively for the free education of the children in the commonwealth."

CHAPTER III.—TAXATION.

§ 14. **Subjects of taxation.**—School districts levy taxes by direction of the legislature and for school purposes only.[1] They are to be levied on districts as they exist at the time of the levy, rather than as they were when the tax was voted.[2] A legal tax may be levied on a person or property coming into a district after the tax has been voted.[3] In New Hampshire the court said: "So far as regards the equity of the thing there is no substantial difference between this case and the case of one annexed against his will to a school district which is already owing debts contracted before the annexation, and, that this may be done, I suppose no one doubts." Where a farm situated in an adjoining town had been annexed to a school district in a city and subsequently the city had been constituted one school district, it was decided that the city, as existing for school purposes at the time it became a single district, constituted that district, and that the farm belonged to it for purposes of taxation for the support of schools.[4]

§ 15. **Purposes of taxation.**— School districts can tax for corporate purposes only,[5] *i. e.*, "such as have a legitimate connection with their objects and a manifest relation thereto."[6] Under this class come the erection of buildings, even though more extensive than immediately necessary;[7] the erection of an alleged unnecessary school-house;[8] the maintenance of a high school;[9] and the instruction of pupils in other languages than the English.[10]

School districts have no right to raise money to build a school-house upon a lot other than that legally designated.[11] Trustees cannot levy a tax for railroad purposes.[12]

---

[1] "In the absence of special constitutional restriction, the legislature may confer the taxing power upon municipalities in such measure as it may deem expedient; in other words, with such limitations as it sees fit, as to the rate of taxation, the purposes for which it is authorized, and the objects (that is, the property) which shall be subjected to taxation." 2 Dillon's Municipal Corporations, sec. 740. See § 3, *ante*.
[2] School District 9 *v.* School District 6, Hamilton Co., 9 Nebr., 331.
[3] Fifield *v.* Swett, 56 N. H., 432, 435.
[4] Pickering *v.* Coleman, 53 N. H., 424.
[5] Board of Trustees *v.* People *ex rel.* T., W. & W. Railway Company, 63 Ill., 299.
[6] People *v.* Dupuyt, 71 Ill., 651, 656.
[7] Greenbanks *v.* Boutwell, 43 Vt., 207.
[8] Power's petition, 52 Mo., 218.
[9] Stuart *v.* Dist. 1 of Kalamazoo, 30 Mich., 69; Richards *v.* Raymond, 92 Ill., 612.
[10] Powell *v.* Board of Education, 97 Ill., 375; s. c., 37 Am. Rep., 123.
[11] Marble *v.* McKenney, 60 Me., 332.
[12] People *v.* Dupuyt, 71 Ill., 651, 656.

In New Jersey the purposes for which money is to be raised by taxation must be declared by the voters in school meeting. Unless the exact objects are specified and the sum to be devoted to each is determined, the tax is void.[1]

A tax levied by the school trustees of a town or city for school purposes is not a tax for "general city or town purposes."[2]

§ 16. **Powers of taxation.**—When discretionary power of taxation has been vested in a board of school directors or supervisors and has been exercised for the year, the power is exhausted for the year in which the levy is made; and neither the officers levying the tax nor their successors can levy a different school tax for that year;[3] yet, if that power has not been used to the full extent, courts might allow a supplementary tax for a special purpose to be raised.[4] In Illinois the directors of school districts, under some circumstances, may levy a special tax without a vote of the people.[5] Where they built a school-house without a vote from the district, the levying a tax, accepting the building, and having a school taught therein did not legalize the act nor bind the people to pay the tax.[6] When county authorities are empowered to levy such a tax, not to exceed a certain amount, as may be determined by the qualified electors of the several school districts, they cannot forestall the action of the electors by assessing a school tax.[7] Authority to levy a tax on property does not authorize the levy of a poll tax.[8] Where it is the duty of one officer to direct another to levy a tax, any written communication is sufficient.[9]

§ 17. **Collection of taxes.**—The illegal formation of a district will afford no ground for resisting the collection of taxes levied by its directors, they being *de facto* officers.[10] Nor can such resistance be offered on the ground that the title to the land purchased as a site for the school building for whose erection the tax was levied is defective, so long as the possession remains undisturbed.[11] Although a school tax is invalid if the notices of election fail to specify the questions to be voted on, its validity cannot be questioned by one who participates in the election and seconded the motion to raise the money.[12] Personal chattels outside of the district to which a tax is due should not be dis-

---

[1] State *v.* Greenleaf, 34 N. J. L., 441; State *v.* Sullivan, 36 N. J. L., 89; State *r.* Duryea, 40 N. J. L., 266.

[2] South Bend *v.* University of Notre Dame du Lac, 69 Ind., 344.

[3] Oliver *v.* Carsner, 39 Texas, 396.

[4] Furniture Company *v.* Harvey, 45 Iowa, 466.

[5] Pennington *v.* Coe, 57 Ill., 118.

[6] School Directors *v.* Fogleman, 76 Ill., 189.

[7] Cairo and Fulton R. R. Co. *v.* Parks, 32 Ark., 131; Murphy *v.* Harbison, 29 Ark., 340.

[8] Board of School Commissioners of Indianapolis *v.* Magner, 84 Ind., 67.

[9] Dent *v.* Bryce, 16 S. C., 1.

[10] Trumbo *v.* People, 75 Ill., 561.

[11] People *v.* Sisson, 98 Ill., 335.

[12] Thacher *v.* People, 98 Ill., 632.

trained for school taxes, even though the district seeking to distrain included, when the tax was levied, the territory within which the chattels are found. A tax levied is not a lien upon personal property.[1] It is well settled in many States that money paid by compulsion on account of a void tax may be recovered in an action against the municipality receiving it. It is equally well settled that if a person voluntarily pays a void tax, with knowledge of the facts which render it void, he cannot recover back the money thus paid.[2]

§ 18. **Exemption of school property from taxation.**—Statutes and constitutional provisions for the exemption from taxation of property used for educational purposes are strictly construed,[3] and are sometimes declared to be directions not to tax rather than grants of a right not to be taxed.[4] Where the constitution of a State exempted property used *exclusively* for educational purposes, it was held that neither land owned by a college with the intention that it should become in future a permanent site,[5] nor a farm used by the owners of a school for supplying produce and illustrating instruction in agriculture,[6] was exempt. In the latter case the court said:

"If a farm be used for the purpose of raising produce to sell and get money to carry on a school, it will not be exempt. The use for educational purposes is in such a case too remote. The immediate or primary object for cultivating the farm in such a case is to obtain the produce, the secondary object is to obtain the money that the produce will bring, and the remote object is to aid and foster the school." The property affected by a clause exempting all deemed necessary for school purposes is much more extensive.[7] In an opinion in the United States Supreme Court, Mr. Justice Miller said:[8] "The distinction is, we think, very broad between property contributing to the purposes of a school, made to aid in the education of persons in that school, and that which is directly or immediately subjected to use in the school. The purposes of the school and the school are not identical. The purpose of a college or university is to give youth an education. The money which comes from the sale or rent of land dedicated to that object aids this purpose. Land so held and leased is held for school purposes in the fullest and clearest sense." It has been decided that a professor's house, owned by a college, is included in an exemption of the grounds and buildings of literary institu-

---

[1] McKay v. Batchellor, 2 Colo., 591. "Municipal power to collect by distress and sale cannot be implied because the State collects its taxes in this manner. It must be given, if not in express terms, yet by the clearest and most indubitable implication." 2 Dillon's Municipal Corporations, sec. 818.

[2] Powell v. Board of Supervisors of St. Croix County, 46 Wis., 210, 213.

[3] South Bend v. University of Notre Dame du Lac, 69 Ind., 344, and nearly all cases cited in this section.

[4] Probasco v. Moundville, 11 W. Va., 501.

[5] Washburn College v. Commissioners of Shawnee County, 8 Kans., 344.

[6] St. Mary's College v. Crowl, 10 Kans., 442, 450.

[7] Chicago v. People, 80 Ill., 384, 387.

[8] University v. People, 99 U. S., 309, 324.

tions "devoted solely to the appropriate objects of these institutions." The reasons assigned for the decision were that the house was erected with money of the college that might otherwise have been exempt, that it was used to sustain the college, that it was for an object peculiarly fitting and appropriate, and that it was not leased or otherwise used with a view to pecuniary profit. Two judges dissented on the ground that the house was owned and used for the purpose and object of reducing salary expenses, and consequently for a pecuniary profit.[1]

§ 19. Same.—Two cases involving the exemption of school property are mentioned in a recent number of a prominent law journal.[2] In one it was held that a building used partly as a dormitory and boarding house for students of an academy and partly as a public house is not exempt from taxation as land "for the use of the academy," the court saying that "the phrase 'for the use of' is not to be taken in the same sense as 'for the profit of.'"[3] In the other case[4] a female seminary was originally located upon a tract of eight acres of land, upon which were erected the buildings of the institution. Afterward the corporation acquired three other small tracts of land. All are included in the common inclosure of the seminary grounds, with dividing fences within that common inclosure. The several tracts are used, a portion for walks and lawns for the exercise and benefit of the scholars, a part for gardening to supply the institution with vegetables, a part for an orchard to supply necessary fruit for the institution, a part for raising feed for stock, for pasturage, and for wood land, all for the exclusive use of the institution, and not "otherwise used with a view to profit." These lands were held exempt from taxation under the statute of exemption relating to property of institutions of learning. The court said: "The evidence further shows that all this property is necessary for the proper carrying on of the institution; that said tracts of land are used exclusively for the purposes of the institution, and that no part of the same has been leased or otherwise used with a view to profit; that it is necessary in connection with the institution to have cows to supply milk for the scholars and teachers, all of whom (numbering about 175 persons) reside and live within and upon the grounds of the institution; that horses are required to do the necessary hauling connected with the seminary, and that all the hay, corn, and oats raised on the place go to the feeding of the stock thereon; that nothing is ever sold off the premises, and that what is raised is but a partial supply for the institution; that the object of the institution is, as far as possible, to make it a self-sustaining one, and that what is realized over and above actual expenses is used as a fund for the education of indigent females. We do not see why the facts of this case do not bring these lands within the very words of

---

[1] Trustees of Griswold College v. State, 46 Iowa, 275, 281, 283.
[2] Albany Law Journal, vol. 28, p. 205.
[3] Trustees of Phillips Exeter Academy v. Exeter, 58 N. H., 306; s. c., 42 Am. Rep., 589.
[4] Monticello Seminary v. People, 106 Ill., 398.

the exemption from taxation of the constitution and the legislation upon the subject. They form one connected body of land, upon which the seminary buildings are situated. They are not lands which are leased by the institution or otherwise used with a view to profit, but they are used strictly in the carrying on of this seminary of learning, and are used exclusively for that purpose." Chief Justice Scott dissented on the ground that land used as a farm was "used with a view to profit."

§ 20. **Same.**—Schools established by private donations, and carried on for the benefit of the public and not with a view to profit, are "institutions of purely public charity" within the meaning of the provision of the Ohio constitution which authorizes such institutions to be exempt from taxation.[1] Such schools are not exempt as being "free public schools."[2] The term "school-houses and seminaries of learning" evidently includes the buildings and the lots upon which they stand.[3] How much is included in an exemption of lots whereon school buildings are erected was discussed at considerable length in New York a few years ago (1875).[4] An academy for ladies owned extensive grounds in the upper part of New York City and had its buildings near the centre of them, occupying about five acres. Eight acres were used as a vegetable garden for the academy, one acre as a cemetery, and the residue, thirty-six acres, more or less, was for recreation and walking. It was decided that the property was exempt. The court said:[5] "The propriety of the exemption is precisely the same, whether it relates to the buildings themselves and the lots on which they stand, or to the ground required to promote and secure the recreation and health of the pupils of the schools and those engaged in teaching and guarding them. A well ordered, prosperous school requires the one as much as it does the other. It would be very unwise and indiscreet to allow young persons to be confined in school buildings upon grounds affording no reasonable opportunity for exercise or diversion." "The property claimed by the relator to be exempt from taxation was all shown to be a portion of the lots or parcel of ground on which its school buildings are situated. What they

---

[1] Gerke v. Purcell, 25 Ohio St., 229.
[2] St. Joseph's Church v. Assessors, 12 R. I., 19.
[3] Warde v. Manchester, 56 N. H., 508; s. c., 22 Am. Rep., 504. "An exemption of all colleges, academies, or seminaries of learning extends to the houses and lots provided by a college for the residences of president, professors, and steward as part of their compensation." Hilliard's "Law of Taxation," sec. 35.
[4] People ex rel. Academy of the Sacred Heart v. Commissioners of Taxes and Assessments of New York City, 6 Hun (N. Y.), 109. The statute under consideration provided that "The following property shall be exempt from taxation: * * * Every building erected for the use of a college, incorporated academy, or other seminary of learning, every building for public worship, every school-house, court-house, and jail, and the several lots whereon such buildings are situated, and the furniture belonging to each of them." Rev. Stat., 5th ed., vol. 1, p. 906.
[5] Ibid., 112, 114. Union College holds exempt 130 acres; Madison University, 140 acres; Vassar College, 210 acres; and Cornell University, a still greater area.

do not occupy has been devoted to the promotion of the convenience of the occupants of the buildings, supplying their wants, and affording them the means of recreation, health, and exercise."

§ 21. **Local assessment of school property.**—It has been frequently stated that school property, exempt from taxation, was nevertheless liable to local assessments for the construction of streets, sewers, and the like.[1] A recent case in Connecticut has been decided to the contrary. Under the charter of the city of Hartford all land specially benefited by a city improvement was liable to be assessed for the expenses of such improvement. A school house and lot, used solely for school purposes, was assessed for a street improvement, and the court held that the benefit to the school district was too contingent and remote to render it liable to pay the assessment.[2] The court said: "The assessment was undoubtedly made upon the idea that the intrinsic value of the property was increased, but, if that were so as a matter of fact, does it follow that it was increased in value as school district property, bought and used solely for school purposes? and did the district, or could it, from the nature of things, derive any immediate, direct, or special benefit from the laying out of the street? We are unable to see how the district as a corporation could be so benefited, or that their property was rendered any more valuable for the purpose for which they use it, and for which they must continue to use it, if not for all time, at least for a very long period."

The following statement of the exemption of school property from taxation appeared in the Report of the United States Commissioner of Education for 1880, pp. cclv–cclvii:

The exemption of school property is either determined by the constitution of each State or else impliedly or expressly delegated by it to the legislative body. The States whose constitutions prescribe the rule of exemption are Arkansas, California, Kansas, Louisiana, Minnesota, Missouri, Ohio, and Pennsylvania. The property which is exempted is, in Pennsylvania, public property used for public purposes, which includes schools aided by the Commonwealth; in Ohio, public school-houses, by which is meant "such as belong to the public and are designed for schools established and conducted under public authority." [Gerke v. Purcell, 25 Ohio St., 229, 240.] The term has been made to cover not only the houses themselves, but their furniture and the books properly belonging with them. In California property used exclusively for public schools is required to be exempted. In Missouri, lots in incorporated cities or towns, or within one mile of the limits of any such city or town, to the extent of one acre, and lots of one mile or more distant from such cities or towns, to the extent of five acres, with the buildings thereon, may be exempted from taxation when the same are used exclusively for religious worship, for schools, or for purposes purely charitable. In Minnesota, public school-houses,

---

[1] "It is no objection to an assessment for a local work that the property assessed is used for a purpose that will not be specially advanced by the improvement; as, for instance, that it is * * * devoted to school or charitable purposes." Cooley on Taxation, p. 458.
"A general statute exempting certain property * * * from 'taxation by any law of the State' does not exempt it from liability for a street assessment." 2 Dillon's Municipal Corporations, sec. 777.

[2] City of Hartford v. West Middle District, 45 Conn., 462; s. c., 29 Am. Rep., 687.

academies, colleges, universities, and all seminaries of learning are exempted from taxation; in Arkansas, school buildings and apparatus, libraries, and grounds used exclusively for school purposes; and in Kansas and Louisiana, all property used exclusively for educational or school purposes. The constitution of Colorado exempts lots, with the buildings thereon, used exclusively for schools, "unless otherwise provided by general law," and that of South Carolina requires the general assembly to enact laws for the exemption of public schools, colleges, and institutions of learning, provided the exemption shall not extend beyond the buildings and premises actually occupied. In the other States the exemption of school property is a matter for independent legislative action, though many constitutions give special permission to legislatures to exempt property of certain kinds or property used for specific purposes.

The latest compilations of the statutes of the several States show substantially the laws regulating the exemption of school property as they now exist. There may have been a few changes, but it is not a subject upon which there has been much fluctuating legislation. In Illinois, Maine, Maryland, Massachusetts, Mississippi, North Carolina, Oregon, South Carolina, and West Virginia, all school property, with some few limitations, has been exempted. In Maine and Maryland all the property of literary institutions is designated as exempt. In Illinois this broad exemption is limited by the provision that it shall not extend to real estate leased or otherwise used with a view to profit. In Massachusetts exemption of real estate does not extend beyond that occupied by the educational institutions and their officers for corporate purposes. In Mississippi it extends, not only to property used for the benefit and support of institutions for the education of youth, but also to that held and occupied by the trustees of schools and school lands for the use of public schools.

* * * * * * * *

The exemption of school property is almost as general in Iowa, Kentucky, Michigan, Minnesota, Nebraska, Nevada, New Jersey, New York, and Texas as in the States previously mentioned. In all of them, buildings, grounds, and furniture are exempt so far as they are actually necessary for the use and enjoyment of the institutions owning them. Books or libraries are expressly included in the exempt property in all these States except Nevada, New Jersey, and New York; and apparatus, equipments, or other general terms are used in all these States to designate personal property commonly found in schools, and which is usually exempted by direct words or by implication. The exemption of these kinds of property is on condition oftentimes that they be used for strictly educational purposes and be not in excess of specified amounts. The real estate exempted is limited to three acres in Nebraska and five acres in Kentucky and New Jersey. In Minnesota, Nevada, and New York it must be immediately connected with the buildings of the institution to which it belongs. In Connecticut, Georgia, New Hampshire, and Vermont it is known that the buildings of educational institutions are exempt, and it is to be presumed that the term "buildings" includes the lots upon which they are erected. In Florida and Indiana public school property is exempted. The laws in Rhode Island and Wisconsin have peculiar features which will best be understood by presenting them *verbatim*. The law of Rhode Island exempts "buildings for free public schools, buildings for religious worship, and the land upon which they stand and immediately surrounding the same to an extent not exceeding one acre, so far as said buildings and land are occupied and used exclusively for religious or educational purposes; the estates, persons, and families of the president and professors, for the time being, of Brown University, for not more than ten thousand dollars for each such officer, his estate, person, and family included."

In Wisconsin exemption extends to "personal property owned by any religious, scientific, literary, or benevolent association, used exclusively for the purposes of such association, and the real property, if not leased or not otherwise used for pecuniary profit, necessary for the location and convenience of the buildings of such association and embracing the same, not exceeding ten acres, and the lands reserved for grounds of a chartered college or university, not exceeding forty acres."

CHAPTER IV.—SCHOOL PROPERTY.

§ 22. **School funds.**—The State is the owner of public school property and school funds; and this is one reason why such property is exempt from taxation.[1] In the case of certain lands held in the name of the city of Chicago exclusively for the use of its public schools and derived mediately from public school lands, the court said:[2] "No act of the general assembly has ever granted the title to the school property and fund irrevocably to any body of persons. They have created corporate bodies to handle and control the fund for the use of the people, but that body has not parted with the power to control the fund in any mode they may choose for the use of schools. They could, if disposed, deprive those to whom its management is intrusted of the fund, and intrust it to others. Whilst the increase of the fund should be expended in the support of schools, the manner or the agency employed may be at all times controlled or changed by the State at pleasure. The State is virtually a trustee of the fund for the use of the people, and the municipalities and officers are but the agencies employed by the State in executing its trust." The general assembly has no power to abdicate its control over the school fund.[3] Such a fund must be applied to the exact purposes for which it was created and exists.[4] But although the State may not have the constitutional power to divert school moneys from the purposes for which they are set apart, she may change the administrators of the funds, and, in her wisdom and discretion, direct the mode and manner of the administration of the trust, and how, by whom, and to whom the moneys are to be paid and applied.[5] If a fund is provided by the constitution for free public schools it can only be applied to such schools as are within the uniform school system required, are free from religious and sectarian control, and open to children of school age; though this freedom of admission does not preclude the classification of the schools according to the ages, sex, race, or mental acquirements of the pupils.[6] In a case in Massachusetts, under a constitutional provision requiring moneys raised for the public schools to be applied only to those under the charge of the public authorities, it was denied that a town could appropriate moneys raised for public schools to the support of a school founded by a bequest, under which the charge of the school was vested in trustees who, though most of them elected by the town, must be connected with certain religious societies.[7] A tax for building purposes cannot be used for ordinary ex-

---

[1] City of Chicago v. People, 80 Ill., 384. See Illinois Industrial University v. Supervisors of Champaign County, 76 Ill., 184, and § 3, *ante*.
[2] City of Chicago v. People, 80 Ill., 385.
[3] Auditor v. Holland, 14 Bush (Ky.), 147.
[4] Wiley v. School Commissioners of Alleghany Co., 51 Md., 401.
[5] Mobile School Commissioners v. Putnam, 44 Ala., 506.
[6] Otken v. Lamkin, 56 Miss., 758. On race classification, see § 44, *post*.
[7] Jenkins v. Andover, 103 Mass., 94.

penses; but the exemption of the surplus of the annual taxes from the payment of debts contracted for buildings would not seem a rule of law or justice, if payment would not prevent the schools from being kept open the required period in the subsequent year.[1] When real estate is conveyed to school trustees for school purposes, and this is so expressed in the deed, the land itself must be so used; the directors and trustees have no right to sell the land and apply the proceeds to school purposes, but they may rent it or use it as a school site.[2] If the power of loan of school funds is regulated, the lending of them on other securities than those mentioned and prescribed is a misapplication, but does not discharge the borrower.[3] Such funds in the hands of a county treasurer are not secured by his general bond, but only by his distinct bond for their payment, this being not cumulative to his general bond, but separate from it.[4]

§ 23. **Same.**—A school district can take by will.[5] Money bequeathed to a township goes to the territory which was included in the specified township at the time of the execution of the will.[6]

There was a bequest in New York City to the board of trustees of each of the several wards as they might exist at the time of the final distribution of the estate, and in construing the clause the court said:[7] "I do not think the provision can be extended to embrace schools in wards created in territory annexed to the city limits since the testator's death. Whilst he did contemplate that by increase of population old wards might be divided and in this way new ones created, he did not provide for schools in territory to be after acquired."

A due proportion of all moneys intended for the education of the children that resided in an original district ought to be given by it to a new one formed partly out of its territory prior to its reception of the moneys, although the new district was not organized until afterward.[8] Where territory is set into an adjoining county or township, or attached to an independent school district in an adjoining county or township, for school purposes, or is restored from an independent district to the district township to which it geographically belongs, there must be an equitable apportionment of all the assets and liabilities.[9] If money is willed to a village to build a suitable structure for a high school, without further direction as to its maintenance and without endowment, the village may build the house, use it temporarily for graded school purposes, and delay for a reasonable time the organization of a higher

---

[1] German Township School District v. Sangston, 74 Pa. St., 454.
[2] Trustees, &c., of Morgan County v. Branor, 71 Ill., 546.
[3] Littleworth v. Davis, 50 Miss., 403.
[4] State v. Young, 23 Minn., 551; State v. Johnson, 55 Mo., 80.
[5] Estate of Bulmer, 59 Cal., 131.
[6] Board of Education v. Ladd, 26 Ohio St., 210.
[7] Betts v. Betts, 4 Abbott's New Cases (N. Y.), 412.
[8] Johnson v. Smith, 64 Ind., 275.
[9] Albin v. Directors of Independent District of West Branch, 58 Iowa, 77. See § 5, *ante*.

department.[1] Fines imposed by municipal ordinance are not included in those accruing to the State, such as in some States are added to the school fund.[2]

§ 24. **Sites and buildings.**—A public school-house is a building belonging to the public and designed for schools established and conducted under public authority.[3] A district contracting for the erection of a house within a stated time is bound to furnish a suitable site within such reasonable time that the contractors may not be delayed in the performance of their agreement.[4] A site may be obtained by condemnation.[5] While the law was silent on the subject of obtaining sites otherwise than by purchase, certain counties of Pennsylvania successfully tried compulsory condemnation; then the State passed a law allowing it, and the law was pronounced constitutional.[6] The court said: "The common school system pervades the whole Commonwealth and is its creature, acting in the several school districts by its boards of directors or controllers, who are simply the agents of the State in carrying out the wise, benevolent, and foresighted policy of the government. Every man, woman, and child in a republic should be able to read and write, and this is the object aimed at by the common school law. School-houses are an essential part of the system, and the compulsory power is as necessary to it as the taking of land for a public highway." In a case in Maine the court assumed that land might be taken under the right of eminent domain, against consent, and the compensation therefor fixed by others, without the participation of the owner, under a statutory clause authorizing school districts " to determine where their school-houses shall be located."[7] Proceedings to condemn are invalid where there has been no legal determination of the site.[8] A petition asking the condemnation of a site should designate the same and show disagreement with the owner as to compensation. When the owner of a proposed site is represented at the proceedings to condemn it, he is deemed to waive objections to jurors if he does not challenge them at the time.[9] If a lot is taken illegally, no allowance will be made for improvements put upon it.[10] The fact that a lot has already been im-

---

[1] Hathaway v. New Baltimore and Lake School District, 48 Mich., 257.
[2] Commissioners v. Raleigh, 88 N. C., 120.
[3] Gerke v. Purcell, 25 Ohio St., 229.
[4] Todd v. School District 1 of Greenwood, 40 Mich., 294; Township Board of Education v. Hackman, 48 Mo., 243.
[5] "Land may be appropriated for the erection of a school-house and for a school yard. The use proposed is not local and limited, but public. Schools are a public necessity, and as taxation for schools is supported the exercise of eminent domain is equally justified in providing suitable locations." Mills on Eminent Domain, § 17.
[6] Long v. Fuller, 68 Pa. St., 170, 172.
[7] Norton v. Perry, 65 Me., 103.
[8] Heck v. Essex School District, 49 Mich., 551.
[9] Smith v. School District 2 of Milton, 40 Mich., 143.
[10] Spalding v. Chelmsford, 117 Mass., 393.

proved does not prevent its condemnation.[1] If a location is void by reason of insufficient and defective description of premises taken, proceedings must be begun anew in order to make a valid location.[2] If a site is purchased the deed of conveyance must be without any defeating condition, such as that the land shall revert to the grantor on a change in the school system. Such a limitation is inconsistent with the objects of the grant and must be rejected as surplusage.[3]

In New York it was held that a deed made and received by a school district trustee on the express condition "that the title and estate of the grantee [trustee] and his successor in the said premises should cease when the said use [as a public school site] should cease, and should thereupon be vested in the grantor, his heirs, and assigns; the district to build the fence and keep it in repair," was such a conveyance as a school district might accept, and that the last clause imposed on the district an obligation differing only in extent from that which the law imposes with regard to division fences, which the district might enter into before voting a tax for building or repairing the fence.[4]

§ 25. **Same.**—A school-house erected on the land of a private citizen by his oral consent will be considered personal property.[5] In the case referred to, the court said: "Although it is a general principle of law that a building permanently annexed to the freehold becomes a part of it and is real estate, yet if it is erected by the builder with his own money, and for his own exclusive use, as disconnected from the use of the land, and with an agreement to that effect between the owner of the land and the builder, it will, as between the parties, be considered personal property." A committee of a board of school directors appointed to get up plans for a new school building from some architect and submit the same for approval, has authority to contract with an architect for plans and specifications as well as a preliminary sketch.[6] Before a building can be paid for, in Nebraska, at least, the district must not only raise the money, but distinctly authorize its expenditure.[7] School-houses and sites are "assets" within the meaning of a statute providing for an equitable division of assets in case of the division of districts.[8]

§ 26. **Use of buildings.**—A public school-house is to be used for public school purposes.[9] A lease of one continuing during a specified time and based on a valuable consideration by a board of education vested with

---

[1] Ferree v. School District, 76 Pa. St., 376.
[2] Norton v. Perry, 65 Mo., 183.
[3] School Committee of Providence v. Kesler, 67 N. C., 443, 447.
[4] Albright v. Riker, 22 Hun (N. Y.), 367.
[5] District Township of Corwin v. Morehead, 43 Iowa, 466, 468.
[6] School District of McKeesport v. Miller, 1 Pa. Sup. Ct., 510.
[7] School District of Dickson County v. Stough, 4 Nebr., 357.
[8] Williams v. District Township of Jackson, 36 Iowa, 216.
[9] Spencer v. School District, 15 Kans., 259. Statutes allow some other uses in several States.

the property of a district in trust for the use of public schools, for the purpose of having a private or select school taught therein, is in violation of trust.¹ Charter authority to a village council, as a board of education, to purchase grounds, erect buildings, borrow money to establish a school of a high grade, and levy taxes for the erection and support of the same, does not authorize the conveyance or leasing of the buildings when completed, without pay or rent, to an individual or private corporation, for the purpose of having a school taught therein for pay. The school contemplated by such a charter is one free to all children of suitable age and advancement residing in the district, and anything else is a perversion of the property from its intended uses.² But if a town is specially empowered to own and use a school-house for educational purposes, it may open a free public school, or rent the premises to private parties,³ or procure an interest in existing schools,⁴ as may seem best to provide for the educational wants of the public. In the case last cited a town purchased a controlling interest in two established schools. In deciding that it had a right to do so, the court, not relying on a statute, and simply referring to the article of the constitution requiring the maintenance of a thorough system of general education, said:⁵ "No student of the history of this country from the earliest settlement to the present day can fail to see that, to furnish facilities for the education of the people, it has not only been the constant practice of both the State and the corporate [municipal] organizations to engage in projects for the advancement of education, but that this has been a favorite and preferred object; and it seems to us that more permanent good has come to the country from this application of municipal funds than from any other use of such funds." "The trustees in this case undertook to keep up the school. No profit accrues to them. The house is the necessary thing; the public may well furnish that, leaving the school to support itself." The use of a school building for the purposes of a Sunday school has been disapproved in Missouri, on the grounds that the school law does not justify or authorize it and that "if the precedent be established it may lead to great abuses and disagreeable altercations between different religious denominations, which it is the purpose of our common school to avoid."⁶ Such a use has been allowed in Iowa under a clause in a statute authorizing the electors to direct the disposition to be made of the school-house;⁷ and the use of the school-house for Sabbath school and religious services is not affected by a clause in the constitution exempting all persons from paying taxes for building

---

¹ Weir v. Day, 35 Ohio St., 143.
² Sherlock v. Winnetka, 68 Ill., 530.
³ Fleishell & Kimsey v. Hightower, 62 Ga., 324.
⁵ Danielly v. Cabaniss, 52 Ga., 211.
⁴ Ibid., 222.
⁶ Dorton v. Hearne, 67 Mo., 301.
⁷ Townsend v. Hagan, 35 Iowa, 194.

or repairing places of worship. The use for the purposes named does not convert the school-house into a building for worship within the meaning of the constitution, since it is only temporary, occasional, and enjoyed only by permission.[1] In Illinois it has been decided that the temporary use of a school-house for religious worship is not repugnant to clauses in the constitution forbidding the use of public funds for sectarian purposes and requiring school moneys to be faithfully applied to school purposes.[2] "Religion and religious worship," said the court, "are not so placed under the ban of the constitution that they may not be allowed to become the recipients of any incidental benefit whatsoever from the public bodies or authorities of the State."

§ 27. **Insurance, repair, and furnishing of school-houses.**—A provision that a school officer shall have the control and management of the school-house does not empower him to bind the district by a contract of insurance,[3] nor to purchase lightning rods.[4] A district can obtain the insurance on a school-house burned, although it had been nominally sold on credit by officers authorized to sell, because such sale on credit was void without ratification by the district.[5] If a house be burned the insurance money cannot be obtained by the creditors by garnishment;[6] for the property of a school district cannot be garnished,[7] nor subjected to a mechanics' lien.[8] Neither a stereoscope with views[9] nor charts containing the multiplication tables, forms for business contracts, and prominent historical events,[10] are " necessary appendages " to a school-house. A board authorized to purchase school apparatus may buy an organ for a school in which music is taught as a recognized branch of education.[11]

[1] Davis v. Boget, 50 Iowa, 11.
[2] Nichols v. School Directors, 93 Ill., 61; s. c., 34 Am. Rep., 160.
[3] American Insurance Company v. District Townships Willow and Grand Meadow, 55 Iowa, 606.
[4] Monticello Bank v. District Township of Coffin's Grove, 51 Iowa, 350; Wolf & Son v. Ind. District, 51 Iowa, 432.
[5] School District v. Ætna Insurance Company, 62 Me., 330.
[6] Fleishell & Kimsey v. Hightower, 62 Ga., 324.
[7] See § 6, *ante*.
[8] State of Missouri v. Tiedemann, 3 McCrary, U. S. Cir. Ct., 399; Whitney & Keemer v. Story County, 54 Iowa, 81; Abercrombie v. Ely, 60 Mo., 23.
[9] Bourbon County, &c., v. Perkins, 21 Kans., 536; s. c., 30 Am. Rep., 447.
[10] Gibson v. School District 5 of Vevay, 36 Mich., 404. A mathematical chart may come within the description of "school apparatus and appendages." The court said: "Now it is certain that all kinds of school apparatus are not included among the articles properly denominated 'appendages;' for instance, we would think that blackboards, outline maps, and mathematical charts, to be hung upon the walls of the school-house and to remain there permanently for the purpose of illustrating such lessons in science, history, or geography as might be taught in the schools, might properly be denominated both 'school apparatus' and 'appendages.' A mathematical chart might be hung upon the walls of the school-house and become an appendage; and it might also be used for the purpose of illustrating the science of mathematics, and thereby become a part of the apparatus used by the school." School District v. Swayze, 29 Kans., 211; Al. L. J. 28, p. 424.
[11] Bellmeyer v. Independent District of Marshalltown, 44 Iowa, 564.

Seats may be bought under a resolution directing a board to "fix the school-house ready for the winter term."[1] The mere fact that seats, maps, globes, &c., have been used by the district does not ratify an illegal purchase and bind the district for payment.[2] A statute providing that a director shall keep the necessary school-house furniture in proper order, and that his expenses shall be subsequently audited and paid, does not intend that money shall be put into his hands previous to such auditing.[3]

CHAPTER V.—OFFICERS.

§ 28. **Quasi-judicial powers of officers.**—School officers are usually possessed of specially defined powers and should exercise no others, except such as arise by fair implication from those granted.[4] In many States certain school officers are clothed with authority to decide controversies and hear appeals. An appeal is not a suit; and a statute providing for the employment of counsel in case of suits by or against a district does not warrant such employment in case of a hearing before a county or State superintendent.[5] The hearing of an appeal and the decision of controversies and disputes arising under the school law are exercises of "a visitatorial power of the most comprehensive character."[6] The decisions of an officer or board clothed with such power are entitled to great weight with the courts[7] and are of value in construing the school law when it admits of different constructions.[8] In Maryland they are summary and conclusive.[9] The manner of conducting the hearing of cases by school officers may be determined by them in the absence of statutory regulation. A superintendent may require evidence to be submitted in the form of affidavits and the arguments of parties or counsel to be in writing, and may refuse a personal hearing of witnesses and an oral examination of them before him.[10] A board of education need not require testimony to be given under oath.[11] "The delicate nature of the duty devolved upon the trustees," said Judge Noah Davis,[12] of New York, in a case involving the discharge of a teacher, "to see to it that unfit or incompetent persons are not put or kept in charge of the children who attend the common schools forbids the idea of a trial with the formality and strictness that belong to

---

[1] McLaren v. Township Board of Akron, 48 Mich., 189.
[2] Johnson v. School Directors, 67 Mo., 319; Kane v. School District, 52 Wis., 502.
[3] Hamtramck Board v. Holihan, 46 Mich., 127.
[4] Peers v. Board of Education, 72 Ill., 508; School District 4 of Rush v. Wing, 30 Mich., 351. The legislative power of a State board of education is discussed in Mobile School Commissioners v. Putnam, 44 Ala., 508.
[5] Templin & Son v. District Township of Fremont, 36 Iowa, 411.
[6] Wiley et al., Trustees, v. School Commissioners of Alleghany Co., 51 Md., 401.
[7] State ex rel. Burpee v. Burton, 45 Wis., 150; s. c., 30 Am. Rep., 706.
[8] Appeal of Cottrell, 10 R. I., 615, 617.
[9] Wiley et al., Trustees, v. School Commissioners of Alleghany Co., 51 Md., 401.
[10] State ex rel. Moreland v. Whitford, 54 Wis., 150, 155.
[11] People ex rel. Murphy v. Board of Education, 3 Hun (N. Y.), 177.
[12] Ibid., p. 181.

courts. It is only necessary to suggest that they must often act upon moral convictions rather than established facts, and upon evidence of unfitness, physical, mental, or moral, that would not in courts be such proof as would justify a verdict of guilt of specific offences or immoralities." If an appeal is taken under a statute, the party appealing waives those questions which require a judicial review and submits himself to the discretion of the appellate body.[1] The wisdom of intrusting school controversies to school officers has been approved in several of the opinions cited, as will be seen by the following brief quotations: "We are satisfied that this supervision of the State superintendent over the affairs of schools and school districts, commonly very fruitful sources of litigation, has been most wisely conferred upon him for the public interest, as well as for the peace and prosperity of the schools and districts themselves."[2] "If every dispute or contention among those intrusted with the administration of the system, or between the functionaries and the patrons or pupils of the schools, offered an occasion for a resort to the courts for settlement, the working of the system would not only be greatly embarrassed and obstructed, but such contentions before the courts would necessarily be attended with great costs and delay, and likely generate such intestine heats and divisions as would in a great degree counteract the benevolent purposes of the law."[3] "A quarrel or a lawsuit in a school district is generally not long confined to the original parties. It spreads among all the families, it goes into the selection of teachers, and injures the discipline of the schools; and if the difficulty once takes the shape of a lawsuit, and the parties have expended money as well as temper upon it, it is still more difficult to settle. Hence the provision for a cheap and speedy decision avoiding the delay and expense of a lawsuit."[4]

§ 29. **Same. Limitation of appeals.**—A clause in the code of Iowa provides that "any person aggrieved by any decision of or order of the district board of directors, in matter of law or fact, may, within thirty days after the rendition of such decision or the making of such order, appeal therefrom to the county superintendent." The directors of the independent school district of West Des Moines had made a rule that scholars guilty of defacing or injuring school property should not be allowed to attend school until payment of damages or adjustment of the case. A child accidentally broke a glass in a window. Neither he nor his parents paid for it. Consequently the child was refused admittance. The case was brought before the courts, and the question of jurisdiction considered. Three judges of the supreme court believed that it had jurisdiction; two, one of them the chief justice, dissented. Rothrock, J., in dissenting, said: "It seems to me that this is a case where

---
[1] Brody v. Penn, 32 Mich., 272.
[2] State ex rel. Moreland v. Whitford, 54 Wis., 154.
[3] Wiley et al., Trustees, v. School Commissioners of Alleghany Co., 51 Md., 406.
[4] Appeal of Cottrell, 10 R. I., 618.

RECENT SCHOOL LAW DECISIONS. 49

the remedy by appeal is peculiarly appropriate. The controversy is one concerning the proper government of the school, and it should be determined by the tribunal appointed by law to settle such questions. If resort can be had to the courts without first appealing to the county superintendent, and from him to the State superintendent, the law allowing an appeal becomes a dead letter and wholly useless and inoperative." The majority decided that the subjects of appeal are limited. Beck, J., giving the opinion, said: "It cannot be held that decisions and orders refusing the allowance and payment of claims against the district, or construing contracts, or affecting the possession of or right to property, when the interest of a citizen is affected thereby, may not be questioned except upon appeal. * * * It was certainly never the intention of the legislature to confer upon school boards, superintendents of schools, or other officers discharging judicial functions exclusive authority to decide questions pertaining to their jurisdiction and the extent of their power. All such questions may be determined by the courts of the State. Hence, when the rights of a citizen are involved in the exercise of authority by a school officer the courts may determine whether such authority was lawfully exercised."[1]

§ 30. **County superintendents.**—The powers and duties of a county superintendent of public instruction are derived entirely from statute. He can only exercise such powers as are especially granted or are incidentally necessary to carry the same into effect. Any proceedings on his part beyond the scope of his authority, or where he has no jurisdiction, are absolutely void.[2] If he has discretionary power with regard to granting certificates, the court may compel him to act upon an application, but it cannot control his discretion.[3] He may sue for and recover moneys due the officers whom he has superseded.[4] He cannot draw a warrant for the minimum salary allowed by law when his salary is to be fixed by a board of supervisors.[5] If he accepts through ignorance a less sum than that to which he was entitled, he cannot recover the remainder.[6] If the amount of the salary is to be determined by a body and that body has acted, the decision is final, though it acted on its own motion, in the absence of the superintendent, and allowed him but half he claimed.[7]

§ 31. **Directors, trustees, &c. Organization.**—The first business of a school board composed of continuing and newly-elected members is to organize. This is best accomplished ordinarily by effecting a temporary organization; whereupon the returns of the election are read or the certificates

---

[1] Perkins v. Directors Ind. Dist. of West Des Moines, 56 Iowa, 476.
[2] Ratcliff v. Faris, 6 Nebr., 539, 544.
[3] Bailey v. Ewart, 52 Iowa, 111.
[4] Simmons v. Holmes, 49 Miss., 134.
[5] Peachy v. Redmond, 59 Cal., 326.
[6] Campbell v. Board of Commissioners of Monroe Co., 71 Ind., 185.
[7] Haile v. Young, 6 Lea (Tenn.), 501.

of the directors elect are presented; and thus all the members participate in the permanent organization. If a permanent organization cannot be accomplished, however, because no one of the members can obtain a majority of votes for president, it is such neglect of duty as will justify the proper court to declare the seats of the directors vacant and appoint others in their stead. The official functions of newly elected members attach when the full term of their predecessors has expired; they are then entitled to meet with the continuing members and participate in both the temporary and permanent organization of the board.[1] When a board is clothed with authority to decide upon all questions relative to the qualifications, elections, and returns of its members, its decision that a person is not entitled to a seat as a member is final; and a statement of the reasons, upon its records, cannot confer on the courts any authority to consider a question which the legislature has made it the duty of the school board to decide finally and without appeal.[2] A member appointed to fill a vacancy until the next election, "when such vacancy shall be filled by electing a person from the district in which the vacancy occurs to supply the same," does not hold his office till the time ordinary directors chosen at that election would begin to act, but his official relations cease with the occurrence of the election.[3] A member appointed to serve until the municipal election next ensuing and the election and qualification of his successor continues in office notwithstanding an illegal election of a successor.[4] An unaccepted resignation does not create a vacancy. It is the right and duty of a member to act until the acceptance of his resignation.[5]

§ 32. Same. **Requisites to valid action.**—"Trustees can act only in pursuance of law; they cannot be compelled to act unless the law is complied with in every substantial particular, nor are they permitted to act until it is so complied with. They have no power to waive anything that is necessary to compel their action. They may not as a matter of grace or favor take territory from one district and add it to another. They may do this [and similar acts] only in the cases provided by law; and whatever is essential to be done before they are bound to act, they must require before they do act."[6] If a board of education is made a body corporate, individual members, acting separately, although a majority, cannot contract a debt nor direct the issuance of an order to pay it.[7] The president and secretary cannot act for the board and without its concurrence in matters of contract.[8] The concurrence of a majority

---

[1] Bouton v. Rice, 10 Phil. Reports, 559.
[2] Peabody v. School Committee of Boston, 115 Mass., 383.
[3] Commonwealth v. Thomas, 10 Phil. Reports, 600.
[4] People v. Harvey, 58 Cal., 337.
[5] Townsend v. School Trustees, 41 N. J. L., 312.
[6] Potter v. Board of Trustees, 10 Ill. App., 343, 346, per Wall, J.
[7] State *ex rel.* Steinbeck v. Treasurer of Liberty Township, 22 Ohio St., 144; Aikman v. School District of Denison, 27 Kans., 129.
[8] School District v. Padden, 89 Pa. St., 395.

when duly assembled is required to constitute a valid act;[1] the instruction of the court below to the jury, that, "If you find from the evidence that two of the [three] subdirectors * * * told the plaintiff that she could continue to teach the school under the contract, and that they would call a meeting to approve the same, this would be a ratification of said contract, and the defendant [district] would be bound thereby," has been declared an error.[2] In New Jersey it is one of the duties of incorporated trustees to employ teachers; and, in commenting upon it, the court said:[3] "The duty of these trustees, in the selection of teachers, was not ministerial merely; they were obliged to examine into the qualifications of teachers and to exercise judgment and discretion in their selection; it was the performance of an important public duty, in the execution of which conference and comparison of judgments were necessary in reaching proper results. It was an act judicial in its nature, and the rule governing such bodies so acting is, unless special provision of law is otherwise made, that all must meet, or have notice to meet, when official action is intended." The action of a majority of a school board will not bind the district when other members of the board had no notice of the action and did not participate in it.[4]

§ 33. Same.—A majority of the votes cast will not be construed a majority of those present.[5] If all members have had due notice, a majority of those present can legally authorize or perform an act, and a contract made by two of three members of a committee, where the third member either authorized them beforehand to make it or consented to it afterward, is valid.[3] It was held in the last case cited[6] that it was correct to instruct a jury that the contract of two members of a committee would be valid "if the third member was notified and requested to act and authorized the others to act without him; that there was no necessity of the committee assembling in a formal meeting at any particular place; that they were not a board, with a clerk, having stated times and places of meeting; and that, if they all consented to and had knowledge of the acts of the majority, that was sufficient, even if the third member had no notice to be present at the time the contract was executed." The proceedings of school boards will not be treated as void and set aside in collateral proceedings for mere irregularities which do not affect the substantial rights of parties.[7] In a Missouri case the

[1] Hazen v. Lerche, 47 Mich., 626.
[2] Herrington v. District Township of Liston, 47 Iowa, 11.
[3] Townsend v. School Trustees, 41 N. J. L., 313. See, also, School Directors v. Jennings, 10 Ill. App., 645, and State v. Leonard, 3 Tenn. Chan., 177.
[4] People v. Peters, 4 Nebr., 254.
[5] Commonwealth v. Wickersham, 66 Pa. St., 134.
[6] Wilson v. Waltersville School District, 46 Conn., 400, 403. A school district committee is not a specially incorporated body in Connecticut, as are customarily boards of trustees, directors, &c., in other States.
[7] Rice v. McClelland, 58 Mo., 116.

court said :[1] "There is no doubt that the action of the township board was irregular; but if all of their proceedings which are had in good faith can be set aside and treated as void in collateral proceedings for irregularities which do not affect the substantial rights of the parties interested, the whole beneficial objects of our school system will be paralyzed and rendered inefficient. The schools must necessarily in many townships be conducted by men not accustomed to legal certainty and forms, and their action should be upheld when good faith has been exercised unless it is in very glaring cases of wrong or where direct proceedings are instituted at the time to set their action aside."

§ 34. Same. Power to employ and dismiss teachers.—A board of school directors, though a corporation, is possessed of certain specially defined powers, and can exercise no others, except such as result by fair implication from the powers granted.[2] A board of education cannot delegate its powers. This was decided in interpreting an Ohio provision "that in each township district the local directors shall employ teachers of the schools in the subdistrict in which they reside," "have power to fix the salary or pay of said teachers," and "shall certify the amount due any teacher for services to the township clerk," &c. The court said :[3] "The local directors of a township school district are not authorized to permit any person to teach or assist in teaching a public school under their control unless employed by them for that purpose. They have no power to delegate the employment of teachers for such schools to any other person or persons, nor to provide for the payment of a teacher thereof, in any other manner than that pointed out." A board authorized to establish and maintain a graded school system has power to appoint a superintendent of schools if his services are needed.[4] If a board is empowered to hire teachers and is given the general care of the affairs of a school or a district, it has by implication the right to dismiss a teacher for good cause,[5] not otherwise.[6] Whether boards or committees can make a contract with a teacher for a longer time than to the end of their term of office has been generally decided in favor of such a contract.[7] In a Connecticut case the court said : "It would be a novel and most mischievous doctrine that the officers who manage the governmental corporations of the State could have no power to make a contract which was not to be performed within the time for which

---

[1] Rice v. McClelland, 58 Mo., 121.
[2] Peers v. Board of Education, 72 Ill., 508.
[3] State ex rel. Werden v. Williams, 29 Ohio St., 161, 163.
[4] Spring v. Wright, 63 Ill., 90; Stuart v. District 1 of Kalamazoo, 30 Mich., 69.
[5] Bays v. State, 6 Nebr., 167; City of Crawfordsville v. Hays, 42 Ind., 200.
[6] McCutcheon v. Windsor, 55 Mo., 149. See § 56, post.
[7] Wilson v. East Bridgeport School District, 36 Conn., 280; Gillis v. Space, 63 Barbour (N. Y.), 177; Wait v. Ray, 5 Hun (N. Y.), 649; Stevenson v. School District, 87 Ill., 255; Davis v. School Directors, 92 Ill., 293; Loomis v. Coleman, 51 Mo., 21.

they were elected to office."[1] The court, in a New York case, said:[2] "To limit the right to employ a teacher for a time not beyond the incumbent's term of office would lead at times to great embarrassments and deprive the district of the opportunity to receive the services of desirable teachers. An indiscreet or corrupt officer may impose on the district, it is true. The inhabitants of a district and patrons of the school must confide this power somewhere, and their protection is in selecting competent and honorable officers." In the case from which this quotation is taken a sole trustee hired a teacher for a school year commencing six days after the expiration of his term of office, and the contract was sustained. In Illinois a similar contract was not sustained, the court saying:[3] "There is doubtless no objection to contracts for the teaching of terms extending for a reasonable time beyond the current school year when such contracts are entered into in good faith, and not for the purpose merely of forcing upon the district an unsatisfactory teacher or defeating the will of the voters at the annual election. But we think the spirit and intent of the law are clearly repugnant to the idea that one board of directors may by contracts wholly to be carried out in the future divest future boards of directors of the power to select the teachers they shall desire for the terms to be commenced after their organization." In Pennsylvania and Missouri it has been said that a contract for the employment of teachers should not extend beyond the current year.[4]

§ 35. Same. Power to repair, expend money, &c.—A board can bind a school district by a contract for repairs to a school-house, and that notwithstanding a given sum was voted at the annual meeting for specified repairs and had been so expended;[5] the direction that "the district board shall have the care and keeping of the school-house," the court said, "may not imply the right to remodel or improve, but it implies the right to do all that may come fairly and strictly within the term 'repair.'" "'Care and keeping,' when used in connection with a trust like this, imply the right to preserve the building in the condition in which it is placed in their custody, to make good the waste and injury to which all buildings, and especially public buildings like a school-house, are subject."[6] A trustee, in purchasing a school site, may agree that the district shall build and repair the entire division fence.[7] A board may bind a district for expenses incurred in securing the location of a highway by its school-house, such expenditures being allowed as "contingent

---

[1] Wilson v. East Bridgeport School District, 36 Conn., 282.
[2] Gillis v. Space, 63 Barbour (N. Y.), 180.
[3] Stevenson v. School District, 87 Ill., 255, 258.
[4] School District of Dennison v. Padden, 89 Pa. St., 395, 398; Loomis v. Coleman, 51 Mo., 21.
[5] Conklin v. School District, 22 Kans., 521.
[6] Ibid., p. 526.
[7] Albright v. Riker, 22 Hun (N. Y.), 367.

expenses necessary for keeping the schools in operation."[1] A school board cannot create a debt by erecting a school-house. The charter of the St. Joseph (Mo.) board of public schools authorized it to make an annual estimate of the amount of money to be raised for the purpose of building, repairing, and furnishing school-houses, and required the county court to cause the same to be levied and collected. It was held that this provision was a limitation upon the power of the board to build school-houses, and that neither this clause nor another empowering the board "to do all lawful acts which may be lawful and convenient to carry into effect the objects of the corporation," authorized the board to create a debt for that purpose and issue bonds for its payment.[2] When the qualified electors of school districts are intrusted with the power to determine what sort of school-houses shall be built and the extent of the expenditure therefor, a school board cannot increase the expenditure and bind the district for its payment.[3] A board may ratify an informal contract for the erection of a school-house, if it is one they had power to make in the first instance.[4] A contract for the erection of a school-house should be made with reference to the funds in the treasury for that purpose. The district board has no authority to draw orders for the payment of claims so arising on a fund which has been proposed but not raised.[5] A board must provide for the payment of claims justly due and judgments, so far as it can, or the courts will be justified in compelling them to do their duty in the premises.[6] Trustees or equivalent officers may take personal property by bequest for their schools. "Devises or bequests to trustees for the purposes of founding a library or school create legal and valid trusts."[7] Public officers cannot contract with themselves as individuals and cannot act judicially on their own interests. They should not occupy two conflicting offices.[8] It is a violation of a trust for several persons holding together a fiduciary relation to others to contract with one or more of their own number in matters relating to such trust. The members of a school board being both public officers and trustees of school property, a contract between it and one of its members for the building of a school-house is voidable in equity by the district.[9] It should not employ one of its number to

[1] Flint River Independent District v. Kelley, 55 Iowa, 568.
[2] Erwin v. St. Joseph Board of Public Schools, 2 McCrary (U. S. Circ. Ct.), 608.
[3] Gehling v. School District No. 56 of Richardson Co., 10 Nebr., 239. See School Directors v. Miller, 54 Ill., 338.
[4] Stevenson & Rice v. Township of Summit, 35 Iowa, 462.
[5] School District 2 of Dixon Co. v. Stough, 4 Nebr., 357.
[6] Boynton v. Newton, 34 Iowa, 510; Stevenson & Rice v. Summit District Township, 35 Iowa, 462; Dannat v. Mayor, 6 Hun (N. Y.), 88.
[7] Betts v. Betts, 4 Abb. N. C. (N. Y.), 317, 409.
[8] Clement v. Everest, 29 Mich., 21.
[9] Pickett v. School District 1 of Wiota, 25 Wis., 551. A school committee can make a legal contract, and thereby bind the district, for a teacher's board, although the district voted at the annual meeting that the teacher should "board around in proportion to the grand list." The court did not apply the rule that public officers can-

oversee the completion of a school-house abandoned by the contractor.[1] Public policy will not allow property held in trust by committees for public school purposes to be taken in execution at the suit of a creditor.[2]

§ 36. Same. General liability.—School officers are not personally and individually liable for the violation of contracts made in the course of their official duty. Where trustees had violated their contract with a teacher the court said "that the mere violation of the contract by the trustees in their official capacity, which they had entered into for the corporation, did not render them personally and individually liable."[3] Being public officers and contracting as such, they are not personally responsible, it being the law that public officers are not liable on any contract they may make within the line of their duty.[4] Suit will not lie against an unincorporated board of subdirectors.[5] An agreement signed by directors in an official capacity and attested by their secretary does not bind the directors as individuals and is binding upon the district.[6] School officers, in matters requiring the exercise of discretion, are not answerable in damages for honest errors of judgment. In Massachusetts it has been said that ordinarily school officers are not accountable to individuals who may be aggrieved for the manner in which they exercise their public functions.[7]

In Missouri the court said:[8] "School directors are elected by the people, receive no compensation for their services, are not always or frequently men who are thoroughly informed as to the best modes of conducting schools. They are authorized, and it is their duty, to adopt reasonable rules for the government and management of the school, and it would deter responsible and suitable men from accepting the position if held liable for damages to a pupil expelled under a rule adopted by

---

not contract with themselves, to a school committee; but held that for boarding the teacher or furnishing supplies, &c., if there is no fraud, recovery for their value can be had from the district. Brown v. School District, 55 Vt.; 28 Al. L. J., 276.

[1] Moore v. Independent District of Toledo City, 55 Iowa, 654.
[2] State v. Tiedemann, 69 Mo., 306.
[3] Morrison et al. v. McFarland, 51 Ind., 206, 210. See, also, Butler v. Haines, 79 Ind., 575.
[4] Robinson v. Howard, 87 N. C., 151.
[5] Board of Directors v. Burton, 26 Ohio St., 421. See, also, Puterbaugh v. Township Board of Education, 53 Mo., 472.
[6] Independent District of Mason City v. Reichard, 50 Iowa, 98, 102.
[7] Learock v. Putnam, 111 Mass., 499.
[8] Dritt v. Snodgrass, 66 Mo., 286; s. c., 27 Am. Rep., 343. This case is sometimes cited as sustaining the doctrine that a school board cannot make rules governing the home conduct of pupils. The court said: "While this court might, on mandamus to compel the board and teacher to admit a pupil thus expelled [for attending a party, contrary to a rule of school], review the action of the board, and pass upon the reasonableness of the rule, *which we do not, however, decide here,* yet the doctrine that the courts could do this is very different from that which would hold the directors liable for damages for enforcing a rule honestly adopted."

them under the impression that the welfare of the school demanded it, if the courts should deem it improper."

In an Illinois case the court said:[1] "A mere mistake in judgment, either as to their duties under the law or as to facts submitted to them, ought not to subject such officers to an action. They may judge wrongly, and so may a court or other tribunal, but the party complaining can have no action when such officers act in good faith and in the line of what they think is honestly their duty. Any other rule might work great hardship to honest men who, with the best of motives, have faithfully endeavored to perform the duties of these inferior offices. Although of the utmost importance to the public, no considerable emoluments are attached to these minor offices, and the duties are usually performed by persons sincerely desiring to do good for their neighbors without any expectation of personal gains; and it would be a very harsh rule that would subject such officers to an action for damages for every mistake they may make in the honest and faithful discharge of their official duties as they understand them." It is not in the line of duty for trustees to refuse a person expelled from a school the quiet enjoyment of an exhibition held by a literary society of the school in the school building. In charging the jury in such a case[2] the judge gave an instruction that "to say that a student expelled from a school for disobedience to some municipal regulation should be excluded from attending a prayer meeting or public lecture in the school-house or college premises for all time to come, without any evidence of improper conduct or suspicion of improper purposes, would be an exercise of tyranny over his private rights not vested in the trustees, directors, or professors of our educational institutions." If a committee use violence in dispossessing a teacher, the person or persons so doing are individually liable.[3]

§ 37. **Same. Liabilities for negligence.**—A school board is not liable in its corporate capacity for negligence in the discharge of its official duty in the erection and maintenance of a common school building.[4]

In the case cited the court, in an opinion by Judge Ashburn, said:[5] "Owing to the very limited number of corporate powers conferred on them, boards of education rank low in the grade of corporate existence, and hence are properly denominated *quasi*-corporations. This designation distinguishes this grade of corporations from municipal corporations, such as cities and towns acting under charters or incorporating statutes, which are vested with more extended powers and a larger measure of corporate life. This superior grade, from the nature of their organization, benefits received, and power to raise needed funds, are

---
[1] McCormick v. Burt, 95 Ill., 263, 266; s. c., 36 Am. Rep., 163. Opinion by Scott, J.
[2] Hughes v. Goodell, 3 Pittsburgh (Pa.), 264, 267. Per Johnson, J.
[3] McCutcheon v. Windsor, 55 Mo., 149.
[4] Finch v. Board of Education, 30 Ohio St., 37. Otherwise in New York.
[5] Ibid., p. 46. See *ante*, § 9 and note.

held responsible by the common law for private personal injuries caused by their own negligence of that of their servants, whilst the inferior grade of public *quasi*-corporations are liable for damages resulting from their negligence only where made so by express legislation. This grade includes the defendant [board of education]. It possesses but limited powers and small corporate life; a corporation in some sense political, but in no sense a municipal corporation." A different line of argument has been taken in New York, substantially as follows: In addition to being a governmental agency a board of education is also a corporation. This being so the courts have held it responsible for its own contracts;[1] being subject to such obligations, it is difficult to see why it should not be liable to an action for the neglect of a duty imposed upon it by law.[2] When it is specially incorporated it must be so; for in that way it is raised from a *quasi* into a responsible corporation. Its members become the living agents through which the corporation manifests itself, exercises its powers, and is liable for neglects.[3] Thus the law stands in New York that a specially incorporated board of education is liable for negligence in the performance of its duties.[4] As to what would constitute negligence in permitting a hole in the school-house floor to remain open, Judge Folger, in a case already cited, said:[5] "If, in the proper discharge of their duty, they had gone to the building, and, looking for defects threatening immediate danger, had found this hole, then they would have had actual and personal knowledge of it, and would have been in fault, if having public means to do it they had not amended it. If so going they had made so careless an inspection as not to see what was so plain, then they would have been faulty. If they did not go at all and took no heed of the liability to danger from the general and particular defects of a building in their charge, which they kept open for the use of many people, then they egregiously failed in doing their duty."

§ 38. **Same. Removal from office.**—Proceedings to remove a school officer cannot justly be taken until the action of the proper authorities has been invoked by complaint of some definite violation of

---

[1] Daumat *v.* Mayor of New York, 6 Hun (N. Y.), 88.
[2] Donovan *v.* Board of Education, 44 N. Y. Sup. Ct., 53, 62.
[3] Bassett *v.* Fish, 75 N. Y. App., 303, 312.
[4] The difficulties in the way of obtaining damages may be illustrated by the case of Thomas Donovan. He fell into a hole in a school yard in New York City. His first suit was against the board of education. The case was dismissed, but a new trial was granted by the court in general term. The second appearance of the case in the reports (46 Sup. Ct., 111) was in a suit against ward trustees individually, in which it was decided they were not so liable, but were liable as a body; yet as a body they were a *quasi*-corporation, and thus not liable. At the third appearance of the suit (46 Sup. Ct., 565) Donovan was nonsuited in an action against the board for not showing any legal connection between it and the acts of the trustees through which the injury occurred. The fourth appearance of the suit was when the last decision was affirmed by the court of appeals. Donovan *v.* McAlpin, 85 N. Y. App., 185; s. c., 39 Am. Rep., 649.
[5] Bassett *v.* Fish, 75 N. Y. App., 310.

duty.[1] The notice of the time and place of the hearing may be agreed upon and issued by the board having the power of removal without a meeting of its members.[2] A wilful refusal to sign a contract made with a teacher, or to accept and file it, or to draw orders for a teacher's pay during the currency of the contract, and an obstinate neglect to furnish necessary school-house supplies may be taken into account in proceedings for a removal;[3] for, as Judge Campbell said,[4] "Nothing is more likely to injure schools than meanness and unfairness in dealing with teachers." An act authorizing the removal of a school officer by the township board for illegal use of school moneys and for the neglect or refusal to discharge a duty does not warrant the removal of an officer for hiring her husband and agreeing to pay him more than was necessary to secure a good or better teacher,[5] nor the removal of a director for conspiring with her to do so.[6] In such cases the township board is the exclusive judge of facts, and its proceeding can be reviewed by courts only on questions of law.[7] If charges set up against a school officer are admitted by him, and he expressly desires the board to act on them without delay, he cannot afterwards complain that they did so.[8]

§ 39. **Treasurer.**—The reception of a treasurer's bond by the board of education is a sufficient approval of him.[9] He may not receive for school moneys anything which the law has not authorized to be so received, and if he does so and receipts for taxes on that account he must make good the amount.[10] He is the only proper custodian of school moneys.[11] His liability is absolute for all funds which come into his hands in his official capacity, regardless of the cause of, or circumstances attending, loss.[12] He is not entitled to credit for sums paid to a township in excess of the funds he has received for it.[13] The failure of a bank where he had deposited funds does not release him, though he was not guilty of any want of care or prudence in failing to ascertain its financial condition.[14] The school district has no authority to release him from liability for money lost or misapplied by him.[15] A stipulation in his bond against

---

[1] Geddes v. Thomastown, 46 Mich., 316.
[2] Wenzel v. Dorr Township Board, 49 Mich., 25.
[3] Geddes v. Thomastown, 46 Mich., 316.
[4] Ibid., p. 319.
[5] Hazen v. Town Board of Akron, 48 Mich., 188.
[6] McLaren v. Town Board of Akron, 48 Mich., 189.
[7] Hamtramck v. Holihan, 46 Mich., 127.
[8] Geddes v. Thomastown, 46 Mich., 316.
[9] Bartlett v. Board of Ed., 59 Ill., 364. See, also, § 30, *ante*.
[10] Jones v. Wright, 34 Mich., 371; Lovingston v. School Trustees, 99 Ill., 564.
[11] Adams v. State, 82 Ill., 132.
[12] Dist. Township of Bluff Creek, v. Hardinbrook, 40 Iowa, 130.
[13] State v. Cook, 72 Mo., 496.
[14] State v. Powell, 67 Mo., 395; Ward v. School Dist. 15 of Colfax Co., 10 Nebr., 293.
[15] Ward v. School District 15 of Colfax Co., 10 Nebr., 293. For certain duties of county and district treasurers in Nebraska, relative to school funds, see Donelly v. Duras, 11 Nebr., 283.

RECENT SCHOOL LAW DECISIONS. 59

liability for non-performance occasioned by inevitable accident does not protect him or his sureties.[1] The liability of a township treasurer is distinct from his ordinary liability for township moneys, and he cannot be released from duties or any way affected by the action of the township, board.[2] In an Iowa case, the court commented on the necessity of a strict compliance with the terms of the bond of a treasurer, as follows:[3] "He is bound by the obligation of the bond, not to exercise due care and diligence in the discharge of this duty, but to perform it absolutely, without conditions or exceptions. He is to hold the money of the district. This is the provision of the law. His contract, expressed in the bond, binds him to the discharge of this duty. He will not be relieved from the contract by showing any degree of diligence or care which falls short of absolute compliance with the terms of his contract. His liability rests upon the conditions of his bond, and if by them he is required to do an act which, without his fault, becomes impossible on account of anything occurring subsequently to the contract, he will not be released. These rules are applicable to all contracts, and the public interest demands that, at this day, when public funds in such vast amounts are committed to the custody of such an immense number of officers, they should not be relaxed when applied to official bonds. A denial of their application in such cases would serve as an invitation to delinquencies which are already so frequent as to cause alarm."

§ 40. **Assessors.**—The duties customarily assigned to treasurers are sometimes performed by assessors.[4] In such a case a showing of want of funds is a complete answer to an application for an order of court requiring the assessor of a school district to pay an order drawn on him in favor of a teacher.[5] An assessor cannot lawfully withhold district funds from his successor on the ground that he is entitled to be previously personally notified officially. If he does so, suit may be brought against him personally as well as upon his bond; for "the bond is required in order to afford other and greater security than the individual responsibility of the person serving, but not to supersede his separate individual responsibility."[6] He cannot defend his refusal to turn over to his successor the funds in his official custody on any questions of the regularity

---

[1] District Township of Union v. Smith, 39 Iowa, 9   Sureties on a county treasurer's general bond, conditioned according to the statute for the performance of his official functions, are not liable for his default in relation to the school fund, which is protected by the special bond prescribed by the statute imposing his duties respecting this fund. State v. Felton, 59 Miss., 402.
[2] Jones v. Wright, 34 Mich., 371.
[3] District Township of Taylor v. Morton, 37 Iowa, 553.
[4] For instance, the Michigan school law provides that "the assessor shall pay all orders of the director, countersigned by the moderator, out of any moneys in his hands belonging to the fund upon which such orders may be drawn." Com. Laws, 1871, p. 1196.
[5] Allen v. Frink, 32 Mich., 96.
[6] Mason v. Fractional District, Scio and Webster, 34 Mich., 230.

of the proceedings whereby the funds came into his possession.[1] If the school district was not legally established, assessors are liable for assessing and issuing a warrant for the collection of a school district tax, although it was certified to them by one acting as clerk of the district that the tax had been voted by the district.[2]

§ 41. **Collector.**—A collector has no right to execute a warrant until he has given a bond. He is not in default for not giving a bond before the trustees have limited the time and fixed the amount in which it is to be given; nor is he in default concerning moneys until a proper order is drawn upon him.[3] If he sell property for an unpaid tax without fulfilling the requirements of the law, he is liable as a trespasser, and the sale is void.[4] His sureties are not liable for any breach of condition happening after the expiration of his term of office, although the officer may be continued under the same or a new appointment or election.[5]

CHAPTER VI.—SCHOOLS AND STUDIES.

§ 42. **Public schools in general.**—A public institution of learning is one which is controlled by the State through its agents, in which the State has a paramount interest and right of property, and which depends upon the State for its existence.[6] The word "common" used in connection with schools has no reference to the studies taught, but means "open to all, belonging to the public."[7] Parochial schools, though gratuitously opened to all, are not free public schools; for they are not established, maintained, and regulated under the statute laws of the State.[8] Some light is thrown on the question of what constitutes a school by the following statement in a recent New York case:[9] "Although two departments are in the same building and each is recognized by the number which marks the building, these departments are, in fact, entirely separate schools, as much so as if they occupied separate buildings. Each has its own principal, vice principal, and teachers, and occupies its distinct part of the building, as does a primary school when in the same building with the grammar school."

An institution principally supported by a State must administer its affairs according to the principles of the educational system of the State. This was affirmed in a recent case in Indiana. The court, by Niblack, J., said:[10] "Purdue University constitutes no part of our system of common schools and has no direct connection with that system;

---
[1] Mason v. Fractional District, Scio and Webster, 34 Mich., 228.
[2] Judd v. Thompson, 125 Mass., 553.
[3] Woodhull v. Bohenblost, 4 Hun (N. Y.), 399.
[4] Bedell v. Barnes, 17 Hun (N. Y.), 353. See, also, § 17, *ante*.
[5] Overton v. Garrett, 5 Lans. (N. Y.), 156.
[6] State *ex rel.* Straight University v. Graham, 25 La. Ann., 440.
[7] Roach v. St. Louis School Board, 7 Mo. App., 567.
[8] St. Joseph's Church v. Assessors, 12 R. I., 19.
[9] Betts v. Betts, 4 Abbott's New Cases, 414.
[10] State *ex rel.* Stallard v. White *et al.*, 82 Ind., 283; s. c., 42 Am. Rep., 496.

but it is an institution of learning primarily endowed by Congress [under the agricultural college land grant of 1862], and continued in existence very largely by appropriations made by the general assembly of this State. It is, therefore, an educational institution sustaining relations to the people at large analogous to those occupied by other public schools and colleges of the State maintained at public expense, and one in which all the inhabitants of the State have a common interest. The general principles underlying the educational system of the State are, consequently, applicable to the government and control of Purdue University, and, in the absence of express legislative provisions, must be invoked in determining the powers which that institution may exercise."

§ 43. **High schools.**—A decision sustaining the right of a school district to levy taxes for the support of a high school in which ancient and modern languages were taught was rendered in Michigan not long ago. In giving the opinion of the court, Judge Cooley said:[1] "Neither in our State policy, in our constitution, nor in our laws, do we find the primary school districts restricted in the branches of knowledge which their officers may cause to be taught, or the grade of instruction that may be given, if their voters consent in regular form to bear the expense and raise the taxes for the purpose." In Illinois it has been decided that the high school is a legitimate part of the system of schools established by virtue of a clause in the constitution which says: "The general assembly shall provide a thorough and efficient system of free schools whereby all the children of this State may receive a good common school education." The court remarked:[2] "While the constitution has not defined what a good common school education is and has failed to prescribe a limit, it is no part of the duty of the courts of the State to declare by judicial construction what particular branches of study shall constitute a common school education." Similar ground has been taken in Mississippi.[3] If an act proposed to be done by the proper officers in establishing a high school be within the scope of the authority delegated, it is not competent for even a court of equity to interfere with the exercise of discretion given by statute, unless it be clearly shown that the power has been or is about to be corruptly used.[4]

§ 44. **Colored schools.**—The decisions relative to the right to establish separate schools for colored children appear to justify the following propositions: First, that no person can be deprived of equal educational privileges with the whites because he is colored.[5] Second, that the estab-

---

[1] Stuart v. District 1 of Kalamazoo, 30 Mich., 69, 84.
[2] Richards v. Raymond, 92 Ill., 612, 618. See Roach v. St. Louis School Board, 7 Mo. App., 567.
[3] Otken v. Lamkin, 56 Miss., 758.
[4] Wiley v. School Commissioners of Alleghany Co., 51 Md., 401.
[5] State v. Duffy, 7 Nev., 342; s. c., 8 Am. Rep., 713; Ward v. Flood, 48 Cal., 36; s. c., 17 Am. Rep., 405; United States v. Buntin, 10 Fed. Rep., 730; People v. Easton, 13 Abb. Pr. N. s. (N. Y.), 159, and other cases.

lishment of separate schools for colored youth is not a question to which the provisions of the fourteenth amendment to the Constitution of the United States apply.[1] Third, that States can direct or allow the existence of such schools.[2] Fourth, that school boards cannot establish such schools when the legislature has not favored their existence.[3] Quotations are given sustaining and explaining these four propositions:

"The exclusion of colored children from schools where white children attend as pupils cannot be supported except * * * where separate schools are actually maintained for the education of colored children; and unless such separate schools be, in fact, maintained, all children of the school district, whether white or colored, have an equal right to become pupils at any common school organized under the laws of the State."[4] "If, as has been contended, you find that said colored school was so remote from the prosecuting witness's residence that he could not attend it without going an unreasonable and oppressive distance; that he was thus placed at a material disadvantage with his white neighbors; that the school did not offer substantially the same facilities and educational advantages that were offered in the school established for the white children, and from which he had been excluded — then and in that event he was entitled to admission in said last named school, and his exclusion therefrom was a denial and a deprivation of his constitutional right."[5]

§ 45. Same. Separate schools for the colored race not forbidden by the fourteenth amendment.—"It is not within the sphere of the National Government to regulate education."[6] "Conceding that the fourteenth amendment not only provides equal securities for all, but guarantees equality of rights to the citizens of a State as one of the privileges of citizens of the United States, it remains to be seen whether this privilege has been abridged in the case before us. The law in question [establishing separate schools for colored children] surely does not attempt to deprive colored persons of any rights. On the contrary it recognizes their right, under the constitution of the State, to equal common school advantages and secures to them their equal proportion of the school fund. It only regulates the mode and manner in which this right shall be enjoyed by all classes of persons."[7] "It will

---

[1] State v. McCann, 21 Ohio St., 198; Dallas v. Fosdick, 40 How. Pr. (N. Y.), 249; Ward v. Flood, 48 Cal., 36; contra, Commonwealth (Pa.) v. Davis, 10 W. N. C., 156.

[2] Cory v. Carter, 48 Ind., 327; s. c., 17 Am. Rep., 738; People v. Gallagher, 11 Abb. N. C., 187; and cases above. The case of People v. Gallagher was affirmed by the New York court of appeals, October 9, 1883, two judges dissenting.

[3] People v. Board of Education, 101 Ill., 308; s. c., 40 Am. Rep., 196; Board v. Tinnon, 26 Kans., 1; Dove v. Independent School District, 41 Iowa, 689, following Clark v. Board of Directors, 24 Iowa, 266; Kaine v. Commonwealth (Pa.), 27 Al. L. J., 283. The last case was decided in December, 1882.

[4] Ward v. Flood, 48 Cal., 56; s. c., 17 Am. Rep., 417. Opinion by Wallace, C. J.

[5] United States v. Buntin, 10 Fed. Rep., 735. Charge to jury by Baxter, C. J.

[6] People v. Gallagher, 11 Abb. (N. Y.) N. C., 245.

[7] State v. McCann, 21 Ohio St., 210. Opinion by Day, J.

indeed be readily conceded that the privilege accorded to the youth of the State, by the law of the State, of attending the public schools maintained at the expense of the State is not a privilege or immunity appertaining to a citizen of the United States as such ; and it necessarily follows, therefore, that no person can lawfully demand admission as a pupil in any such school because of the mere status of citizenship ; and it is perhaps hardly necessary to add that assuredly no person can be said to have been deprived of either life, liberty, or property because denied the right to attend as a pupil at such schools, however obviously insufficient and untenable be the ground upon which the exclusion is put. The last clause of so much of the amendment as has been recited [last sentence, section 1, fourteenth amendment], however, forbids the State to 'deny to any person within its jurisdiction the equal protection of the laws.' * * * The protection of law is indeed inseparable from the assumed existence of a recognized legal right, through the vindication of which the protection is to operate. To declare, then, that each person within the jurisdiction of the State shall enjoy the equal protection of its laws, is necessarily to declare that the measure of legal rights within the State shall be equal and uniform ; * * * and in the circumstance that the races are separated in the public schools there is certainly to be found no violation of the constitutional rights of the one race more than of the other, and we see none of either, for each, though separated from the other, is to be educated upon equal terms with that other, and both at the common public expense."[1] "Any classification which preserves substantially equal school advantages is not prohibited by either the State or Federal Constitution, nor would it contravene the provisions of either."[2]

§ 46. Same. Separate schools for the colored race a subject for State legislation.—"The classification of scholars on the basis of race or color and their education in separate schools involve questions of domestic policy which are within the legislative discretion and control, and do not amount to an exclusion of either class. In other words, the placing of the white children of the State in one class and the negro children of the State in another class, and requiring these classes to be taught separately, provision being made for their education in the same branches, according to age, capacity, or advancement, with capable teachers, and to the extent of their pro rata share in the school revenue, does not amount to a denial of equal privileges to either or conflict with the open character of the system required by the constitution. The system would be equally open to all. The tuition would be free. The privileges of the schools would be denied to none."[3] "It must be remembered that, unless some statute can be found authorizing the establishment of sep-

---

[1] Ward v. Flood, 48 Cal., 49, 50, 52; s. c., 17 Am. Rep., 411, 412, 414.
[2] State v. McCann, 21 Ohio St., 211.
[3] Cory v. Carter, 48 Ind., 362; s. c., 17 Am. Rep., 764. Opinion by Buskirk, J.

arate schools for colored children, no such authority exists."[1] "All the youth are equal before the law, and there is no discretion vested in the board of directors or elsewhere to interfere with or disturb that equality. The board of directors may exercise a uniform discretion, equally operative upon all, as to the residence, or qualifications, or freedom from contagious disease, or the like, of children, to entitle them to admission to each particular school; but the board cannot in their discretion, or otherwise, deny a youth admission to any particular school because of his or her nationality, religion, color, clothing, or the like."[2] " Under our law [requiring directors to secure to all children the right and opportunity to an equal education in free schools], aside from the fourteenth amendment, directors of schools and boards of education, like defendants in error, have no discretion to deny a pupil of the proper age admission to the public schools on account of nationality, color, or religion."[3]

§ 47. **Studies.**—The principal questions under this head which have been before the courts recently are how far a parent can control the studies of his child and whether "other branches," mentioned in a statute after an enumeration of English studies, would include German. The court answered the latter question affirmatively, taking judicial notice of the practice and policy of the State to allow the study of German and of the omission of the legislature to prohibit the instruction of pupils in that language.[4] The former question has been answered in two States, Illinois and Wisconsin. In Illinois the court said:[5] "No parent has the right to demand that the interests of the children of others shall be sacrificed for the interests of his child; and he cannot, consequently, insist that his child shall be placed or kept in particular classes, when by so doing others will be retarded in the advancement they would otherwise make; or that his child shall be taught studies not in the prescribed course of the school or be allowed to use a text book different from that decided to be used in the school, or that he shall be allowed to adopt methods of study that interfere with others in their study. * * * The policy of our law has ever been to recognize the right of the parent to determine to what extent his child shall be educated during minority, presuming that his natural affections and superior opportunities of knowing the physical and mental capabilities and future prospects of his child will insure the adoption of that course which will most effectually promote the child's welfare. The policy of

---

[1] Board of Education v. Tinnon, 26 Kans., 23. Per Valentine, J., Brewer, J., dissenting.

[2] Clark v. Board of Directors, 24 Iowa, 277. Opinion by Cole, J. Wright, J., dissented.

[3] People v. Board of Education, 101 Ill., 316; s. c., 40 Am. Rep., 201. Opinion by Craig., C. J. Walker, J., dissented. See State v. Grubb, 85 Ind., 213.

[4] Powell v. Board of Education, 97 Ill., 375; s. c., 37 Am. Rep., 123.

[5] Trustees of Schools v. People, 87 Ill., 303, 307; s. c., 29 Am. Rep., 55.

the school law is only to withdraw from the parent the right to select the branches to be studied by the child to the extent that the exercise of that right would interfere with the system of instruction prescribed for the school, and its efficiency in imparting education to all entitled to share in its benefits. No particular branch of study is compulsory upon those who attend school." In Wisconsin the court said:[1] "Now, we can see no reason whatever for denying to the father the right to direct what studies, included in the prescribed course, his child shall take. He is as likely to know the health, temperament, aptitudes, and deficiencies of his child as the teacher, and how long he can send him to school. All these matters ought to be considered in determining the question what particular studies the child should pursue at a given term."

§ 48. **Text books.**—It has been decided in Minnesota that the legislature may order a contract to be made with a single individual to supply the ordinary common schools of the State with text books of prescribed kinds and qualities at rates not to exceed a specified limit. The contract is not invalid, though it may deprive the patrons of the schools of the benefits of an open and competitive market in which to make purchases, and thus impose an additional burden upon the enjoyment of public school privileges, because it invades no legal rights and violates no constitutional provisions.[2] When text books are to be changed due notice should be given; the publication of the proposed change as a matter of news is not sufficient.[3] A clause inserted in a newly adopted constitution, declaring that certain officers "shall adopt a series of text books for the use of the common schools within their respective jurisdictions," is self executing and supersedes all previous statutes on the subject.[4] The duty imposed by such a regulation concerning text books ought to be performed without unnecessary delay.[5] A recent Kansas case seems to take the ground that the adoption by a board of a series of readers, of which there were several widely varying editions, would be void for uncertainty, and that the court would hear an application for an injunction of the use of a later adopted series, not from a private citizen, but only from the proper public officer; but an injunction might, under some circumstances, be allowed at the instance of a private individual to restrain the use of the later series so far as it interfered with the use of the former series by the complainant's child.[6]

---

[1] Morrow v. Wood, 35 Wis., 64; s. c., 17 Am. Rep., 741.
[2] Curryer v. Merrill, 25 Minn., 1, 7; s. c., 33 Am. Rep., 450.
[3] People v. State Board of Education, 49 Cal., 684.
[4] People v. Board of Education of Oakland, 55 Cal., 331.
[5] State v. School Directors of Springfield, 74 Mo., 21.
[6] School District v. Shadduck, 25 Kans., 467.

CHAPTER VII.—TEACHERS.

§ 49. License prerequisite to a valid contract.—A contract to employ a person to teach who has not a certificate or license is void in Illinois,[1] Indiana,[2] and Minnesota;[3] and procuring a certificate after entering into such an agreement does not render it a valid contract. In Ohio it has been decided that a statutory provision similar to the one prohibiting the employment of unlicensed teachers in the States above mentioned does not render invalid a contract of employment entered into with a teacher before he obtains a certificate, provided he obtains it before commencing to teach. The court said:[4] "The law forbids the *employment* of a teacher who has not a certificate. The teacher is not 'employed,' within the meaning and intent of this provision, until he engages in the discharge of his duties as teacher. The mischief intended to be guarded against was the teaching of a school by an incompetent person, and not the making of the contract by an incompetent person." In Vermont, if a person commences teaching without a certificate and continues to teach after obtaining one, he is considered to have made a new contract, commencing at the time when the certificate was obtained and having the same terms as the one under which teaching was begun.[5] In Minnesota a person commenced teaching under a verbal contract. He taught three weeks, then obtained a certificate and made a written contract to run three months from the time he commenced teaching. It was held that he was entitled to wages at the stipulated rate after the certificate was obtained and the written contract made, and to no remuneration for the previous three weeks.[6] In an Illinois case a certificate was not obtained until the middle of the term. A new contract was entered into at that time to pay the teacher double wages for the remainder of the term. This was considered an attempt to do indirectly what there was no power to do directly; and therefore the contract was held void, as was the original contract.[7]

§ 50. Contracts.—A contract is to be construed in reference to contemporaneous laws and usages. For example, in Michigan the law directs that a contract of hiring to teach "shall require the teacher to keep a correct list of the pupils and the age of each attending the school, and the number of days each pupil is present, and to furnish the director with a correct copy of the same at the close of the school." The court

---

[1] Wells *v.* People, 71 Ill., 532; Stevenson *v.* School Directors, 87 Ill., 255; School Directors *v.* Jennings, 10 Ill. App., 643.
[2] Putnam *v.* Town of Irvington, 69 Ind., 80; Butler *v.* Haines, 79 Ind., 575.
[3] Ryan *v.* School District 13, 27 Minn., 433. See Blondon *v.* Moses, 29 Hun (N. Y.), 606.
[4] School District 2 of Oxford *v.* Dilman, 22 Ohio St., 194.
[5] Scott *v.* School District 2 of Fairfax, 46 Vt., 452.
[6] McKinney *v.* School District 45 of Dakota Co., 20 Minn., 72.
[7] Wells *v.* People, 71 Ill., 532.

thought that it could not be doubted these requirements, though not mentioned in his contract, imposed upon the teacher of every public district school the duty of compliance with them, and that they become a part of a teacher's contract, whether inserted in it or not.[1] The contract of a teacher is for his own personal services.[2] The nature and quality of those services were admirably described by Judge Worden in an Indiana case. In giving the opinion of the court, he said:[3] "A teacher doubtless, like a lawyer, surgeon, or physician, when he undertakes an employment, impliedly agrees that he will bestow upon the service a reasonable degree of learning, skill, and care. When he accepts an employment as teacher in any given school, he agrees by implication that he has the learning necessary to enable him to teach the branches that are to be taught therein, as well as that he has the capacity in a reasonable degree of imparting that learning to others. He agrees, also, that he will exercise a reasonable degree of care and diligence in the advancement of his pupils in their studies, in preserving harmony, order, and discipline in the school, and that he will himself conform as near as may be to such reasonable rules and regulations as may be established by competent authority for the government of the school. He also agrees, as we think, by a necessary implication, that while he continues in such employment his moral conduct shall be in all respects exemplary and beyond just reproach."

The hiring of a substitute by a teacher under any ordinary circumstances is a breach of contract, though the competency of the substitute is unquestioned.[4] A teacher may not ordinarily absent himself by leave of individual members of a school board.[5]

§ 51. **Same.**—A teacher's contract is oftentimes binding upon a district though it is irregular in some respect, as when it was made with part of a board[6] or was verbally made with a subcommittee instructed by the board to employ a teacher.[7] The law implies a contract from the doing and accepting of work, and a district cannot, on the ground that he has not complied with the law requiring a written contract,[8] have the benefit of a teacher's services without remunerating him. Where there is a written contract it cannot be orally contradicted.[9] A contract with a township board to teach in a subdistrict over which a lower court has decided that the board has control, is not invalidated by the

---

[1] Everett v. School District 2 of Cannon, 30 Mich., 249, 252.
[2] School Directors v. Hudson, 88 Ill., 563.
[3] City of Crawfordsville v. Hays, 42 Ind., 209, 210.
[4] School Directors v. Hudson, 58 Ill., 563.
[5] State v. Leonard, 3 Tenn. Chan., 177.
[6] Adkins v. Mitchell, 67 Ill., 511.
[7] Wilson v. Board of Education, 63 Mo., 167.
[8] Jones v. School District 47 of Neosho County, 8 Kans., 362; Monaghan v. School District, 38 Wis., 100.
[9] Mann v. Independent School District of Le Grand, 52 Iowa, 130.

reversal of that decision by the supreme court.¹ Contracts with *de facto* officers are binding upon the body they represent;² but contracts entered into with a number of persons acting as a board are not binding upon the school district when there is in existence at the same time another acting board who are so *de jure* and who have notified the persons contracting with the other board not to carry out their contracts. Which of the boards is such of right is a question for the courts to decide.³ The part performance of an oral contract, in a case where the law requires a written one, is a ratification of it and renders a district liable for any breach of it.⁴ There is no contract, express or implied, between a teacher and a pupil, and, in the absence of trespass, the latter cannot sue the former for refusing to hear his recitations. The teacher's contract is with the directors alone.⁵ A minor who possesses the essential qualifications in regard to moral character, learning, and ability, and who has obtained the requisite certificate, may, with the assent of his parents, enter into a valid contract to teach school. A father is charged with certain duties as respects his child, as education, support, and protection, and, as some compensation for these duties, he has a right to claim the earnings of his child in the absence of proof of relinquishment.⁶

§ 52. **Recovery of wages. When impossible.**—A teacher cannot recover for services rendered after the appropriation out of which payment of them must be made is exhausted when the law of the place "is clear that no contract or debt can be created without the authority of the

---

¹ Hall & Julins *v.* District Township of Pleasant Valley, 41 Iowa, 494.

² School District 25 of Hall County *v.* Cowee, 9 Nebr., 53; Woodbury *v.* Knox, 74 Me., 462; Burditt *v.* Barry, 6 Hun (N. Y.), 657. "The doctrine is everywhere declared that the acts of *de facto* officers, as distinguished from the acts of mere usurpers, are valid." 1 Dillon's Municipal Corporations, § 276.

³ Genesee Township *v.* McDonald, 98 Pa. St., 444.

⁴ Cook *v.* Independent School District of North McGregor, 40 Iowa, 444. A dissenting opinion by Beck, J., held that a verbal contract, being unauthorized by law, was a nullity and could not be made of effect by subsequent ratification.

⁵ Stuckey *v.* Churchman, 2 Ill. App., 584.

⁶ Monaghan *v.* School District 1 of Randall, 38 Wis., 100. The following notes will be of value in connection with this decision:

(1) "In general, when a contract is not manifestly for the benefit of an infant, he may avoid it as well in equity as at law, and when it can never be for his benefit it is utterly void." Schouler's Domestic Relations, § 401.

(2) "All other things being equal, the father is actually entitled to the value of his child's labor and services until the latter becomes of age." Ibid, § 252.

(3) "The parent may emancipate his child, and this may be done by refusing him support, or denying him a home, or compelling him to labor abroad for his own living." Taylor on Infancy and Coverture, p. 200.

(4) "And if the parent authorize a third person to employ and pay the child, payment to the child and not to the parent will be a sufficient discharge. Such an agreement may be in express terms or it may be implied from circumstances." Schouler's Domestic Relations, § 252 *a.*

councils and an appropriation to meet it."[1] Wages cannot be recovered on a void contract. In Iowa a contract must be approved by the president of the school board; and where he refused to do so a teacher was not allowed to recover although she proceeded to teach under control of the subdirector hiring her and completed her term of instruction.[2] If a teacher is discharged on the ground of incompetency he must use all proper means for his vindication and reinstatement before the courts will entertain a suit for the recovery of wages.[3] Then the question of competency will be one for the jury.[4] Of course he cannot recover if found incompetent; for, "if a teacher, although he has been employed for a definite length of time, proves to be incompetent and unable to teach the branches of instruction he has been employed to teach, either from a lack of learning or from an utter want of capacity to impart his learning to others, or if in any other respect he fails to perform the obligations resting upon him as such teacher, whether arising from the express terms of his contract or by necessary implication, he has broken the agreement on his part."[5] For teaching done in defiance of a decision of removal no right whatever accrues to compensation out of the public fund.[6] In a Mississippi case a teacher recovered wages for services rendered after the revocation of his license by the county superintendent in opposition to the wishes of the contracting board of trustees, the court saying that "after the vacation of the certificate the relator was not competent to make a new engagement to teach, but could continue to execute an existing contract, unless the local trustees coöperated with the superintendent to vacate the contract."[7]

§ 53. Same.—The failure to make required reports destroys the right to recover wages, and a statute requiring teachers to make specified entries in a register applies to a principal of a number of schools, although he has done no actual teaching.[8] If the omission of entries is through no fault of the teacher, it will not prevent the recovery of wages. This rule was stated as follows in a case in which a teacher did not complete her school and made none of the entries required by

---

[1] Perrott v. Philadelphia, 83 Pa. St., 479.
[2] Place v. District Township of Colfax, 56 Iowa, 573. Adams, C. J., dissented on the grounds that it was the ministerial duty of the president of the board to approve the contract and that the district, by receiving the teacher's services, became liable for her wages.
[3] Kirkpatrick v. Independent School District of Liberty, 53 Iowa, 585; Pierce v. Beck, 61 Ga., 413.
[4] McCutcheon v. Windsor, 55 Mo., 149; Ewing v. School Directors, 2 Ill. App., 458.
[5] City of Crawfordsville v. Hays, 42 Ind., 210. See § 24, ante.
[6] Pierce v. Beck, 61 Ga., 413.
[7] Jamison v. Senter, 56 Miss., 194. This decision was under a law providing that a county superintendent alone might revoke a license but could annul a contract only with the concurrence of the trustees.
[8] School Commissioners of Alleghany Co. v. Adams, 43 Md., 349.

statute to be made at the close of a school:¹ "The close of school there meant must be the close of the term of school; for the answers to the inquiries required to be entered relate to the whole term, and could not be answered till the close of it. If the school stopped before the close of the term through the fault of the teacher, then the plaintiff would not be entitled to recover, whether she made the necessary entries in the register or not; but if the prudential committee, by his own conduct, without her fault, prevented the close of the term being reached by her, so she could make the entries, then the want of them would not prevent the recovery of the wages."

§ 54. Same. When possible.—A teacher can recover wages for services rendered while he holds a certificate irregularly given. The certificate is in the nature of a commission, and cannot be attacked collaterally, though it does not correspond to the form in which the statute says it *may* be drawn and was given without an examination of the candidate.[2]

In a Nebraska case a teacher was without a certificate three months during a term of nine months and recovered wages. "It is true," said the court, "that the statute prohibits the school board from paying from the school fund any but qualified teachers and makes a certificate or diploma, issued in the manner directed, the only evidence of such qualification. The prohibition of the statute is, however, upon the district board and not upon the teacher."[3]

If a teacher lawfully employed is dismissed without just cause, he may recover wages for the whole time for which he was employed. The court in Wisconsin laid down the rule as follows: "Unless the discharge of the teacher be justified by proof of the fact that he is not properly performing his contract on his part, the district becomes liable to the teacher for such damages as he may sustain by such discharge in the loss of wages for the residue of his term."[4] Where a teacher was kept from rendering services by the burning of the school-house, but was ready to teach whenever a place should be provided and filled out her register at the end of the time specified, it was held that full wages could be recovered.[5]

---

[1] Scott v. School District 2 of Fairfax, 46 Vt., 452, 457. Under an indictment charging a school teacher with perjury in swearing to his monthly report to the county superintendent, which represented that certain named pupils each attended school a certain number of days, whereas none attended as stated, he can be convicted on evidence that one did not attend. Page v. State, 59 Miss., 474.

[2] School District v. Sterricker, 86 Ill., 595. In Missouri the forging of a teacher's certificate is a penal offence. State v. Grant, 74 Mo., 33.

[3] School District v. Estes, 13 Nebr., 52.

[4] Scott v. Joint School District, 51 Wis., 554, 557. A teacher can only recover as damages the difference between the stipulated wages and what he earned, or might have earned, at a similar employment in his own vicinity during the time covered by his contract. See 2 Greenleaf on Evidence, § 161 *a*; 2 Chitty on Contracts, 11th Am. ed., p. 855, *note*.

[5] Cashen v. School District 12 of Berlin, 50 Vt., 30.

§ 55. **Same.**—A teacher can recover wages for time included in legal holidays. Chief Justice Campbell, of Michigan, said in a recent case:[1] "In regard to deductions for holidays we are of opinion that school management should always conform to those decent usages which recognize the propriety of omitting to hold public exercises on recognized holidays, and that it is not lawful to impose forfeitures or deductions for such proper suspension of labor. Schools should conform to what may fairly be expected of all institutions in civilized communities. All contracts for teaching during periods mentioned must be construed of necessity as subject to such days of vacation, and public policy as well as usage requires that there should be no penalty laid on such observances." If a teacher is employed for a definite time, and during the period of his employment the district officers close the schools on account of the prevalence of contagious disease, and keep them closed for a time, the teacher continuing ready to perform his contract, he is entitled to full wages during such period.[2] Wages have been recovered by a teacher who stipulated in the contract of employment that she would not instruct certain children in the district,[3] and by a teacher who was obliged to give up her school because the committee insisted on her allowing a disobedient and unmanageable boy to attend.[4] The court said: "The teacher could not perform the duties of her employment without maintaining proper and necessary discipline in the school, and when all her other means for doing so failed in respect to the boy it was her right, and might be her duty, to expel him, to save the rest of the school from being injured by his presence. It was not the duty of the teacher, under the contract, to teach the school without maintaining proper and necessary discipline in it; and if the committee insisted that she should have the boy there, when she could not have him there and have the discipline too, it was equivalent to insisting that she should teach the school without the discipline, which she was not bound to do."

§ 56. **Dismissal.**—If a teacher in a public school, although employed for a definite time, fails to perform the obligations resting upon him, he has broken the agreement on his part, and the trustees are clearly authorized to dismiss him from such employment.[5] When the school law empowers a city board of education to employ teachers and *remove them at pleasure*, the provision enters into and forms a part of the contract with a teacher for his services for a specified period; he may be discharged before its expiration, notwithstanding the terms of his employment.[6] But where the power of discharge is limited it ought not to be exercised

---

[1] School District 4 of Marathon v. Gage, 39 Mich., 480.
[2] Dewey v. Union District of Alpena, 43 Mich., 480.
[3] State v. Blain, 36 Ohio St., 429. Johnson, J., dissented.
[4] Scott v. School District 2 of Fairfax, 46 Vt., 452; *contra*, Parker v. School District, 5 Lea (Tenn.), 525.
[5] City of Crawfordsville v. Hays, 42 Ind., 200; Bays v. State, 6 Nebr., 167.
[6] Jones v. Nebraska City, 1 Nebr., 176. See § 24, *ante*.

until notice has been given the teacher and proper testimony heard against him.[1] If, at a hearing, he does not object to the sufficiency of the notice, he will not be allowed to do so afterward.[2] It has been held, generally, that the power to discharge teachers could not be enlarged by stipulations introduced into the contract of hiring.[3] A school board in Wisconsin included in such a contract the clause " We reserve the right to close the school at any time if not satisfactory to us." The court, in commenting on it, said:[4] " We think the good order and usefulness of the schools would be greatly prejudiced by holding that the boards had such power. If the power claimed for the board in this case exists and may be enforced, then the public schools must be taught to suit the whims, caprices, and peculiar notions of the hiring board, and not as the teacher, in the conscientious discharge of his duty, should teach the same."

§ 57. **Same.**—In New York the State superintendent has general supervision and direction of the normal schools, and it is one of his discretionary duties to approve the hiring of teachers for them. It has been decided that these powers do not authorize him to qualify his approval with the words " To continue in force during the pleasure of the board and the superintendent;" for "it is not within the power of the superintendent, by annexing conditions to his approval of the employment, to change the law regulating the discharge of the teachers of these schools."[5]

In Kansas a school district board employed a school teacher, and the contract of employment contained, among others, a stipulation that, if by the inability or neglect of the said A (the teacher) the interests of the school shall suffer, the district board shall have full power to annul this contract after one month's written notice. The court, the chief justice dissenting, held that the stipulation was valid, notwithstanding a clause in the school law providing that the district board in conjunction with the county superintendent may dismiss a teacher for incompetency, cruelty, negligence, or immorality, and that under the contract the school district board might alone, without any formal trial, and not in conjunction with the county superintendent, dismiss the teacher for incompetence and negligence from which the interests of the school suffer. " The object of the statutes," says the court,[6] " was simply to provide that the school district should not so bind itself by contract that a school teacher could not be discharged at any time by the school board acting in conjunction with the county superintendent, for

---

[1] Morley v. Power, 5 Lea (Tenn.), 691. See § 19, ante.
[2] Woodbury v. Knox, 74 Me., 462.
[3] Tripp v. School District, 50 Wis., 651; People v. Hyde, 89 N. Y. App., 11; Armstrong v. School District, 28 Kans., 345, Horton, C. J., dissenting.
[4] Tripp v. School District, 50 Wis., 651.
[5] People ex rel. Gilmour v. Hyde et al., 89 N. Y. App., 11.
[6] Armstrong v. School District, 28 Kans., 345; following School District v. Colvin, 10 Kans., 283.

incompetency, cruelty, negligence, or immorality; and it was not intended to prohibit the school board from making other provisions for the discharge of an incompetent, cruel, negligent, or immoral teacher."

§ 58. **Complaints against candidates for teachers' positions.**—A communication made by persons interested in a particular school to the superintendent having jurisdiction over it for the sole purpose of preventing him from issuing a license to teach the school to a particular individual on the ground that he was of bad moral character and wholly unfit to teach and have the care of a district school, is a privileged communication, and was abundantly justified by proof that he was an habitual blasphemer and profane person and an open violator of the Sabbath.[1] The court said:[2] "We do not think any superintendent would need vindication for being dissatisfied with the moral character of a teacher who has the faults complained of by these parties who opposed the licensing of plaintiff. A superintendent who should subject young children to such influences would be very censurable." The right to remonstrate must not be made the means of gratifying malice and enmity, and inquiry may be made as to the motives and private purposes of petitioners.[3]

CHAPTER VIII.—ADMINISTRATION.

§ 59. **Rules and regulations.**—Every student upon his admission into an institution of learning impliedly or expressly promises to submit to and be governed by all the necessary and proper rules and regulations which have been or thereafter may be adopted for the government of the institution.[4] Rules for the good conduct of a school are not invalidated because the board making them (though it must record votes, orders, and proceedings) does not adopt them formally and record them.[5] Courts will interfere to prevent the enforcement by a school board of any rule which manifestly reaches beyond their sphere of action, and relates to subjects in nowise connected with the management or successful operation of the school, or which is plainly calculated to retard the leading objects of legislation on educational affairs;[6] or, as another court expressed it, which is found to be unauthorized, against common right, or palpably unreasonable.[7]

§ 60. **Regulations respecting studies.**—Under the power to prescribe necessary rules and regulations for the management and government of schools, directors (or trustees) may require of pupils prompt attendance, diligence in study, proper deportment, and classification with respect to

---

[1] Wieman v. Mabee, 45 Mich., 484.
[2] Ibid., p. 486.
[3] Van Arsdale v. Laverty, 69 Pa. St., 103.
[4] State ex rel. Stallard v. White et al., 82 Ind., 286; s. c., 42 Am. Rep., 496.
[5] Russell v. Lynnfield, 116 Mass., 365.
[6] King v. Jefferson City School Board, 71 Mo., 628; s. c., 36 Am. Rep., 499.
[7] State v. White, 82 Ind., 286; s. c., 42 Am. Rep., 496.

the branches of study they are respectively pursuing, and with respect to proficiency or degree of advancement in those branches.[1] The following quotation is from an exposition of this doctrine in an Illinois case:[2] "In the performance of their duty in carrying the law into effect the directors may prescribe proper rules and regulations for the government of the schools of their district and enforce them. They may, no doubt, classify the scholars, regulate their studies and their deportment, the hours to be taught, besides the performance of other duties necessary to promote the success and secure the well being of such schools. But all such rules and regulations must be reasonable and calculated to promote the objects of the law : the conferring of such an education [one which includes the branches required by law] upon all, free of charge. The law having conferred upon each child of proper age the right to be taught the enumerated branches, any rule or regulation which, by its enforcement, would tend to hinder or deprive the child of this right cannot be sustained." In Ohio it has been decided that authority to make and enforce all necessary rules and regulations for schools, and to determine "the various studies and parts of studies" in which instruction shall be given in the departments of the schools, included the power in a board of education to adopt a rule that if any pupil, unless excused, should fail to be prepared with a rhetorical exercise at the time appointed he should be immediately suspended.[3]

§ 61. **Regulations respecting attendance.**—Regulations discriminating against the attendance of a certain class of inhabitants entitled to the privileges of the schools are unauthorized and cannot be sustained.[4] Rules requiring regularity of attendance are reasonable. Suspension for six half-days' absence in four consecutive weeks has been upheld in Missouri;[5] for six half-days' absence and two instances of tardiness in the same time, in Iowa;[6] and for a single day's unexcused absence to attend a religious service, in Vermont.[7] Judge Beck, in giving the opinion of the court in Iowa, said:[8] "It requires but little experience in the instruction of children and youth to convince any one that the only means which will assure progress in their studies is to secure their attendance, the application of the powers of their minds to the studies in which they are instructed. Unless the pupil's mind is open to receive instruc-

---

[1] Trustees of Schools v. People, 87 Ill., 303; s. c., 29 Am. Rep., 55. In Illinois, township high school trustees and district directors have power to adopt and enforce all necessary rules and regulations for the management and government of the schools; to direct what branches of study shall be taught, &c. Rev. Stat. 1880, p. 1377.

[2] Rulison v. Post, 79 Ill., 567, 570. This case and the preceding one decided that a rule compelling a pupil to pursue a study against the will of his father was not reasonable. See § 35, *ante*.

[3] Sewell v. Board of Education of Defiance, 29 Ohio St., 89.

[4] State v. White, 82 Ind., 278; s. c., 42 Am. Rep., 496. See § 34, *ante*.

[5] King v. Jefferson City School Board, 71 Mo., 628; s. c., 36 Am. Rep., 499.

[6] Burdick v. Babcock, 31 Iowa, 562, Miller, J., dissenting.

[7] Ferriter v. Tyler, 48 Vt., 444; s. c., 21 Am. Rep., 133.

[8] Burdick v. Babcock, 31 Iowa, 566.

tion, vain will be the effort of the teacher to lead him forward in learning. This application of the mind in children is secured by interesting them in their studies. But this cannot be done if they are at school one day and at home the next, if a recitation is omitted or a lesson left unlearned at the whim or convenience of parents. In order to interest a child he must be able to understand the subject in which he is instructed. If he has failed to prepare previous lessons he will not understand the one which the teacher explains to him. If he is required to do double duty, and prepare a previous lesson, omitted in order to make a visit or do an errand at home, with the lesson of the day, he will fail to master them and become discouraged. The inevitable consequence is that his interest flags and he is unable to apply the powers of his mind to the studies before him. The rule requiring constant and prompt attendance is for the good of the pupil and to secure the very objects the law had in view in establishing public schools. It is therefore reasonable and proper.

"In another view it is required by the best interests of all the pupils of the school. Irregular attendance of pupils not only retards their own progress, but interferes with the progress of those pupils who may be regular and prompt. The whole class may be annoyed and hindered by the imperfect recitations of one who has failed to prepare his lessons on account of absence. The class must endure and suffer the blunders, promptings, and reproofs of the irregular pupil, all resulting from failure to prepare lessons which should have been studied when the child's time was occupied by direction of the parent in work or visiting.

"Tardiness, that is, arriving late, is a direct injury to the whole school. The confusion of hurrying to seats, gathering together of books, &c., by tardy ones, at a time when all should be at study, cannot fail to greatly impede the progress of those who are regular and prompt in attendance. The rule requiring prompt and regular attendance is demanded for the good of the whole school."

In the Vermont decision it was said that in case of casual sickness of the scholar; of sickness or death in the family of the scholar; of some impediment, like fire or flood; and in case of various incidents of current life, giving occasion for temporary detention, the enforcement of the penalty of exclusion for unexcused absence would be adjudged to be unauthorized.[1]

§ 62. Same.—A rule which excludes from school a pupil for failure to pay for injuries accidentally done the school-house is not authorized by a clause permitting suspension of a pupil for a breach of discipline or an offence against good order. The court said:[2] "The State does not deprive its citizens of their property, or their liberty, or any of their rights except as a punishment for a crime. It would be very harsh and obvi-

---

[1] Ferriter v. Tyler, 48 Vt., 444, 477; s. c., 21 Am. Rep., 133.
[2] Perkins v. Directors of Independent School District of West Des Moines, 56 Iowa, 476, 479.

ously unjust to deprive a child of education for the reason that through accident and without intention of wrong he destroyed property of the school district. Doubtless a child may be expelled from school as a punishment for breach of discipline or for offences against good morals, but not for innocent acts." A rule that would bar the doors of a schoolhouse against little children, who come a great distance in cold, winter weather, for no other reason than that they are a few minutes tardy, is unreasonable and therefore unlawful.[1]

§ 63. **Suspension of pupils in the absence of rules.**—The law governing the suspension of pupils by a teacher in cases where no rule requiring it exists has been clearly stated recently in Wisconsin in an opinion by Judge Lyon, from which the following extended quotation is taken:[2] "While the principal or teacher in charge of a public school is subordinate to the school board or board of education of his district or city, and must enforce rules and regulations adopted by the board for the government of the school, and execute all its lawful orders in that behalf, he does not derive all his power and authority in the school and over his pupils from the affirmative action of the board. He stands for the time being *in loco parentis* to his pupils, and, because of that relation, he must necessarily exercise authority over them in many things concerning which the board may have remained silent. In the school, as in the family, there exist on the part of the pupils the obligations of obedience to lawful commands, subordination, civil deportment, respect for the rights of other pupils, and fidelity to duty. These obligations are inherent in any proper school system, and constitute, so to speak, the common law of the school. Every pupil is presumed to know this law, and is subject to it whether it has or has not been reënacted by the district board in the form of written rules and regulations. Indeed, it would seem impossible to frame rules which would cover all cases of insubordination and all acts of vicious tendency which the teacher is liable to encounter daily and hourly.

"The teacher is responsible for the discipline of his school and for the progress, conduct, and deportment of his pupils. It is his imperative duty to maintain good order and to require of his pupils a faithful performance of their duties. If he fails in this he is unfit for his position. To enable him to discharge these duties effectually he must necessarily have the power to enforce prompt obedience to his lawful commands. For this reason the law gives him the power, in proper cases, to inflict corporal punishment upon refractory pupils. But there are cases of misconduct for which such punishment is an inadequate remedy. If the offender is incorrigible, suspension or expulsion is the only adequate remedy. In general, no doubt, the teacher should report a case of that kind to the proper board for its action in the first instance, if no delay

---

[1] Thompson v. Beaver, 63 Ill., 353, 357.
[2] State v. Burton, 45 Wis., 150, 155; s. c., 30 Am. Rep., 706. See, also, Parker v. School District, 5 Lea (Tenn.), 528.

will necessarily result from that course prejudicial to the best interests of the school. But the conduct of the recusant pupil may be such that his presence in the school for a day or an hour may be disastrous to the discipline of the school and even to the morals of the other pupils. In such a case it seems absolutely essential to the welfare of the school that the teacher should have the power to suspend the offender at once from the privileges of the school; and he must necessarily decide for himself whether the case requires that remedy."

§ 64. **Same.**—Persons having the general charge and superintendence of public schools have power to exclude a child for sufficient cause, as, for example, that his conduct, not in violation of prescribed rules, tended to injure the discipline and impair the usefulness of the school.[1] The view that acts, to be within the authority of the school board and teachers for discipline and correction, must be done within school hours is narrow and without regard to the spirit of the law and the best interest of common schools.[2] But the publication of an article ridiculing school officers and tending to create insubordination in a school cannot be punished by the expulsion of the offender, when the statute only authorizes dismissals for gross immorality and persistent violation of school regulations.[3] If a person would recover damages for exclusion from a school he must first appeal to school officers who have authority to reinstate him,[4] if there be such, and, if the case come to trial, prove the action of the officers excluding him to have been wanton and malicious.[5]

§ 65. **Corporal punishment.**—In the absence of statutory enactments, the authorities upon the right of a teacher to inflict reasonable chastisement upon a pupil are not numerous, but they are sufficient to prove its existence.[6] The law is well settled that the teacher has the right to exact from his pupils obedience to his lawful and reasonable commands, and to punish disobedience, with "kindness, prudence, and propriety."[7] Any punishment with a rod which leaves marks

[1] Hodgkins v. Rockport, 105 Mass., 475.
[2] Burdick v. Babcock, 31 Iowa, 567. See Lander v. Seaver, 32 Vt., 114; and § 36, *note, ante.*
[3] Murphy v. Board of Directors of Independent District of Marengo, 30 Iowa, 429.
[4] Davis v. Boston, 133 Mass., 103.
[5] McCormick v. Burt, 95 Ill., 263; s. c., 35 Am. Rep., 163.
[6] State v. Mizner, 45 Iowa, 248.
[7] Danenhoffer v. State, 69 Ind., 295; s. c., 35 Am. Rep., 216. In the case of Lander v. Seaver, 32 Vt., 114, it was decided that a schoolmaster is not relieved from liability in damages for the punishment of a scholar which is clearly excessive and unnecessary by the fact that he acted in good faith and without malice, honestly thinking that the punishment was necessary, both for the discipline of the school and the welfare of the scholar. In Commonwealth v. Seed, 5 Pa. L. Jour. Rep., 78, Judge Parson said: "The law does not permit a court to invade the sanctuary of the domestic circle and usurp the parental authority in every family because we may think the punishment is severe. It is only when from the surrounding circumstances of the case there is strong reason to believe that the parent has been actuated by bad and malevolent motives, using his legal parental authority for the gratification of a mind

and welts on the person of the pupil for two months afterward, or much less time, is immoderate and excessive.[1] Proof that the punishment was for an insufficient cause or in an unreasonable manner will be received to rebut the presumption to the contrary. In no case can the punishment be justifiable unless it is inflicted for some definite offence which the pupil has committed and the pupil is given to understand why he is punished. "Punishment inflicted when the reason of it is unknown to the punished is subversive, and not promotive, of the true objects of punishment." It must not be inflicted for obedience to the lawful directions of a parent.[2] The authority to chastise extends to a pupil who has attained his majority; for by voluntarily attending school he waives any privilege and submits himself to like discipline with those that are within school age.[3] A member of a school committee may eject a pupil from the school-house for insulting conduct toward him. This was decided in a Connecticut case, stated by the judge in his opinion, as follows:[4] "The defendant, being at the school-house performing certain duties connected with the school, called the attention of the plaintiff to certain acts, not specially culpable in character, which he acknowledged he had committed. His bearing and manner were insolent and offensive, and the language in which he indulged was grossly profane. Such language, reprehensible at all times, should not have been allowed to pass with impunity from a school boy of the older class, within the walls of a school-house, in the presence and hearing of younger pupils. After being told to leave, he so conducted that it was proper to remove him, no unnecessary force being used to attain that object."

---

bent on mischief, that the law has given the court the right to interpose for the protection and safety of the child. Such is the rule relative to the school teacher, whom the parent, for the time being, has placed in his stead." See, also, Burke's Law of Public Schools, pp. 119-132.

[1] State v. Mizner, 50 Iowa, 145, 149; s. c., 32 Am. Rep., 128.
[2] Morrow v. Wood, 35 Wis., 59; s. c., 17 Am. Rep., 471.
[3] State v. Mizner, 45 Iowa, 248, 250; s. c., 24 Am. Rep., 769.
[4] Peck v. Smith, 41 Conn., 442, 446.

County School Fund.

No. _____
A.

$ _____ _____ School District,

_____ County, _____ 188 _____

THE TREASURER of _____ County, _____

will pay to _____ or Order,

_____ Dollars, and _____ Cents,

out of the County School Fund for 188__, being the amount due _____ as a Teacher of Public

School No. _____, for _____ month __, ending _____ 188 _____

By order of the Board of School Trustees:

_____ Clerk. _____ Chairman.

COUNTY SCHOOL FUND.

No. _____

$ _____ _____ 188 __

Dated, _____

Issued to _____

For _____

State School Fund.

No. _____
B.

$ _____ _____ School District,

_____ County, _____ 188 _____

THE TREASURER of _____ County

will pay to the order of _____

_____ Dollars and _____ Cents, out of the

State School Fund for 188__, being the amount due _____ as a Teacher of Public School No. _____

for _____ month __, ending _____ 188 __

By order of the Board of School Trustees:

_____ Clerk. _____ Chairman.

STATE SCHOOL FUND.

No. _____

$ _____ _____ 188 __

Dated, _____

Issued to _____

For _____

DISTRICT SCHOOL FUND.

No. _____
C.

_____ 188_

To _____

_____ 188_ _____ School District,
_____ County,
$ _____

District School Fund.

THE TREASURER of _____ County,
will pay to _____ , or order,
_____ Dollars and _____ Cents, out of the
District School Fund for 18__, being the amount due _____ for _____ 188_
Public School No. _____

By order of the Board of School Trustees:

_____ Clerk. _____ Chairman.

Order by letter,

These warrants are recommended by Hon. R. R. Farr, Superintendent of Public Instruction.
Books of 200 Warrants (printed on good white paper,) will be mailed, post-paid, on receipt of $1.00.
thus, "A," "B," or "C," and we will know the kind you want.
A full supply of Public and Private school Books and Stationery.

J. W. RANDOLPH & ENGLISH,
BOOKSELLERS, & STATIONERS,
1302 and 4 Main Street, RICHMOND, VA.

INDEX.

	Page.
Absence, justifiable grounds for	75
Accidents, child not to be expelled for	75–76
Administration of school affairs	73–78
Alteration of districts	27
Annexation of districts, effect of, on property	31–32
Apparatus, articles considered as	46
Appeals to school officers	47–49
Appendages "necessary" to a schoolhouse	46
Apportionment of funds on change of district	42
Appropriation, new districts entitled to share of	27
Appropriations, powers of legislatures to make	24
Ashburn, J., on liability of school boards	56
Assessment of school property for local purposes	39
Assessors	59
Assets, adjustment of, on division of districts	32
include school-houses and sites	44
Attendance, regulations respecting	74–76
Barrett, J., on the nature of building school district may erect	28
Beck, J., on the limitation of appeals to school officers	49
on regularity of attendance	74
Bequests, district may accept	29
distribution of	42
Board of education, trustees, or directors, organization of	49
membership in	50
requisites to valid action by	50–52
corporate nature of	56
liabilities of	55–57
cannot change the law of discharge of teachers	72
Bond, nature of treasurer's	59
Bonds, power to issue	30
vitiated by irregularities in proceedings to issue	31

	Page.
Campbell, J., on presumptions of district organization	26
on effect of meanness to teachers	58
on payment of wages through holidays	71
Care of school-house	53
Cases, table of	7–20
Certificate, teacher must obtain	60
Claims must be presented to school officer	32
overdue, may be paid	25
Collection of taxes	35, 60
Collector	60
Colleges, what property of, exempt from taxation	36, 37
Colored schools	61–64
Colt, J., on transfer of property by modification of school system	23
Commissioner of Education, letter of	5
Complaint, who may not bring	25
Condemnation of land for schoolhouse	43
Constitutional law, questions of	21–25
Contagious disease, wages due for time school closed on account of	71
Contracts embody existing laws	24, 66–67
of school board, how long valid	52–53
respecting school-house	54
of teachers	66–68
implied	67
Controversies, wisdom of settlement of, by school authorities	48
Cooley, J., on the maintenance of high schools	61
Corporal punishment	77, 78
Corporations, power of legislature over public educational	23
liabilities of quasi	33, 56
County superintendents	49
Courts will not control the exercise of discretionary power	22, 27
Dalrimple, J., on district liability	32
Damages for breach of contract of hiring	70

237

	Page.		Page.
Davis, J., on judicial action of school trustees	47	Hunt, Mr. Justice, on contracts "subject to law"	24
Debts for building purposes	30, 54	Incompetency of teacher prevents	
effect of change of district on	31–32	recovery of wages	69
Directors. See Board of education, &c.		Independent district. See Districts (independent).	
Discipline	77–78	Industrial schools, commitment to	22–23
Dismissal of teachers	71	Infancy, effect of, on contracts	68
Duties of teachers	67, 76	Injuries, liability of district for	33–34
Districts (independent), power of legislature to create	21	Insurance of school-houses	46
		Irregularities in organizing district	26
Districts, various kinds of, may exist in a uniform school system	22	in meetings and elections	31
		in action of school boards	52
power of legislature over	23	in teacher's contract	67
organization of	26	Krekel, J., on establishment of normal schools	22
organization of, cannot be collaterally attacked	26	Land conveyed for school purposes must be so used	42
alteration of	27		
powers of	28	condemnation of, for schoolhouse site	43
effect of alteration of, on property and debts	31–32	for school purposes should not be conveyed with defeating conditions	44
liabilities of	31–34		
nature of corporate powers of	33		
power of, to tax	34–35	Lawsuits, effects of	48
liability of, for wages of teacher	70–71	Legislature, powers of	21–25
Eaton, John, letter of	5	Liabilities of districts	31–34
Education, propriety of using municipal funds for	45	of school officers	55–57
		of treasurer	58, 59
Equality of school privileges required	62	License fees not taxes	25
		License necessary to valid contract by teacher	66
Errors of judgment, school officers not liable for	56	Lightning rods	46
Exemption of school property from taxation	36–40	Local assessment of school property	39
		Local legislation, evils of	21
Folger, J., on negligence of school board	57	Lyon, J., on school government	76
		Meetings, school district	30
Funds, school, must not be diverted from school purposes	25, 41	rules about calling special	30, n
		of school board	51
the State the owner of	41	Miller, Mr. Justice, on the exemption from taxation of land used for school purposes	36
apportionment of, on change of district	42		
use of municipal, for education	45	Minors, contracts of, to teach	68
duty of treasurer respecting	58	Moneys. (See Funds.)	
Furniture of school-houses	46	Moral character, complaints of, to proper officer, privileged communications	73
Garnishment, district not subject to	28		
German, study of, in public schools	64		
Hall may be built for school purposes	28	Negligence, liability of school board for	56–57
Hearing, form of conducting	47	Normal schools may be established, when	22
teacher entitled to, before dismissal	72	duty of State to provide for	25
High schools, right of districts to establish	22, 61	Notes, district may make promissory	29
Holidays, wages recoverable for	71	Notice of district meeting	31

RECENT SCHOOL LAW DECISIONS.

	Page.
Officers, school, must not contract with themselves	54–55
quasi-judicial powers of	46–48
liabilities of	55–57
removal of	57
Officers *de facto*, contracts of	68
Orders, qualities of school	29
Organization of school districts	26
presumed after continued existence	26
Organization of school board	49
Parents, nature of their authority.	23
rights of, to children	23
right of, to determine a child's studies	64–65
Powers of school boards	52–54
Promissory note, district may make.	29
Property, school	41–47
distribution of, on change of district	27
Public schools, definitions of	41, 60
Pupils, home conduct of	55, n, 77
regulations respecting	73–76
Railroads, school districts cannot aid	24
Rapallo, J., on the support of normal schools	25
Record of clerk best evidence of proceedings	31
Reform schools	22
Regulations must be reasonable	73
respecting studies	73–74
respecting attendance	74–76
Removal from office	57
Repair of school-houses	47, 53–55
Reports, teacher must make, as prescribed	69
Rothrock, J., on appeals to school authorities	49
Rules and regulations	73–76
Ryan, C. J., on reform schools	22
School-houses, the erection of	28, 42–44
use of	44–46
powers of board to build and repair	53–54
negligence, in care of	57
School meetings, boards, officers, &c. See Boards, meetings, officers, &c.	
Schools and studies	60–65
Schools may be maintained longer than the State constitution requires	22

	Page.
Scott, C. J., on what constitutes use "with a view to profit"	38
Sites for school-houses, condemnation of	43
Special meetings, rules about calling	30, n
State, the owner of public school funds	41
Students, implied promise of, respecting conduct	73
Studies	64–65
regulations respecting	73–74
Substitute may not be employed	67
Sunday school, use of public school-house for	45
Superintendent, county	49
Superintendent, State, may be given quasi-judicial powers	22
Superintendent of schools, power of board to appoint	52
Sureties, liability of	60
Suspension of pupils in the absence of rules	76–77
Tardiness, ill effects of	75
Taxation, powers of legislatures respecting	24
by school districts	34
purposes of	34
exemptions from	36–40
Taxes for educational purposes are "for the defence and benefit of the people"	24
what constitutional provisions respecting, are self-executing.	25
may be levied on what	34
collection of	60
Teachers, the selection of, a judicial act	51
power of school boards to employ and dismiss	52
time for which board may employ	52–53
committee may not use violence in dispossessing	56
contracts of	66–68
payment for services of	68–71
dismissal of	71
responsible for good discipline.	76–77
Text books	65
Town system, effects on districts of creating	23, 24
effects on districts of abolishing	27
Treasurer	58
Trunkey, J., on district liability	33

	Page.		Page.
Trustees. See Board of education.		Village, effect of incorporating....	27
Universities, State, power of legislature over......................	24	Vories, J., on presumption of school district organization.............	26
principles applicable to.......	60–61	Wages, recovery of...............	68–71
Use of school buildings...........	44–46	Worden, J., on duties of a teacher.	67

www.ingramcontent.com/pod-product-compliance
Lightning Source LLC
Chambersburg PA
CBHW032008230426
43672CB00010B/2294